Home Is Where The Truth Is

Is

Why You Can and *Should* Homeschool Your Child

By: Maeve Jemison

For my husband Mat...
Make me laugh.

Table of Contents

Introduction

FLASHBACK TO JANUARY 1, 2021. Coming out of the unprecedented amount of times the word 'unprecedented' was used over the dumpster fire year 2020, it seemed that all of my luck would continue to spiral downward as my dishwasher promptly decided to conk out on New Year's Day. Happy New Year to me! My patience would soon be chipping away along with my gel nails during the hand-washing of dishes for five hours a day. Let's get this truth out on the table quickly. When multiple people eat six meals a day under the same roof you get a deluge of dirty dishes. Those dishpan hands are worth the effort though to look into your family's face and hear their sweet, sticky little smacking lips. Especially when eating meals together around the table leads to less chance that you'll raise drug addicts or violent, depressed teens with eating disorders. Add to that a side of better vocabulary and more self-esteem[1], "Sure I'll have another helpin', please." It turns out that there's a lot you can do *from* home to not only raise good citizens but also raise people who have strong faith, less teenage sex, and drink less alcohol[2]. It's called *homeschooling*. Now, I know that is a scary word fraught with inaccurate social stigmas and some parents' worst nightmares—like being home with their kids all day, every day, *and* being responsible for their education, but please read on as I dispel those myths.

Today's generation of children has a lot going against them as they trudge onto their school campuses. Depending on how young they are, they may have seldom seen their teachers or peers ever smile at them, as they were hidden behind mandated masks for years during crucial developmental phases of childhood. The anxieties and fears of an armed shooter kicking down their classroom door constantly loom in the back of their minds. But the very entities that provide peace and security through stressful times, God and prayer, have long since been barred from classrooms. This is the loneliest, most anxious, and depressed young generation our world has possibly ever seen. Constant comparison and isolation through social media add to the problems. Preventative measures like lots of vitamin D, time in nature, and face-to-face playtime aren't used nearly enough because of crammed schedules, blue-glowing screens, and overworked parents (who depend on those handy babysitting devices and the much-needed break they provide). Sadly, more young girls are depressed[3] and more young boys are addicted to pornography than ever. These stats are linked directly back to the ubiquitous phones in their pockets. College freshmen now report the highest stress levels and worst mental health conditions in 25 years[4]. College counseling centers are seeing growing numbers in serious psychiatric conditions like stress-related eating disorders, substance abuse, and self-injury.[5] Sitting in cold, hard desks in the lecture room they are told many lies by the teachers that they trust. For one thing, there's no real truth, everyone can make up "their truth". Another lie, their success in America hinges on how much melanin their skin produces. Students with more melanin are doomed as oppressed victims and will never rise out of their lot in life due to lighter-skinned people holding them down. Oh, and on top of all that...you might not really be a boy or a girl.

If the Department of Education gets its way, female athletes, it really sucks for you. It doesn't matter how hard you train, a biological male with his denser bones, larger heart, and greater amount of fast-twitch muscle fibers can now race against you simply because he likes to wear dresses. Your feeling of safety and privacy in your locker rooms and bathrooms will be no more. He's going to invade those as well and walk around naked with his junk hanging out if he so desires. He will not only beat you at your sport but also take your scholarship and then turn around and sue you for sexual harassment if you speak out against him.

Lots of parents don't realize there is a war waging right now and our children are the main target. They're being groomed with gender ideology without parental knowledge or approval. They're being indoctrinated with so much misinformation that it's no wonder our youth are confused about who they are, that 57% of teens seek out porn monthly[6], and half of them admit to being addicted to their mobile device[7].

You've picked up this book though. You are on the right path for finding the solution that will save your child from all that, and I believe, will save America for future generations. Your growing disenchantment with your local school board and the Department of Education is prompting you to search for and provide something better for your darlings and kudos to you for listening to the call!

Dissatisfaction with government education is growing fast, not like a wave building as it gets closer to shore, but more like a tsunami rising steeply. COVID lockdowns and the blatant sexualization of our children through school curricula are just a couple of the myriad reasons on which I will shed light. Today, at least 3.7 million Americans are learning at home. It's the fastest-growing form of education in the United States and is growing globally in countries like Australia, Canada, France, Hungary, Japan, Kenya, Russia, Mexico, South Korea, Thailand, and the United Kingdom. [8] As a homeschool mom, who started in 2009, I could choose to stay in my bubble and ignore it, or I could tell the truth to every disgruntled parent I can reach about the wonderful, family-bonding, educational adventure that is homeschooling.

Whether you have already made the decision to homeschool, or are in the researching and praying phase, this book is going to help you along. When all of America, nay all the world became homeschoolers, we who were already homeschooling got our brains picked *A LOT*. It seemed as though every parent I knew, even mere acquaintances, had questions for me. I didn't mind it. Actually, I loved it because it led me to one of my greatest callings—writing this book. I'm happy to give any parent all my knowledge in hopes that they will get to experience all the extraordinary benefits of homeschooling.

The appliance repairman, Keith, diagnosing my decrepit dishwasher felt about the same way you might. He could see that there might be *some* benefits to homeschooling over public or private schools. But he couldn't see past all the misconceptions. How do I know this? Well, as an outgoing homeschool mom, I befriend anyone who comes within my realm. We're talking pest control guys, delivery people, and religious folks that come knocking on the door. They are all fair game with which to socialize. I mean, how else are you going to get out of the homeschool bubble and socialize, right? (Pshhhh, more on socializing in Chapter 1.)

As I chatted with Keith, he brought up his Catholic school education and said that he hoped he could provide that for his baby girl when she is school-aged. "However, my wife really wants to homeschool," said he.

Wait, what?

"OMG, I HOMESCHOOL!!"

I say with the enthusiasm of a high school cheerleader.

The poor guy didn't even know what he'd just walked into as he blurted out the number one homeschool fallacy that I hear: "How do you socialize them?"

I promptly served him up rebuttal after rebuttal on that topic until he said to me, "Wow, your point of view just completely changed my perspective on that, I think that's a notch in my wife's favor."

Unfortunately, Keith couldn't fix my dishwasher. And I don't know what he and his wife decided about their daughter's education. I'll be sure and ask him when my 'fridge craps the bed. But he was certainly not the only person to ask me about homeschooling. Soccer moms, running buddies, church ladies, even dads at the gym have questions, and this book's purpose is to answer them.

Please don't let me come off cocky, I must let you know that I am not an all-knowing academia expert. My parents did not educate me at home, I am 100% a product of government school. I am quite impressed by public school teachers battling daily in the trenches, trying to educate kids in a system that's not designed to keep the joy of discovery thriving, but for the dulling of children (I will explain this in-depth in chapter six). Neither did I help the homeschool movement to become legal back in the 1990s, like those courageous, trailblazing parents who did what they knew was best for their children despite the risk of the cops pounding on their door and the scary, real possibility of losing legal custody.

I do not write my own curriculum when I don't find one that fits. Shoot, I can't even pull my own *unit study* together, after attending a break-out session on how to do just that. It's all too overwhelming for my distractible brain. And it's much easier to go online and print out a pre-made unit! I'm a whiz on scarcely any curriculum, as I like trying new approaches and discarding those that are boring or hard to stick with. I don't even pretend to know the intricate details of the differences between the Classical Model vs. the Principle Approach to home education. I don't have 14 kids, 12 of whom turned out to be rocket scientists, doctors, lawyers, or the developer of the best fishing jig that caught the world record bass. Nope, I *only* have five kids. (None of my friends who send their kids to school can believe that I had to type '*only*' before the number 5, but a handful of homeschool moms just threw this book down and scoffed at me because I'm not quite to cargo van status.)

As a homeschool parent with fourteen years in the game, plus five years experience as a high school journalism teacher and Yearbook adviser at our county's largest high school, I have wisdom that I truly feel compelled to share with you. There is no person on this planet who will do for your kids' success what you are willing to do. Perhaps more importantly, I'm a mom who wants to teach her kids their faith and how to defend it. Don't you? That's a feat much easier to do when the whole secular world doesn't get to babysit and indoctrinate them for eight hours a day.

Just like you, I've made many awful parenting mistakes, read on for juicy details. But thanks to my homeschooling journey and the Holy Spirit, every once in a while, I will do something with my children so wonderful, so good-habit-forming, so naturally mind-broadening, I have to sit and relish in the moment of winning with my kids *in my own living room*. Maybe this is a hint of what you're yearning for.

Ahead of you are some lies that well-meaning people have conceived and spread as their beliefs about homeschooling. If you homeschool now or decide to in the future, you will eventually be asked your opinion on them. Maybe you've even accepted these misconceptions. I had to work through them to come out on the side of truth and reality through my own blessed, glorious, tiring, rewarding, calling to homeschool. May the information from my story be a springboard for you on your journey.

LIE #1:

Your Children Won't Be Adequately Socialized.

"I feel ashamed that so many of us cannot imagine a better way to do things than locking children up all day in cells instead of letting them grow up knowing their families, mingling with the world, assuming real obligations, striving to be independent and self-reliant and free."
— John Taylor Gatto, Author, Education reformer, New York City Teacher of the Year 1989, 1990, and 1991 and New York State Teacher of the Year in 1991

"Keep company with the wise and you will become wise. If you make friends with stupid people, you will be ruined." Proverbs 13:20

WITHOUT A DOUBT, THIS is whopper *Numero Uno* that I hear from everyone. I'm talking in-laws, fellow parishioners, curious moms, the nephew's girlfriend, even cashiers. The conversation goes something like this:

"Are you off school today?" The grocer will ask my gaggle because we are clearly grocery shopping at 9 a.m. on a school day.

"No, we homeschool," one of them replies.

And then here it comes: "Oh, but how do you socialize them?"

To which I reply, "I lock them up for 8 hours a day, push them in the hallways, make fun of their clothes, and make sure they have a screen in their face when we go out in public so that don't have to acknowledge or speak to anyone."

Well, o.k. I've never said that, but I swear one day I will! Dictionary.com defines socialization as a continuing process whereby an individual acquires a personal identity and learns the norms, values, behavior, and social skills appropriate to his or her social position. I'm guessing that all these overly curious meddlers really wonder how a child can actually learn social skills within the four walls of his or her home. Perhaps they've become biased after seeing one too many weird bubble-wrapped homeschool kids, unhip to pop culture, fashion, music, and dumbed-down slang. Lacking the precocious influences that come from peers, TikTok, social media, and institutional learning, homeschoolers often do stand out from a crowd of kids that attend school, but y'all act like that's a bad thing or that it's something you see *only* in homeschoolers.

Socialization is a learned skill no matter what type of education you receive. Let me remind you lots of socially awkward kids graduate from public and private institutions just as socially inept as they were the first day that they stepped on campus. In actuality, government high school graduates may be more withdrawn and angrier from years of being picked on because they weren't completely mainstream in all dress, talk, and behavior. Any trip to the fro-yo spot and you'll see a group of teens out together for a cold treat and some of that good 'ol socializing. The only problem is that they're all on their phones, scrolling through virtual loneliness. Ignoring the live, breathing friend that's right next to them. Are those kids properly socialized?

Which does this sound like, socialization or isolation? Every day at exactly the same time you go to the same building, are in the same room with the same peers, read the same textbook, sit in the same spot at lunch and even eat the same thing. To me, that's more like harsh isolation. Indeed, the very framework of government school was inspired by Marxists and Communists who hated traditional values, like God, patriotism, and fathers as the heads of households. Hoping to manufacture a political revolution through the indoctrination and sexualization of our children, and to undermine the importance of family life, they modeled our school system off of Soviet Russia's. In his 1932 book *Toward Soviet America,* William Z. Foster, the national chairman of the American Communist Party, was crystal clear about the party's goal for American education.

"Among the elementary measures the American Soviet government will adopt to further the cultural revolution are... [a] National Department of Education...the studies will be revolutionized, being cleansed of religious, patriotic, and the features of the bourgeois ideology. The students will be taught the basis of Marxian dialectical materialism, internationalism, and the general ethics of the new Socialist society" [1]

Four years earlier in 1928, John Dewey, the Father of Progressive Education, had traveled to Soviet Russia. Dewey was a staunch atheist and one of the original signers of *The Humanist Manifesto,* which introduced a new religion, Humanism, as a movement to transcend and replace previous religions that were based on deities or supernatural revelation. He was enamored with their education system seeing it for the sharp political scythe that it is. He wrote a book of his desire to replicate the ways it embedded collectivist mindsets into children, dismantling the need for a family unit. His book states, "Our special concern here is with the role of the schools in building up forces and factors whose natural effect is to undermine the importance and uniqueness of family life."[2] Dewey believed education should be a tool for social engineering toward activism and, eventually revolution. Through his teaching career at the Teacher's College at Columbia University, Dewey had a profound impact on education, and we as parents have been completely duped into thinking that government schools ever had our children's best interests in mind. As Noelle Mering states in her book, *Awake Not Woke,* "The early goal for the elementary years was to separate children from parents, not only physically, but also by undermining and fracturing the influence and authority of parents by injecting a slow drip of ideology into the school system." Mering continues, "Essential to this effort is the introduction of the child, as early as possible, to adult sexual practices."[3] We will talk more about the sexualization of children through government schools in chapter five. Then, in chapter nine, when I talk about private schools, I'm going to divulge more details about the history of this wretched school style. You are not even going to believe who originally came up with this model (but I'll give you a hint, he's been called the Spiritual Father of Modern Neo-Nazism). I'll also tell you about the other nefarious people who perpetuated it. However, in this first chapter, I wanted you to see the school system for what it was created to do, and that its real goal in "socializing" your child is more like making them into a social*ist.*

Since plenty of American parents have no idea about the history of government schools when they ask about socialization, I can surmise that their true concern is: How competent will homeschooled kids be in communicating with others? Believe me, raising a competent communicator—someone that's able to get their thoughts, words, and writings out to any group of people in any type of forum—is at the very top of my list. Unfortunately, I am here to tell you that a traditional classroom is the exact opposite of a safe and effective learning environment for this subject. Can somebody please tell me in which real-world setting are you in the same twenty by twenty-foot room with forty other people your exact age? Perhaps working on the same project? Or toward the same objectives even? No? Hmm. Let me try...perhaps at the nightclub? And if that's the goal, to have them comfortable to get on a sweaty dance floor and yell over loud music, then I think a couple of shots of Don Julio tequila can help them there. Shots might help *you* on a stressful day of teaching a reluctant reader while corralling a toddler that eats crayons and scribbles on walls with the less-tasty ones.

And I have to seriously ask, do you want to socialize your precious, innocent baby into a higher chance of using illegal substances? Homeschooled kids were significantly less likely to report the use of alcohol, tobacco, and weed than their non-homeschooled counterparts, and are less likely to have access to illicit drugs or even be approached by drug dealers.[4]

Let's think past those school years, even past the young adult stage—like all the way into eternity where the most important thing is instilling our faith, and helping them to know God. Yes, you can do that even if you don't homeschool, but the numbers tell the true story about socialization through school's ill effect when homeschoolers are about 7.5 times more likely to be strong in their Christian beliefs than those attending private school.[5]

So how are you going to socialize them? You'll enjoy doing it without the bad habits, cruel words, cliquish social group standards, and time waste of the traditional classroom. You will socialize them in the real world, in rich experiences guided by you and your spouse, trusted music teachers, coaches, youth ministers, and people whom *you* choose. That's the key, in homeschooling, you get to choose who influences your precious darlings.

When I attended my first homeschool convention, six months after snatching my oldest child from the soul-deadening clutches of middle school, I was astounded at the homeschool children's social maturity. First, there was the teen boy who was helping run his parents' curriculum booth at the expo. He stood there with a strong posture, dressed professionally in a polo shirt and khakis, hair combed and lightly gelled. His hands clasped calmly in front of his chest, he answered my questions directly and capably, looked me in the eye, and called me "Ma'am". I reflected on my career as a government high school teacher. I had seldom to *never* had a student address me with such confidence and professionalism. The farther I ventured serpentinely through the huge ballroom filled with endless rows of homeschool hoard hawkers, I realized that kid was no anomaly in this *hoi polloi*.

I know it's not fair to generalize from my experience, a five-year career in a diverse 3,500-student high school. To this day, some of the most faith-filled, responsible, respectful, goal-achieving people that I've ever met were 15-year-olds. Unfortunately, that was a tiny handful, not the majority. Now,14 years into my homeschooling career, I'm completely convinced that homeschoolers are the BEST socialized children there are. I get compliments on my kids' behavior in public all the time. Nice strangers will come up and tell us how they've enjoyed sitting near our family at dinner and watching us interact. When we have friends over, the kids can talk with them no matter what the guests' ages are. I mean communicating with a proper voice level, making eye contact, adding to the conversation, not just answering questions with a nod and a one-word answer.

What any child needs is to be taught how to make eye contact, and answer, 'Yes, Ma'am' and 'No, ma'am'. To say, "Thanks for asking," when someone asks how their day is going. I've had to teach my kids that it's inappropriate to make the conversation about you every time you add to it.

(Unfortunately, that's a skill that a lot of adults still don't have.)

Before we walked into church, we drilled the kids.

"What's the proper response if someone tells you they like your new haircut?"

Or before we go into the restaurant, "When the waitress talks to you, don't stare at the TV like a zombie. Look at her in her eyes and speak loudly enough for her to hear you."

We run drills with role playing when necessary and the kids do swimmingly when they know what's expected.

What about the not-so-formal run-ins with peers, you ask? Are they going to be able to sociably blend with them? Will they get along with other people? Oh, don't you worry, Mom and Dad, there will be plenty of opportunities to get social credibility. I've found that no matter how tightly I bubble-wrap these homeschooled kids of mine, the world seeps in.

After soccer practice, I am explaining what newly heard cuss words mean and letting my son know that it's not ok to de-pants your friends in front of others, or at all for that matter—as one teammate did to another. On park days, my kids have had skirmishes, tempers flared, and pushing ensued. We still get some street fights in the homeschooling realm. Perhaps that's one of those life skills that the grocer was hoping my kids didn't miss out on.

After elementary night at church, my daughter asked me what one gesture meant that would've made a hardened criminal blush. Heck, the first time my daughter ever heard the F-bomb was from a college-aged swim coach. She has never stepped foot on a school campus, we regulate her media intake and have standards on movie ratings such as no PG-13s. Yet, even I was surprised to know that she had never *heard* the word. Sure, we'd had discussions about cuss words and their meanings, so she recognized it. She was thirteen years old when she heard it, which gave me cause for a little self-back pat, surprising myself that I had never let one fly in front of her. She has, however, heard most other four-letter words from yours truly. In the next chapter, allow me to tell you a little more about letting all that profanity fly, or not fly, which has everything to do with patience.

Let me conclude this chapter by hearkening you, Moms and Dads. We can protect our children's innocence while carefully socializing them under our supervision. We can save them from the need to dumb themselves down to fit in with peers, or if you are a person of color, protect them from hearing "stop acting white" because they show intellectual proficiency. We can plug our children's ears to the poisonous indoctrination of dangerous ideologies that is happening in government and private schools all across our nation (which I'll get into in Chapter 5) while teaching them objective truth and how to defend it. With the Lord's help, we can raise a generation that knows how to put a phone down and pick up a conversation, that loves God, loves their own family, and loves America.

Key Point:
Parents can teach positive socialization at home without the negative influences that happen in government and private schools.

Home is where the truth is:
Adults who were homeschooled are more likely to have Christian beliefs and less likely to use drugs.

Action Item:
Start a conversation with a homeschooled family, and interact with the kids. You might say something to the parents like, "I read that homeschooled kids are some of the best-socialized kids, could I have a casual chat with your family?" I can promise you they've never heard that one before! Keep it light with the kids, ask what book they're reading, or what they like to do for fun. Could you invite them over for coffee or lunch so that you can continue the conversation with the parents and kids on a personal level? Let them know that you're researching and praying about removing your kids from school, and truly appreciate any information they can share. If they're like me, they'll not only be flattered that you value their advice, but will want to minister to you in any way they can.

LIE #2:

I Could Never Homeschool, I Don't Have the Patience.

*"The most difficult thing is the decision to act, the
rest is merely tenacity."*
—Amelia Earhart

*"Fools give full vent to their rage, but the wise
bring calm in the end." Proverbs 29:11*

"**G**OD BLESS YOU! I could never homeschool my kids,
I don't have the patience."

This is the second most common line that I
hear directly after I utter those two words, "We
homeschool." And while I appreciate the blessing followed
by the assumption that I'm a patient person, I don't accept
this as a good enough excuse as to why you won't try to
educate your kids at home. It's so easy to flippantly throw it
out there like any good excuse that allows you to blow off
something you don't really want to do. Like: "No, I'm sorry I
can't help you move. I have a bad back." Or, "Sorry I missed
your one-year-old's birthday party. My plants needed
watering." Homeschooling isn't about patience, it's about
resolve. So, what sounds like a plausible excuse at the time
is not one which is permanent. Just like we can target and
strengthen those back muscles, we can work those patience
muscles for composure and imperturbability when dealing
with our li'l flock.

Let me be the first one to admit that when I started
homeschooling, I quickly saw how unholy, impatient, and

angry I can get, and that's just during a game of checkers with the five-year-old. I also came to another realization though: God called me to homeschool. A favorite platitude definitely holds true here: *God doesn't call the equipped. He equips the called.* After reading this book, you will see without a doubt that the benefits of homeschooling far outweigh the harms of continuing to send them to school. And it's far more beneficial to us parents to work on our poor character traits than to throw our hands in the air and give in to the superabundance of evil that's out to win the hearts and souls of our children.

First, let's talk about our lack of patience. I completely understand where you're coming from! I'm constantly struggling with lack of patience which gives vent to anger. For Lent, I gave up cussing which should give you some indication of my malediction.

To cling to my sanity, I wake up at 4 AM many mornings to get some miles with my running group. Heart-pounding-out-of-my-chest camaraderie and adult conversations are necessary and regenerative for me. Before dawn one muggy morning, I ran down a dimly lit paved fitness trail with my good friend, Carolyn. She's fast, muscular with a six-pack, and an Iron Man triathlete who has a few years of homeschooling experience on me. She's blessed with beauty and a joyful and benevolent personality bubbling over with the love of Christ. When she shows up to a party with her casserole dish, it's healthy *and* a crowd favorite. "Carolyn, we simply must have this recipe," everyone gushes. She moonlights by bringing babies into the world as a full-time delivery nurse and even coached me through the birth of my son—sans pain meds! She's the kind of woman that you look at and say, *How does she do it all, and how does she do it so well?* Therefore, when she spouts wisdom, I listen.

On this particular run, I let on that I didn't think I had the patience to keep all this parent-led education *and* my healthy mind under the same roof. Always quick to get frustrated with my kids at missed words on the easy readers, and getting snippy when I wasn't checking all the items off my to-do list that day, were some emergent patterns of which I was not so proud.

Like the clapping bystanders along the 26-mile run portion of her IronMan triathlon, she urged me on between breaths, "God blessed you with those children. He chose *you*. Therefore, he is going to equip you to teach them."

That's right, Love, out of the seven billion people on the planet, you were chosen by God to raise and mentor that little bundle of joy. No one else. YOU. Did you lose patience when you taught them to speak their first language, or when you taught them to walk or use the potty? (Ok, you probably lost it a couple of times there, but understandably so.)

In her personal writings, Mother Teresa penned this prayer,

"Sweetest Lord, make me appreciative of the dignity of my call and its many responsibilities. Never permit me to disgrace it by giving way to coldness, unkindness or impatience."

It's truly a beautiful thought and a high bar that St. Teresa of Calcutta set. If anyone could achieve those standards, it would have been she. One of the holiest women of the 20th century, Mother Teresa spent hours in silent prayer at the start of every day. The rest of it she spent pulling the forgotten poorest of the poor out of the gutters and trash dumps of Calcutta to nurse their oozing wounds, demonstrating to them the love of Jesus. What an inspiration of holiness!

Alas, I'm no saint. Nor do I have hours of silence every day, so I know that patience is hard. I always joke with friends, *Don't pray for patience, because the Lord will give you plenty of instances to practice it.* You'll get stuck in traffic and have to clean up spilled milk after you're already flustered from refereeing the bickering children. The printer will run out of ink, the Wi-Fi will be down, and the cat will claw your couch to shreds all because you wanted a little practicing of the ol' blessed virtue.

Allow me to share with you some of the best advice I ever got. There we were on a camping trip to Savannah, Georgia, which brought us to the Cathedral Basilica of St. John the Baptist. This striking French Gothic church built in the late 1800s beckons visitors of all denominations and faith backgrounds with its 81 stained glass windows, and gargoyles above twin tower spires that soar hundreds of feet in the air. The iconography is breathtaking and as I took it all in, I was struck by the ornately carved wood on the door of the confessional. And wait...score! They were holding confession in just a few minutes. Now, if you're Catholic, you know to jump at the chance to go to confession when you're out of town to a priest that you'll never see again. It's like the comfortable anonymity of wigs and sunglasses for Jerry Springer guests. Finally, they have the courage to come clean with a heinous sin against a loved one in front of millions on national TV because they won't be recognized in their hometown.

Not hesitating, I stepped into the beautiful confessional and began confessing the same sin that, bar-none I always have to confess: snapping at my kids, losing my temper in impatience. The priest told me something that I immediately started to do, and it helps me every single time I do it.

"When you feel yourself losing your temper, pray in front of them, out loud," he said with his soft Irish accent.

"Something like, Lord, give me calm. Help me with my patience, help me to love these kids like you do, Lord. Make sure that it's in that moment that you're upset and that your children hear the prayer coming off your lips."

Talk about a game-changer! That prayer delivers grace, calms me down, and allows my babies to hear me saying a prayer that is for them as much as it is for me. Now, when I am getting huffy and losing my patience, I will often hear the soft little voice of one of my children slowly saying, "Mommy, *I think you need to pray.*" That innocent little voice is a testimony that prayer works and they know it does because of seeing Mommy calm down so many times through that supplication.

As a wooden rolling pin smoothens a lump of dough across the counter, that small prayer softens my angry ridges so that I can attempt to follow the counsel of the apostle James: "Everyone *(especially parents)* should be quick to listen, slow to speak and slow to become angry, because human anger does not produce the righteousness that God desires."[1]

Parents, we should try with all our might to never angrily rebuke our children because it does not produce the righteousness that God desires. Scolding is an angry and sinful reaction that brings pain and models sinful anger for our children. It's only a matter of time until they are doing that exact thing to their siblings, friends, and perhaps even to you.

How did I not realize that my angry outbursts were forming my children into angry little humans? One of our children became so angry that their siblings couldn't even take a drink of water without getting reamed for swallowing too loudly. If this child, on the constant verge of exploding didn't get their entire way or had to do 30 more seconds of chores, the thunderstorm of stomping, pouting, and harrumphing would go on for hours. Usually well-behaved, obedient, and quiet, this child had me searching for answers to why this was happening and what we could do to stop it. As I scoured podcasts in the parenting genre for tips on dealing with angry children, the Lord worked the algorithm for his glory bringing me to Biblical parenting guru, Ginger Hubbard. Her podcast, which I inhaled like a master class, helped me identify the reasons why that seed of anger had taken root in my child and was now controlling them. Er uh, how do I put this...It was our fault as parents. There are many things that parents do to cause anger to develop in their children, like being inconsistent with discipline. There could be a lack of marital harmony, or if the parents make the child think that the world revolves around them. If parents don't ask for forgiveness when they're wrong anger can fester. Instead of being too heavy on scolding, it's important to have a balance of praise, training, and admonition. The biggie for my spouse and me was that we modeled sinful anger and scolded our children pretty much on a daily basis.

So, you don't have the patience to homeschool? Well, neither do I! I was basically teaching *Anger 101, Snapping As a Way of Life*. This is when we realized that administering Biblical discipline in a loving and gentle manner was one of the best things that my husband and I could do for our family. The wisest man to ever live said, "A gentle answer turns away wrath, but a harsh word stirs up anger."[2] Instead of provoking our children to anger, we have to take those angry thoughts captive and make them obedient to Christ. Hubbard gives us a standard against which to hold ourselves, "We know that we are ready to reprove our children biblically when we can speak to them in a normal tone of voice with carefully measured words."[3] Berating our children in anger makes them "*resent* instead of wanting to *repent"*.[4] Just like the prayer that the priest told me to pray, we must do something in our mind to hold those angry thoughts prisoner and not let them burst forth on our poor kids, even if they did something completely disobedient and rotten. Are we going to blow it? Yes. But I promise you can learn to control your anger and become a more patient parent who seldom loses their temper.

It sounded unbelievable to me when I first heard it. Don't ever yell at your kids? Don't ever scold? My parents certainly scolded me, yelled at me every time I slammed the door during Jeopardy. My grandparents yelled at my parents. It's what we know. Are there truly parents who don't yell in anger after their child has been outright defiant, spilled red Gatorade on the new rug, or hit his defenseless baby brother across the head with a Tonka truck? Yes, there are, and they aren't mythical characters like Kris Kringle, but you might have to go clear to the North Pole to find them.

The Inuit people live in the Arctic tundra, at the top of the world, over a vast territory spanning nearly three thousand miles from the Bering Strait, across Alaska, Canada, and all the way over to Greenland. Over the past millennia, they figured out how to survive in one of the most severe climates on Earth. They thrived because of innovations like waterproof pants made from seal skins, breeding dogs specifically for pulling sleds, and aerodynamic kayaks that allowed them to hunt the planet's biggest creatures. They garden, hunt caribou and seal, and braid fishing lines with caribou sinew. These survival skills are incredible, but there is something about this culture that actually blows my Western-parent mind even more. They never act in anger toward their children! They don't even get flustered. For real, these mothers have so much composure that they labor, without pain medication, so quietly that even in childbirth they won't wake the others in the igloo.[5]

It's uncanny how unshakeable the Inuit parents are. When a kid kicks boiling tea across the abode the adults don't say a thing, they don't even flinch! Even though it's literally melting the floor. Michaeleen Doucleff, author of *Hunt, Gather, Parent*, sought ancient wisdom for parenting. And boy, am I glad that she ventured with her three-year-old daughter to the Arctic village of Kugaaruk to live with and learn from these calm mothers gleaning simple, ancient parenting wisdom. Because of her, we know that it's possible to follow the Golden rule of Inuit parenting which is "Never yell at a child". For generations, Inuit parents have never yelled at their children.

"When you yell at children, they stop listening," said seventy-four-year-old Sidonie Nirlungayuk whose mother also silently gave birth in the middle of the night. Her theory as to why American kids don't listen is because their parents shout at them, "You can tell when a parent yells at a child because the child doesn't listen anymore."[6] Many clinical psychologists in America agree with ancient Inuit wisdom that says yelling at kids has a negative impact on them, and actually trains them *not* to listen.[7]

What the Inuit have known for generations, and we Americans may have forgotten is that parents are the teachers of emotional regulation. If we model composure instead of lashing out, then our kids will see an example of being calm under the pressure of anger. However, if instead we lash out in anger, we are teaching them to yell. Not only that, but we are also sending the message that yelling is a means to an end.

Controlling your anger and never scolding does not mean that you are going to let your kids get away with everything and run all over you. Oh, no no no. Once you're calm, you'll be ready to administer biblical discipline which is more effective than yelling. Teaching biblical character is the prequel to Biblical discipline and when the two go hand in hand, parents can gently and lovingly bring peace to any situation.

We've drilled our children since the age of two that obedience is: "Doing what is expected of me, immediately, cheerfully, and thoroughly." Leaning on the authority of scripture, we made sure that they memorized Colossians 3:20, "Children, obey your parents in everything, for this pleases the Lord." So, when my son ignores my request to stop throwing the ball in the house, I have two choices. I can angrily yell something like, "Son! I told you no kicking or throwing balls, now give me the football!" (Which will cause him to get angry.) Or I can simply stay calm and ask, "Are you being obedient or disobedient?" If he doesn't answer the question correctly, I'll answer it for him. Then we are going to go into a semi-deep little discussion about how much I love him and cannot allow him to sin against God and his Mama. Now, don't even roll your eyes and think I'm being dramatic. We need to teach our kids not to sin and how to live by God's commands. I've prayed for chances to do it like, "Lord, if my child is lying, help me to catch them, so that I can teach them about honesty." The Lord is always faithful!

As we help our kids develop character, we are wise to see it as another beautiful aspect of homeschooling...that *our* character as parents is developing too! It truly is a beautiful phenomenon that occurs, as you pour biblical truth, sacred scripture, morals, and integrity into your babies, you can't help but be transformed. Your spouse and yourself are going to be completely different parents after a few years of homeschooling. The sooner you realize that good character is the most important subject to teach your little brood of hypers, the sooner they'll become more bearable to live with, and enjoyable to teach.

The family won't be free from quarreling and misbehaviors, but more harmony is harnessed when character development is the top priority, which brings us to the next lie to debunk. It's the one about the importance of schoolwork.

Key Point:
Yes, your kids will try your ever-lovin' last nerve on a daily basis, but your patience will grow with prayer, practice, and the teaching of good behavior to your little ones.

"Patience is the root and guardian of all the virtues."
—St. Pope Gregory the Great

Action Item:
Tips for parents to overcome angry outbursts:
The next time you are about to lose your temper in front of your children, pray this prayer out loud in front of them:
"Lord, give me calm. Help me with my patience, help me to love these kids like you do, Lord. Amen."
Then leave the room.
Or—
Don't utter a word. (Pray the prayer in your head.)
Leave the room.

LIE #3:

The Highest Priority Is Getting Our Schoolwork Done.

"Isn't it absurd to send children out to jobs and to school, and to do all you can to prepare them for these, and yet not to 'bring them up in the chastening and admonition of the Lord (Eph 6:4)?' Discipline is needed, not eloquence; character, not cleverness; deeds, not words. These gain a man the kingdom."
— *St. John Chrysostom*

"Love the Lord your God with all your heart, with all your soul, and with all your strength. 6 Never forget these commands that I am giving you today. 7 Teach them to your children. Repeat them when you are at home and when you are away, when you are resting and when you are working." Deuteronomy 6:4-8

THIS MIGHT SOUND A little backward at first, but who cares if your child can read at grade level when there's a risk of losing their heart to evil? Who cares if your high school-aged student can diagram a cell if they don't know and fear the Creator of all cells? So much more important than anything found in a textbook is the foundation of good character and imbuing your faith in your children. "For what is a man profited, if he shall gain the whole world and lose his own soul? Or what shall a man give in exchange for his soul?"[1]

This is so easy to forget as we veer into the rut of, "What math lesson are you on? Did we get grammar done this week?

Are we behind?" Let me share one egregious example of my forgetfulness of this. It was around two p.m., and we were churning toward a very productive day, complete with a ziggurat project that included homemade salt dough (pshhhh....easy, is that all you got?), a trip to tutoring, the library, and the b-ball court. We had edited a seventh-grade level essay to resemble just that, and my house was clean because it was that blessed second Thursday when Tammy comes to clean it. Friend, I had even connected some pieces on my 750-piece Farmer's Market scene puzzle. As far as a homeschool day goes for me, this is bliss, a solid 10 out of 10.

My twelve-year-old had a couple more things on her to-do list when she asked me if she could read her Bible reading for youth group. Do you think I said, "Sure honey, you want to read Blessed Scripture to later discuss with your middle school friends upon your own Spirit-led volition? That's so wonderful! I wish I could be more open to the Spirit like you are!"

Nope. I told her, Go. Finish. Your. Vocabulary.

Why didn't I just tell her to take off those modest shorts with the seven-inch inseam and go throw on some daisy dukes while I was at it, oh, and go have one of Mommy's White Claws, you deserve it!

Major parenting fail y'all! It wasn't until hours later that it dawned on me that I had missed a wonderful opportunity to encourage her in the most important thing, the Word of the Lord.

Obviously, I'm not trying to raise any derelicts, so yes, there is a time and place to get our schoolwork done. But I adhered early and without regrets to the wisdom of Charlotte Mason who says, "The mother who takes pains to endow her children with good habits secures for herself smooth and easy days." Mason was a British educator who devoted her life to improving the quality of children's education at the turn of the nineteenth century, a time when education was relegated to children depending on their social class. The poorer kids had to learn a trade while the hoity-toity feasted on fine arts and literature. Well, her methods were so effective that her dream of a "liberal education for all" came to fruition. Now, her writings and teaching practices, collectively referred to as *The Charlotte Mason Method* are fan favorites in the homeschool world.

Some of her methods include having children play outside for at least two or three hours and doing nature studies through observation. She believed in keeping lessons short, interesting, and fun. She taught her teachers to immerse children in beautiful art and classical music. History came alive through "living books"—quality literature (fiction or non-fiction) written by an author with a passion for the subject which begets wonderfully descriptive imagery and captivating plots— instead of dry textbooks. Of extreme importance for learners is cultivating good habits that will lead to self-governance. These good habits are like the rails on which our children's lives can run smoothly and it's our job as parents to teach those habits.

My husband's and my parenting lives changed when we found and employed a character curriculum written by Marylin Boyer, homeschooling mother of 17 children, called *Character Concepts*. This biblically based homespun product, takes the jewels of wisdom found in Scripture and applies them to all the good qualities young students need to succeed. Starting with preschoolers, it has character-building studies for all ages and we've used it non-stop for *yeeeeaaaars* in our homeschool. While parenting kids toward good character is an arduous and decades-long calling, the earlier you start, the more good behavior sticks, and the more fruitful your efforts.

You can't let up though, the minute that you let character and integrity take a back seat to math worksheets you are just one undone chore, unwanted assignment, or sibling quarrel away from possible meltdown (from you the teacher *or* from your students). That's why there are other things that are also more important than "bookwork."

Outside time, field trips, real-life learning, and one-on-one time to bond with your babies are so important in laying the groundwork for a firm foundation in solid character. Truly, it's about building relationships and teaching their hearts. My kids thrive when I amp up affection like cuddles during read-aloud, or when I help them find their passions through interests and hobbies. There is no "school work" so joyful as sitting on the carpet and building a Lincoln Log fort with my son who is obsessed with historical military battles right now. Strategically placing soldiers, cannons, and horses for mini-military campaigns, his mood flourishes. Through the counting and stacking of little wooden pieces, I am actually helping the Lord to build up my son in discovering his life's purpose and passion. Max Lucado says it beautifully in the letter to parents at the beginning of his children's book *The Oak Inside the Acorn.*

"God prewired your infant. He scripted your child's strengths. He set your teen on a trajectory. God gave you an eighteen-year research project. Ask yourself, your spouse, and your friends: what sets this child apart? Childhood tendencies forecast adult abilities. Read them. Discern them. Affirm them. Cheerlead them.

You've been given a book with no title—read it! A CD with no cover—listen to it! An island with no owner—explore it! Resist the urge to label before you study. Attend carefully to the unique childhood of your child.

Uncommon are the parents who attempt to learn these God-given abilities—and blessed are their children."[2]

Instead of spending too much of that eighteen-year research project worrying about reading levels, copy work, and college admissions, build relationships. Read the Bible and pray together. Attend church as a family. Then all of these tools will interlink to develop a passion-driven, well-rounded citizen with a foundation of faith. All the other subjects will fall much more easily into place than if you never had.

I can't wait to tell you about some more very effective, enjoyable, and simple tools for the homeschool parent's arsenal that will revolutionize the way your kids learn and the way you teach. Pair the aforementioned character work with the tips in the next chapter and you will soon be dominating this homeschool life.

Key Point:
Teaching faith and good character to your children is more important than bookwork.

"The question is not,—how much does the youth know when he has finished his education—but how much does he care?

And about how many orders of things does he care? In fact, how large is the room in which he finds his feet set? And therefore how full is the life he has before him?"
—Charlotte Mason

Action Item:
Set all phones on their charger and forget about them, and without any distractions in the next hour, like having to make dinner or leave for sports practice, engage with your child in the hobby or interest of their choosing. Be there to guide, give tips, and teach where necessary, while keeping the main thing to simply enjoy it with them. (This is how a good day of homeschooling will feel.)

LIE #4:

You Have to Follow A Certain Curricula to Succeed. There's a Perfect One Out There For You. All You Have To Do Is Find It.

"All children are born artists, the problem is to remain an artist as we grow up."—Pablo Picasso

"Trust in the Lord with all your heart. Never rely on what you think you know. Remember the Lord in everything you do, and he will show you the right way." Proverbs 3:5-6

YOU WILL BE DOING yourself and your family a disservice if you are always on the hunt for that curriculum that makes teaching fun and easy—and compels learning to be alluring and addicting. We want every lesson mapped out daily on a handy calendar tucked nicely into a three-ring binder that the kids can't wait to grab off the shelf and dive into; annihilating all the objectives while crushing the comprehension. Right? *That is* until the curriculum arrives and we can't even figure out *how* to set up the Lord-Of-The-Rings-trilogy-sized binder.

I'm not saying to throw all the curriculum out because none of it's useful. There are some great tools out there in the form of curriculum. My kids would've been severely lacking in math, had I not found the wonderful parent-obsolete math curriculum *Teaching Textbooks*. And wow, do I love my *Connecting With History* curriculum that teaches us about ancient cultures, portrays thrilling historical figures, and introduces biblical characters along the Bible's timeline. What an adventure that's been! What I am saying is that there are a couple of tools that prove to be better for your student and much more fun and engaging for you, their teacher, than the right curricula. They are: reading aloud and imaginative play.[1]

READING ALOUD

It turns out that the least expensive, most relaxing, and bonding thing you can possibly do with your child—reading aloud, is also the most beneficial. Experts suggest it's the number one thing that you can do to foster linguistic proficiency, which includes writing and speaking. Today for the vast majority of kids the main sources of input of language are media (television, Internet) and peers, depriving kids of the rich vocabulary that books provide. Even if a child is exposed to great vocabulary, when they are around their counterparts in a classroom setting, they tend to dumb themselves down to blend in with the lowest intelligence level. It's a survival skill, ya' know, so they aren't mocked for their exceptional word use. Another key source of language— parental parlance can still be lacking despite our best efforts to talk to our children with mature and robust language. Bless our hearts, we get so tired we can barely keep our kids' names straight, let alone use multisyllabic words past four p.m. The vocabulary that our children will hear from a great read-aloud are generally not the ones they hear in common conversations.

The benefits of reading aloud are gleaned no matter the age or socioeconomic standing and cannot be overstated. Early on, the single most important activity for building the knowledge for eventual success in reading and broader academic skills, such as persistence and the ability to sustain attention is reading aloud to children. [2] Even for teens, reading test scores show a powerful correlation: the more they were read to as children, the higher the scores at age fifteen, and this holds true regardless of income.[3] Children who are consistently read to or listen to audiobooks become older kids who like reading.[4]

Even older kids who are strong readers reap huge benefits from read-alouds. Words that they might've skipped over because they don't know them, will be heard and meanings more likely inferred from an audiobook or from a parent reading to them. An idiom that would've gone totally over their head can be explained by the more experienced person who's reading aloud.

Aside from the pedagogical pluses are the even more important familial benefits. For my family, the read-aloud has bonded us through stories, grounded us in our nightly routine, and ridden with us on numerous road trips, cinching tighter the memories we share. An emergency room visit that required stitches over an eyebrow was made less frantic by an audiobook. With two adults, four kids, and a hospital bed all packed into a private room, the nervous energy was a bit overbearing, the pepper-spraying of questions from my kids sending me near overload. I grabbed my phone, flipped to the Hoopla reading app, played the story to which we'd been listening for the last few weeks, and suddenly a calm came over the sanitized cell.

The classic *Johnnie Tremaine* written by Esther Forbes accompanied us on our trip to explore Colonial Williamsburg, fascinating us with the Boston Tea Party and other tumults that were happening through the colonies in the 1700s. *The Captain's Dog* written by Roland Smith made the Lewis and Clark expedition come to life through the eyes of its furry hero *Seaman* as we followed their journey 214 years later. The series *Tuesdays at the Castle* by Jessica Day George had us enraptured every night for six months as we all piled in one room—even my manly-man husband was cheering for the 10-year-old heroine and her magical griffin, Rufus.

You don't have to be reading an epic novel to see the mesmerizing effect of reading aloud to all ages. Today, my teen will stop scrolling Pinterest "nail polish ideas" or whatever mature, sassy trend she's pinning and come over and curl up on the bean bag with us as soon as I bust out a beautiful picture book (even if it's aimed for the younger ones). It takes only moments for the story to wash over us all, relaxing us and holding us spellbound.

There are many places to find lists for captivating read-alouds, simplycharlottemason.com has an extensive list of them or what they refer to as "living" books. Sarah Mackenzie over at Read Aloud Revival has an invaluable blog and podcast with booklists for every season, age group, and category of armchair-tested books. These resources are great places to do more research on just how important reading aloud is to your student. The stress-free simplicity will keep you rejuvenated, and your home school on track. There have been seasons of my kids' education when I simply read the books and did the accompanying activities on readaloudrevival.com, like cooking recipes mentioned in the story—and it was enough! The savory smell of onion and cumin wafted through our home as we prepared Nigerian beef stew just like Omu makes in *Thank You, Omu!* By Oge Mora, a meal that has become my daughter's all-time favorite meal, go-to request, and dinner-time staple. Studying the history and geography of a beloved story cements the new information in their brains. Mackenzie rightly calls read-aloud "teaching from rest." I concur! The least stressful, most engaging and rewarding activity I do with my children is a brilliant read-aloud.

IMAGINATIVE PLAY

The other tool that will quite literally foster genius in your sweet babies is imaginative play. In 1957, psychologist and author Dr. Harold McCurdy investigated the lives of twenty geniuses like John Stuart Mill, the most influential English language philosopher of the nineteenth century, and Gottfried Wilhelm Leibniz, a great mind of the eighteenth century, who made important contributions to the fields of metaphysics, philosophy, mathematics, physics, geology, and history, as well as Blaise Pascal, French mathematician, philosopher, writer, and theologian. Dr. McCurdy aimed to find commonalities in their lives that might have aided their intellectual development. Here's what he found in his published study, *The Childhood Pattern of Genius*[5]:

In the geniuses he studied, the typical pattern of development had three common aspects: one, a high degree of attention focused upon the child by parents and other adults through education and abundant love, two, isolation from other children especially outside the family, and three, lots of fantastical imaginative playtime.

If you didn't make the immediate connection, let me clarify, this trifecta is basically the homeschooling recipe! Do you hear that sweet parents? Just the very act of showering love on your child as you educate them disengaged from their peers puts them in the company of greatness. People like the sixth president of the United States, John Quincy Adams, and the greatest German literary figure of the modern era, Johann Wolfgang von Goethe.

You know what else I like about this study? It tells me that boredom is a path to genius. If they are never bored or constantly have a glowing screen in their face, then when will that imagination kick in? For certain seasons of our life, we don't allow recreational screen time during the week. That's only a weekend privilege that must be earned throughout the week by completing all their work and chores. (And ok, let's be totally truthful here, if Dad's in charge, suddenly that rule is lifted and they're all watching a movie together. Or let's say they didn't finish all their priorities, if mama needs some quiet writing time on the weekends, I will just overlook that minor detail of unfinished math assignments for a couple of blessed hours of silence. But that's only when I'm on deadlines for any of my kids that are reading this. So, you could liken our screen restrictions to "the pirate code" *of The Pirates of the Caribbean,* as Captain Barbossa says, "The code is more what you'd call guidelines than actual rules."

It is *totally* worth the parental energy required to enforce the code to restrict glowing screens as a boredom safety net when you witness imagination and creativity kick in. Kids live-action role-play, draw, color, play board games or card games, read, create, play outside, practice their instrument, and interact with their siblings! Of course, I'm not saying that I never hear, "I'm boredddddddddddd." But when I do hear it, the kids know that I am going to respond with my canned answer: "Boredom is good! Imagination and genius are birthed from boredom!"

This genius recipe is going to be rife with opportunities for them to find their own interests which, properly stoked will lead them to creatively discover their passion. Educational experts agree that young children have an "extraordinary capacity for innovation"[6], and that "genius is as common as dirt."[7] A child—or any person that is given a creative license toward their passion will be happier and possibly more knowledgeable than their counterpart that has trudged through the institution, even all the way through college earning a degree in the same discipline.

Have we not all witnessed the trend of degrees becoming useless after seeing the neighbor's kid come home after earning their college degree, to wait tables or work in a job that has nothing to do with their field of study, maybe it's even our own child, or ourselves! UNESCO said that in a mere 30 years (circa 2005-2035) more people worldwide will be graduating through education than since the beginning of history[8]. As technology changes the workforce and global population explodes, suddenly you need a master's or Ph.D., when it used to be a bachelor's degree would get you the job. You could try to help your kids keep up with the rest of the world on this dull track to a good job. Or you can promptly quit the conveyor-belt-to-college mentality, and teach them to develop something that's in danger of disappearing, yet employers and college admissions want it more and more: creativity.

In the most popular TED Talk of all time, *Do Schools Kill Creativity*, International Advisor on Education Sir Ken Robinson contends that as degrees become worthless amid educational inflation, we should quit ruthlessly squandering our children's talents and put creativity up there on a pedestal just as highly as literacy. "If you think of it, the whole system of public education around the world is a protracted process of university entrance. And the consequence is that many highly talented, brilliant, creative people think they're not, because the thing they were good at at school wasn't valued, or was actually stigmatized,"[9] said Robinson. In recent past generations, we were steered away from that which we showed passion and proficiency if it wasn't practical for a job. You're good at painting, but you better major in business administration because who wants to be a starving artist? How can you make a living as a dancer? That's fun for a hobby, but please stop dancing and do your calculus homework," parents, teachers, and other well-meaning people told us.

PASSION DRIVEN LEARNING

When we allow our children to follow their passions, to create their own course of study, our home school will be filled with joy, your child with internal motivation. For it is they who need to find their own path, we can't find it for them. Think tank guru and author of *Passion Driven Education* Connor

Boyack succinctly puts it, "These passions are the ideas that resonate with their soul and augment their sense of wonder. They allow us to speak to our children in language they already know and love. Providing our children with the freedom and time to focus on their passions honors their individuality and validates their positive choices. It allows them to be themselves rather than saying and doing what others tell them."[10]

While you allow your children to be themselves, you are saving them from anxiety that comes from a lack of control of their own life. As you guide them to discover God's path for their life through the passions that he's wired in them, you'll also be keeping them from taking some very dark journeys through anxiety and depression. Dr. William Stixrud and Ned Johnson, coauthors of *The Self-Driven Child,* specialize in helping kids gain control over their own life, to find their inner drive, and make the most of their potential. Thanks to them we know that a low sense of control is enormously stressful and that autonomy is key to developing motivation. It really is a matter of brain science. Giving kids freedom to make their own decisions makes them feel in charge because their brain is learning to make hard choices, while figuring out how to protect itself from that helpless feeling caused by stress. The more struggles they overcome, the better they'll manage their own stress, and the more their prefrontal cortex will be able to regulate their amygdala—the part of the brain that regulates emotions like fear and aggression, reward processing, and decision-making. It's like working a competency muscle, the more control they have, the better decision-makers they will become.[11] Or, as the talented Mark Twain put it, "Good decisions come from experience. Experience comes from making bad decisions."

But my child is too *blank* to make their own decisions. Insert fitting adjective: young, wild, scatter-brained, reckless, irresponsible, obsessed-with-Minecraft-- they all went through my mind too. We simply cannot wait until their prefrontal lobes are fully developed before we relinquish some control to our children over their own life. Not only will we be contributing to an unmotivated, anxious, depressed adulthood—we'd be waiting until their late twenties to early thirties to finally let them think for themselves! *But what if we do give her control, then she fails, wouldn't that cause her to become depressed?* No! Dr. Srtixrud emphasizes that adolescents are more likely to become depressed from a lack of self-control than from failure.[12] Especially when you the parent are a safe base, who teaches them that failures aren't bad, they are learning experiences, opportunities for improvement.

So what if they make some bad choices, there are some great life lessons in consequences. You forgot your lunch? No, I'm not bringing it to you, you'll have to feel the pang of hunger for that lesson. You brought ankle socks to the skating rink after I told you to find some long socks? You'll have to feel the sting of blisters to send that lesson home. You missed the deadline to apply for an internship? I'm sure next time you'll make note of important dates. This is where emotional intelligence starts to mature as well, kids need to know what matters to them. They need knowledge and emotional input. What happens when they experience envy, remorse, admiration, compassion, anger, resentment? They have to work through their emotions and use them to make healthy decisions. We wish we could, but parents, we can't override their emotions for them. They need to work through them in the safety of our love and support. A good amount of control is related to what every parent wants for their kids: physical and mental health, academic success and happiness.

In 2013, a skinny little guy with long locks hanging out of his pink ski beanie, looking cool and comfortable in his jeans and sneakers, stood on stage at the University of Nevada. He gave a TED Talk about his way of educating himself which brought him happiness. Thirteen-year-old Logan Laplante, who would've rather been snow skiing at the time, hoped for maybe a thousand views. So far, it's reached over 10 million views and is the second most-watched TED Talk of all time—out of 40,000! Laplante told viewers how he "hacks his education." With the creativity of a hacker's mindset, he bases his learning on the study and practice of being happy and healthy. His innovative learning methods include learning what he wants in the ways most enticing to him. He peppers in classes and camps, internships, and online resources. He finds balance employing Dr. Robert Walsh's eight therapeutic lifestyle changes, which are exercise, diet and nutrition, time in nature, service to others, relationships, recreation, relaxation and stress management, and religious and spiritual activities.

If you've ever shaken the freshly nuked popcorn bag upside down over the trash with the tiniest opening in the bag to eradicate all the un-popped kernels, then you can imagine how our children can do the same with their education. Dumping the stuff that's too tough to digest—the rubbish that they don't care about, to focus on the tasty morsels that they want to shove in their face by the handful. Unfortunately, government schools use the opposite approach, making them consume all the roughage: stuffing their brains with multitudinous, unrelated facts and forcing them to regurgitate it on a test nine weeks later, or worse nine months later on an end-of-course exam. By the end of high school, most kids have been conditioned to think that there's only one path to success, which looks like this: I must make good grades, accrue lots of activities and club participation for my college resume, get into college, earn a degree. Also, since any little mistake can derail those plans, autonomy has long since been squelched. With room for one or two electives like art, music, speech, or creative writing per year, creativity falls by the wayside, as does the nerve to dare to be different.

As we allow our children freedom to learn about whatever they want, parents can feel some relief that we don't have to be an expert on everything. We're merely their advocates and consultants on *their* journey to proficiency. Exposing them to a gentle feast of subjects, time in nature, sports, and art, we watch their interests grow. We take care to not pooh-pooh their obsessions. Instead seize them as opportunities to imbue your kids with relevant information to that which they're already interested. It's a way to speak to their hearts and in the teen years—believe me, you'll need this no matter how well you get along with them now—it's common ground.

Passion driven learning works for all ages, with more guidance needed in the younger years when they're learning to read and developing their research skills. When my kids were lower elementary level, I would let them choose the subject and we would learn every angle of it—history, math, science, literature all flowing into an interesting river of knowledge about one thing, also known as *unit studies*. I'd download a unit study for about five dollars and with a good bit of printer ink we were off on learning adventures about dolphins, Lewis and Clark, trains, robots, sports, seasons, camouflage in creation, Benjamin Franklin, oceans, eyes, brains, reptiles and more. For years we learned like this, all together, learning the same thing. Peppering in some read-alouds, camping trips, and handi-crafts this served as the foundation to build on as they grew older and became passionate about their own interests.

As those interests start to flourish, we take a step back and become more of a consultant. In the business world consultants offer expert advice, find ways to solve problems, assess the pros and cons of possible strategies, and help implement solutions. You'll remain a valuable asset in their education, allowing them self-governance and time to learn from their mistakes. When your family is cruising along through passion-driven learning you may have to resist the urge to do things that suck the fun right out of it. Don't you go assigning book reports, drawing up a quiz, or requiring a thousand-word report by the end of the week. If they are enjoying reading for the sheer love of knowledge and adventure, then your job is done! Some people like, veteran teachers, government school graduates, and those extrinsically motivated by praise might insist that grades are a necessary paycheck for the learner to continue to work. Most of the time this isn't the case when the learner is intrinsically motivated by passion. Yes, there may be a streak of laziness in all of us, so providing structure, like a consistent daily schedule, time for research, and regular field trips, will serve as the external motivators if they're needed. When given autonomy, your learner will value your feedback, and look to you as a sounding board. There will be copious conversations about that which they are passionate, you might find yourself at times painting on a smile and forcing your own enthusiasm to keep up with theirs.

When I first started allowing my nine-year-old to chart his learning course through his passions, he spent hours studying football teams and their records. I wanted many times to stop him to "come read" or "do math". However, my want of nagging quickly faded when he ran up to me with a watermelon-rind smile saying, "I'm having so much fun!" Hugging me, he immediately turned and ran back to his office chair, flopping seat first and swinging his legs for momentum and a spin, to continue his eager research.

Going out in public with him is like having a Bing search engine for football facts in your pocket. Only this one is completely hands-free, with blonde hair and braces. At the meat counter of our family-owned grocer, the employee wrapping the shish kabobs in bacon had on a Jets hat.

"Quick, Bud, give me a tidbit about the Jets, so I can chat this guy up!"

Instantly my passionate little football-fact-machine responded, "They just lost to the Lions and they're on a three-game losing streak."

Armed with new knowledge, I stepped up to the glass dome counter that housed the seafood.

"How 'bout those Jets huh, on a little bit of a losing streak."

"Yeah, it's tough being a Jets fan, but I'm grateful for the wins we got," he said with a friendly smile.

Now more than just a positive interaction with a stranger, this fellow football fan shared one of his earliest memories, meeting the 1978 Jets team at his dad's mechanic shop. I don't know if you've gotten to tell one of your earliest memories lately, but it's always a poignant conversation of which to be a part.

"We still hold on to hope," he said handing me the package of bacon-wrapped chicken kabobs.

"How long has it been since the Jets won the Super Bowl," I asked Dash when we were out of earshot.

"They haven't won since 1969," he said showing his teeth as he winced at the harshness of the reality.

My son is logic-smart and absolutely thrives on facts and figures and is now an endless font of player and coach's stats, and team records. He's become so knowledgeable, he even caught a mis-fact that a commentator threw out on live TV.

Follow me here, when the Dallas Cowboys beat the Washington Commanders, then the Washington Commanders beat the Green Bay Packers, but the Green Bay Packers beat the Dallas Cowboys in a three-week timespan, he analyzed data like turnovers, interceptions, passing and rushing yards all to figure out this great life's mystery (which is, none of that matters if you don't get the ball into the end zone.) He's having fun with data analytics, something I would be loathed to teach, but is the number one career in terms of increasing demand, and averages six figures.[13] Let's see where this goes.

That's another thing, let's have faith in the God that created our children, that he has them in the palm of his hands. When we rely on him to guide our children's education, he sets up appointments and works out details in divine omnipotence. To illustrate this point and the point that Sir Ken Robinson made in the most popular TED Talk of all time—that creativity is as important as literacy. Allow me to share a story.

As we checked in to the coveted Jetty Park Campground, situated across the inlet from NASA launchpads in Cocoa Beach, I squealed with delight as I read the words scribbled on the whiteboard behind the desk: *Launch Tuesday @ 5:45 AM*. For years we had tried to get a campsite when a launch was scheduled. Retired, lifestyle RVers and other lucky adventurers always seemed to have the upper hand with reservations and once there, would stay through all the launch scrubs until the rocket finally blasted off. This time we had serendipitously landed a site where we could walk out about fifty yards, sit our lawn chairs atop boulders at the water's edge, and see real-life rocket science! It was only about three days till launch, the kids' enthusiasm (and the parents' because of this free and magnificent science lesson) grew daily.

On the eve of the launch my husband and I left the teenager in charge and went on a date to a waterfront bar and grill. We watched the sunset behind the water, a feat that isn't easy on Florida's east coast, but with the angle of the inlet, happened for us that night. The TV screens behind the bar played sporting events, one played NASA TV.

"You work for NASA?" The guy on the barstool next to my husband Mat asked him.

"Oh no, we're camping over at Jetty Park."

"Oh. You here for the launch?"

"Yeah, we're going to watch it."

And just like a Star Wars fanatic gets very animated talking about the Jedi, our new friend Sam, was suddenly engaging us in a probing conversation about our interest in the space program. As my husband and I looked side-eyed at one another, we both wondered, is he a space nerd?

Over the next few drinks, we shared with him our zeal and gratitude that we would be able to watch the launch, that it was a great science and history lesson for us to witness, and basically how great it was to be on a vacation where so much learning was taking place—and that we homeschool, that surely came out pretty quickly. I proudly touted, "We homeschool and this is a science, history and nature immersion all rolled into one!"

Our new friend Sam, nodded enthusiastically, "Oh that's great! So, you like NASA?"

He grilled us on if we'd ever been to Kennedy Space Center, if our kids are interested in Space exploration, and even how we felt about NASA politically, like the handling of funds and it being the newest branch of the military.

He smiled and nodded vigorously at our answers. "Yes, yes, and we are happy about it! Good for America," we answered.

It turns out that Sam worked for Uncle Sam at NASA. Although he didn't have an engineering degree or one laden with sciences, he applied to NASA with his degree in Classical Piano. His job was to work the mathematical equations to figure out the amount of fuel that would be needed for rocket missions. He told us that his classical piano training made him a perfect fit for the math required, that jet engines burned fuel kind of like the rhythm of a classical piano piece. And then he gave us this nugget of wisdom and hope:

"If your kids are interested *at all* in space exploration, or working for NASA. Tell them they can get a job! All they need is to think outside the box. They just need to think *creatively*." Sam continued earnestly. "I went in to my NASA interview with no experience whatsoever. I just had a brain that understood music and was good at math. I then applied it to what NASA needed."

As he gushed about his pension, high pay, great schedule and traveling perks, he went on. "Not only does NASA need more women and minorities, they need people that can think for themselves."

The more the drinks flowed, the more we learned about Sam. After he showed us pictures of scorched launchpads, workstations for Mars and other highly classified things that he probably wasn't supposed to show us, he let on that he actually had two jobs at NASA, his second was to go out into the community and get a pulse for what people think about NASA. The following week he would be at the Kentucky Derby mingling to collect data, his wife bought a derby hat, he would be required to buy a mint julep and stand in line and place a bet. We joked that there were not many of his co-workers that qualified to do that kind of work, what with the engineering mindset. And that's when he reiterated the need for other-minded people.

"We know that kids are interested when they're young, we want to know when they lose that interest and why," Sam said. "Seriously, I want to encourage you to tell your kids we need them. The future of NASA needs them."

Sam was exuberant to meet two homeschool parents that were excited about NASA and making it a priority that our kids experience it. "I'm going back to my hotel room to write a report and your family is going to be the main subject!"

These divine appointments, as I like to call them, are a wonderful sign from God. As Mat and I drove back to the camper, we were both stricken by the message and could not wait to relay it to our children, which we did with the backdrop of a rocket launching into the dark sky on a humid Florida morning. Recounting the story of Sam the NASA worker, we saw a gleam in their eye as the booster rocket fell back to earth encased in a white glowing ball of gas resembling the head of an opaque jellyfish.

What happened later that day could've only been the exclamation point of the Lord driving the message home. Hours later, after lunch, we were driving to the launch pad museum of Cape Canaveral. Suddenly, the sheriff driving in front of us turned his vehicle across the traffic lane, hopped out, and put his hand up to halt traffic. Our car being the first vehicle, we had front row seats to the reason for this traffic stop. "Whoooooooa!" we all said in unison as we gaped at the giant flatbed rocket mover making its turn onto the road a mere 20 yards in front of us. Proceeding at about four miles per hour there was the very burnt-out rocket booster that we watched plummet back to earth a few hours earlier.

"Wow! Oh, wow!" Came the cries from the backseat. We couldn't figure out what was more fascinating, our amazing vantage point, or that NASA workers had already made such progress in bringing it back to the Cape from the barge in the Atlantic on which it landed, the vehicle that was carrying the behemoth, or the scorched rocket booster itself. Suffice it to say that major interest in all things NASA planted in my children's hearts and minds on that trip. All Mat and I did was plan a camping trip. The good Lord did the rest.

What a great gig, right? As a homeschool parent, there will come a time when your main job is giving them a ride to the library for more books on the subject or to a mentorship for professional training. You can be the driver of passions, literally and figuratively. Similar to the cliche: learn to read so you can read to learn; this way of thinking is: Discover your passion, so that you can passionately discover. Can you picture how great learning will occur? Can you see how wonderfully it will keep creativity alive, and curiosity abounding?

Also, I know it's early in our friendship, you're only four chapters in, but I feel like you and I are close enough to tell you something that many parents don't know. Some very sinister curricula are being taught in government schools all around this country, and other countries worldwide. If reading aloud, imaginative play, and passion-driven learning didn't change your mind about government schools, I pray what you read about them in the next chapter does.

Key Idea:
Instead of finding the perfect curriculum, read aloud to them, teach them at home, and give them lots of fantastical imaginative playtime. Allow your children to pursue their interests, and learn through their passions.

Home Is Where The Truth Is:
Reading aloud to your kids is the single most effective thing you can do to help them effectively command language.

Action Item:
Go over to readaloudrevival.com and peruse the age-appropriate book lists and activities for family read-aloud. Choose one to start as a family!

LIE #5:

At Least I Know They're Teaching the Right Things In School.

"Arise, soldiers of Christ, throw away the works of darkness and put on the armor of light." St. Cecilia, virgin and martyr. Circa 200 AD

"But if you cause one of these little ones who trusts in me to fall into sin, it would be better for you to have a large millstone tied around your neck and be drowned in the depths of the sea." Matthew 18:6

OR THE INFORMATION THAT lies ahead, let's first draw a distinction between *education* and *indoctrination*. When you send your child to school to get an education, you hope they learn reading, writing, and arithmetic, right? *Education* refers to enabling the attainment of knowledge, skills, personal development, and habits, using methods like teaching, training, and discussions in formal and informal settings. *Indoctrination*, on the other hand, refers to propagandizing a person with ideas, opinions, beliefs, concepts, principles, and ideologies. [1] For decades now, government schools have been overstepping their jurisdiction and shoving progressive ideologies down our children's throats. This chapter will bring you to an apt realization that you must make the decision: will you or won't you allow your children to be indoctrinated with a godless, divisive, woke agenda? Think gender ideology, Critical Race Theory (CRT), comprehensive sex-ed (CSE), teaching that humans evolved from apes as though it's proven fact and not theory, Relativism—that truth is subjective, and let's throw in Common Core math, to really be a thorn in your side as you help Junior at the homework table after a long day at a stressful job.

You will be outraged to find out what educators are feeding our children's innocent, young, impressionable minds. I will attempt to convey some of the horrors to you, I must warn you that this chapter contains some graphic content, so if you are listening to the audio around children, now is a good time to pause until you are alone. Seriously, we are about to get rated R up in here so turn it off now.

Ugh. This has been the hardest chapter to write *and* research. It'll definitely be the hardest to read. My jaw literally dropped when I read some of the curriculum being pushed by the purveyors of perversity onto innocent children as early as age 5. But that wasn't the only difficult thing about getting these words onto paper. As I wrestled with "parents-have-to-know-these-things", I thought about the people in my life that I work out with, hang out with on weekends, who live a different lifestyle than mine. Are they going to "unfriend" me? Will I be another casualty of the cancel culture? (As if I have something to cancel.) What will the angry mob do to my husband, a hard and honest worker; or to myself, a sinner, who has made many moral mistakes? But you see, that's the problem, and that's why activist groups have gotten such a stronghold on our kids' education. We've been bullied into silence because we don't want to come off as 'mean'. The majority of people disagree with sexualizing young children[2] and do not want schools indoctrinating their children in ideologies with which they disagree, but they won't speak out because of a form of cultural Marxism—a loss of our free speech due to fear of job loss, being labeled a bigot or even worse as a domestic terrorist by the FBI.[3] But fear of man is a snare, and whose approval am I trying to win anyway...God's or man's? Besides, you can't fire me, I work for Jesus.

It's time to stand up for the kids, to stand in the gap and protect them from these life-damaging philosophies, outright lies destroying families, undermining parents, and stripping away their parental rights. So here it goes. *Lord, give me strength.*

Firstly, let's talk about that which we all agree: that no child should be made fun of, bullied, or discriminated against because of their faith, sexuality, clothes they wear, hair texture, skin color, anything. We parents could probably all do a better job at loving our neighbor as ourselves, no matter what the neighbor thinks, looks, or acts like, thus showing our kids kindness, love, and tolerance. But let me be clear, I'm talking about the real definition of tolerance-*the disposition to be patient and fair; freedom from bigotry*. I'm not referring to a hijacked-by-the-woke-mob definition of tolerance which infers that I must teach my children lies as though they are facts, just because other people believe said lies.

Gender ideology has been a slow-dripping poison in our school systems for decades. The ramifications of this have surged to dangerous and absurd levels. Dangerous for the children to the point of irreversible body mutilation in many cases, and absurd for the things that we've stood idle and allowed to happen, like letting natal men—with their bigger hearts and lungs, greater amount of fast-twitch muscle fibers, denser bones, and stronger muscles compete against females—and calling it fair.

Only twenty-three states have enacted laws to protect women's sports by banning males who identify as women from competing against biological females. Sadly, the headlines keep coming in from states like Washington, California, and Maine, showing male athletes dominating females, ousting these hardworking athletes from podiums and possible scholarships.[4] Or worse, shamelessly injuring female athletes like North Carolina volleyball player Payton McNabb, who sustained a neck injury and concussion after a male player spiked the ball at her. Or the field hockey athlete who got her front teeth knocked out by a shot from a male player and was hospitalized with severe facial and dental injuries. [5] Adding insult to this horrific injury, the male player's team won due to the two points that he scored. It's not only unfair and maddening but perplexing when you see the levels to which adults are taking the transgender craze.

In 2019, The California Teachers Association voted to approve and is pushing a policy that will allow self-identified, transgender kids aged 12 and up to leave government campuses to get gender-changing hormones, without their parents' permission or knowledge. [6] They can't even buy marijuana until they're 18 or alcohol until twenty-one, but they should be able to diagnose themselves and get puberty blockers which stunt brain development and cause sterility without their parents' knowledge or consent at 12? Please don't be naive and think, *Oh, that's just one rogue teachers' association, that's not happening around here.* If a kid wants to change their pronouns and name to socially transition, parents lose rights as soon as their child steps foot on campus in states like Washington, New Jersey, Colorado, Pennsylvania, Illinois, and many more. In over one thousand school districts across America, which includes eighteen thousand schools, affecting 10.6 million students[7] policies openly state that district personnel can or should keep a student's transgender status hidden from parents. They will affirm the child's decision and keep it hush-hush from parents. Even if the parents go to the school and demand administrators not to affirm the child, administrators side with the minor. Transition closets—rooms full of clothing and accessories for kids to change into after they're dropped off at school are popping up in public schools across America.

Parental rights are further being eroded by laws like senate bill 5599 signed in May 2023 by Washington Governor Jay Inslee. This law allows transgender kids who are seeking "protected health care services" which include hormones and puberty blockers to live at state-funded youth shelters. When they leave the home of a parent—who loves them and wants to protect them from irreversible damage—and opt instead for the state-funded youth house, that facility will then make referrals on behalf of the minor to receive state-funded counseling (which is a good thing), but also hormone therapy, puberty blockers, and in some cases, surgery. So, if the parents are taken out of the process, then it follows that the state is paying for the transition.

Some of the people to whom we entrust the care of our children on government school campuses, administrators and teachers, along with the staff at state-licensed shelters are essentially telling confused adolescents:

- Let's begin your gender dysphoria make-over through a social transition with new names and pronouns.
- Let's not leave out the physical change we can get for you with puberty-blocking hormones.
- For outward appearance, you can choose from piles of hand-me-downs complete with accessories to change into every morning at school, all without your parents being the least bit privy.
- If your parents don't support you, 'I'll be your new mom,' states a teacher's classroom poster encouraging children to embrace a new 'glitter family'. (I wonder if she's willing to pay college tuition for all her surrogates, or even hold their

hair back when a stomach bug has them puking in the toilet at 1 a.m.)

- Go ahead and leave home if you want this bad enough, we'll even give you a place to live and medical referrals to assist with your transition.

Before you start thinking, 'trans kids do need a safe space', let me tell you about the gender ideology that is being shoved down their throats. Evidence shows it is this very gender training that is ramping up the numbers making gender dysphoria explode like a contagion. This is what Abigail Shrier iterates in her groundbreaking book, *Irreversible Damage*. Before 2012 there was not one shred of scientific literature on girls ages eleven to twenty-one ever having developed gender dysphoria—the feeling like you are a boy trapped in a girl's body. However, in the last decade, the Western world has seen a sudden surge of adolescents claiming to have gender dysphoria and self-identifying as transgender. For the first time in medical history, natal girls are not only present among those so identifying, they constitute the majority.[8] Suddenly, teenage girls, who never showed any signs of gender dysphoria are claiming to be transgender, oftentimes from the same groups of friends. How and why has this happened? As Shrier presents in her book, for a lot of reasons. I will highlight the accomplice of government schools.

Activist groups like GLADD, ACLU, and Planned Parenthood have radicalized teachers' unions and imbued our school systems with curriculum, speakers, and events seeking to "revolutionize curricula and culture in public schools to stamp out 'hegemonic heterosexuality.' Instead of accepting the traditional view that heterosexuality is the norm, these groups are in favor of a new ethos that does not just tolerate homosexuality but instead actively endorses experimenting with it, as well as with a polymorphous range of bisexuality, transgenderism, and transsexuality."[9]

California boasts the most comprehensive state-wide gender identity and sexual orientation instruction, *statutorily mandatory* for all students enrolled in grades K-12 and explicitly barring parental opt-out.[10] Under the guise of anti-bullying, educators are mainstreaming radical gender ideology at every age level. Gender ideologues argued and were successful in many states that in order to protect gay and trans kids from bullying, every child must receive sexual orientation and gender identity training, and parents, it doesn't matter if you like it or not—you cannot opt your child out!

In some schools starting as early as preschool kids are taught that gender is completely fluid, passing through many different phases, and has no connection to your biological sex; confusing kids to the point that they believe that experimenting with a range of homosexual behaviors serves the cause of civil rights. Activists won't stop until every small child thinks that heterosexism -the belief that heterosexuality is the norm, is as repugnant as racism or sexism.

In kindergarten, they start with gender stereotypes asking, "What are some activities, colors, games that boys like? What about for girls?"[11] These stereotypes must be understood for gender identity to take hold. As soon as the little boy who likes to sing or dance realizes that those are things girls like, the more readily he will question if he really is a boy. Books like *Who Are You? The Kids Guide To Gender Identity,* available in the California Board of Education's virtual library, gives kids a plethora of gender options. ("These are just a few words people use: trans, genderqueer, non-binary, gender fluid, transgender, gender neutral, agender, neutrois, bigender, third gender, two-spirit...") Perhaps the most flagrant tenet of *Who Are You,* tells the young reader that it's *their* feelings that are truly the indicator of their gender. "You are who you say you are because YOU know best," the book proselytizes.

Are you kidding me? This age group is still eating boogers and putting their shoes on the wrong feet, yet this author tells them to choose their own gender by feelings. The grooming of young children towards transgenderism is even more blatant when you back that up with a performance from Lindsay Amer, a ukulele-playing educator that identifies as "queer"— outside the gender binary of male and female. Amer goes around to schools playing her ukulele and singing her original song written for preschoolers with lyrics, "It's OK to be gay. We are different in many ways. Doesn't matter if you're a boy, girl, or somewhere in between, we are all part of one big family. Gay means 'happy'."[12]

Amer's YouTube channel is dedicated to teaching LGBTQ+ doctrine to kids ages 3 and up as she uses a teddy bear for a prop, posts videos on pronouns, and reads books like the one entitled *B is for Bisexual*. Amer's story time could almost be called conservative compared to the videos that recently surfaced from "family-friendly" drag queen shows. At first glance it looks like what you'd see at any community story hour geared toward young moms and preschoolers. Babies, no more than five or six months old are sitting here and there on a padded floor, balls and ribbons are strewn about, with moms sitting in a semi-circle in the background. A baby sucks on his fist, such a cute, innocent scene until suddenly, a man in six-inch platform stilettos, and a sheer black negligée struts out and drops down in a straddle-split twerking for all he's worth, between the stunned babies. Mothers whoop and holler for him as he writhes on the floor, swinging his legs inches from the babies' heads, heaving his chest up and down in strip-tease fashion. Another man does a headstand in a chair, spreads his legs, and gyrates on stage in the same room full of young children. Continually upping the shock factor, another man shakes his butt, straddles, splits, and rolls around on the floor, so moms and children all get a close-up of his full leotard bodysuit and tucked-in package.

The comment thread for the drag queen story hour video lights up, "How can parents willingly expose their children to this debauchery meant to sexualize and blur the truth of male and female?" Unfortunately, America has been slow to realize, that the government school system is in cahoots with the lavishly inappropriate drag queens. In October 2022, the Encinitas Union School District posted a flier that invited children to a "queer" and "family-friendly" drag show called "Boo Bash". The sponsors of this event, a San Francisco gender reassignment surgery center, and an over-21 gay nightclub were blatantly targeting young children. The school district was complicit until some irate parents called them out as "groomers" and "pimp activists" and they removed the flier.

The transgender ideology is taught at every grade level. A middle school curriculum asks children, "If a boy acts like a girl, or a girl acts like a boy, does that mean they're gay?" And, "Can you change your sexual orientation or gender identity?" And "How do gay, lesbian, and trans people have sex?"[13]

At the high school level gender ideology gets downright raunchy and explicit. One of the most lascivious curricula available uses vulgar methods to teach about condoms, sexual pleasure, masturbation, and anal and oral sex. It promotes transgender ideology by using terms such as 'gender assigned at birth 'and 'person with a uterus'. And if you get that 'person with a uterus' pregnant, well, abortion is a perfectly acceptable response. The writers of this curriculum classify pornography as a 'normal activity' for teens and promote using it, 'as long as both partners consent.' One twelfth-grade lesson goes so far as to show sexually explicit photos to students in a PowerPoint presentation. [14] The dangerously addictive nature of pornography and the harmful effects it has on the brain are not little-known facts, I don't care what circle you run in or what your beliefs. This illustrates that some adults will stop at nothing to sexualize children.

School calendars are chock full of events all school year[15] to hyper-sexualize our children and drive home the complete acceptance of transgenderism. Kicking off the school year with "Bisexual Awareness Week" in September, October has "Coming Out Day," "International Pronouns Day," LGBTQ History Month, and yet another thing to confuse children: "Asexual (ACE) Awareness Week". This celebrates asexuality defined as a lack of interest in sexual desire. This can be super confusing for prepubescent children—or any for that matter who don't think about sex or have the desire to date or be in a relationship. Why should they be forced into a gender identity and labeled, simply because they aren't boy-crazy, or girl-crazy? November rings in "Transgender Awareness Week" and wraps up with "Transgender Day of Remembrance" a vigil for individuals killed for this identity. December has Pansexual Pride Day for those who are attracted to any and all of the aforementioned sexual deviations. In February, your little tyke may celebrate "Welcoming Schools National Day of Recognition" an afternoon in which they'll be read books that promote transgender ideology. March is "Transgender Visibility Month." April boasts Day of Silence/Day of Action" to raise awareness of bullying and harassment of LGBTQ students. In May there's "International Day of Homophobia, Transphobia and Biphobia", "Pansexual Visibility Day", and "Harvey Milk Day" a day dedicated to remembering one of the first openly gay officials elected in the US. I hope you're not tired of all the celebrating yet because we still have the entire month of June, Pride month, with parades and banners exalting LGBTQ identities and fighting LGBTQ oppression.[16]

As our children are being propagandized throughout the year at school, pride month brings it to every American regardless of whether they're in the private, business, or government sector. However, if we think for ourselves and search for the truth, we quickly uncover the lies behind the banners. Such as the lifting up of people like Harvey Milk, whose death made him the face of the gay rights movement. As an ephebophile, someone with a sexual preference for mid-to-late adolescents, Milk had a penchant for runaway teen boys with drug addictions.[17] He advocated for polyamorous relationships because the "heterosexual model doesn't work for homosexuals." [18] Tragically, that polyamorous model didn't work for two of his discarded lovers. Jack Galen McKinley and Jack Lira both committed suicide, the latter hanging himself on the back porch of Milk's residence. Milk had no qualms about lying for votes, claiming that he was kicked out of the military due to his sexuality. Saying to his campaign manager, "Maybe they'll hear it, feel sorry for me, and vote for me." [19] However, the military records don't support his lie.

You might be thinking, "Big deal, what politician doesn't lie for votes?" But here's a disturbing twist. After losing two elections, Milk won his third run for office. How'd he finally come out with a win? With the help of one of the most notorious cult leaders of the twentieth century, Jim Jones. The leader of "The People's Temple" gave him hundreds of campaign volunteers, a printing press, and publicity in The People's Forum newspaper.[20] Just a few months after Milk's election, Jones forced over 900 of his followers to commit suicide by drinking a fruity concoction laced with cyanide, in the infamous Jonestown Massacre. If you've ever used the metaphor, when someone goes headstrong into a new belief or hobby, "Oh, they drank the Kool-Aid," then you may already be familiar with one of the largest mass murder-suicides in American history.

Milk's unrelated death would come just eight days after the Jonestown Massacre. Don't believe the lie that Milk was killed because of his sexuality as depicted on the silver screen which further cast him as a gay rights martyr. He was murdered by fellow Democrat Daniel White, who supported Milk's agenda with his influence, his vote, and his money. White shot Milk and San Francisco Mayor George Moscone, a heterosexual, due to a fall-out over a land use issue in White's district.

In Milk's eleven months in office, his one historical political contribution was authoring a city ordinance—that dog owners must clean up their pet's mess. Yet President Obama awarded him the nation's highest honor, the Presidential Medal of Freedom, putting him on a pedestal with other recipients John F. Kennedy, Ronald Reagan, and Jimmy Carter to name a few. As if that wasn't enough, a Naval ship was named in his honor in 2016. What ceremonial ship christening is complete if it doesn't have a man dressed in a woman's Naval uniform to break the bottle of champagne over the bow? Certainly not that of the USNS Harvey Milk (T-AO 206). Doesn't this make you stop and think, *Has every American drunk the Kool-Aid?*

This constant stream of lies, propaganda and gender ideology through curriculum and celebrations forces kids to hyper focus on their gender identity. The progressive cult wants kids to constantly look for impulses that they could lean toward genderqueer, non-binary, transgender, or whichever of the 107 gender identities beset the newest list. When teenage crisis hits in one of its many forms—being dumped by the opposite sex, being teased because of your body type, or being ostracized, here's a new identity in which to cling and find comradeship. The truly maddening thing as Shrier points out is, "Schools that administer this instruction never acknowledge that, as a scientific matter, it's gibberish. It is biologically nonsensical that a girl's brain—every cell of it stamped with XX chromosomes—might inhabit a boy's body. No mention is made of the fact that there are no diagnostic or empirical criteria for deciding that a biological girl is in fact 'really a boy.' Nevertheless, this drivel is taught with the same sobriety and apparent thoroughness as facts about human reproduction and sexually transmitted disease."

Neither do they want it known that 70 percent of kids will grow out of gender dysphoria if they are not affirmed,[21] if they are not socially transitioned, not allowed to change their pronouns, or name, or use the opposite sex bathroom, or bunk with the opposite sex on overnight trips (all of which are allowed across America's school districts).

Kenneth Zucker is an international expert on child and adolescent gender dysphoria. As psychologist-in-chief of Toronto's Center for Addiction and Mental Health (CAMH) and head of its Gender Identity Service, he worked for decades helping children affected by gender dysphoria to grow more comfortable in their bodies. He oversaw writing the definition of "gender dysphoria" for the DSM-5[22] and you could say he literally wrote the book on treating trans kids with the "Standards of Care" guidelines for the World Professional Association for Transgender Health (WPATH). In a study of 100 of his patients that had *not* been socially transitioned by parents, a whopping 88 of them had outgrown gender dysphoria. [23] His method looked at the whole kid, probing to see why the child came to believe that a gender change would lead to a happier life; and what beliefs they had about boys and girls in the first place. Often the gender dysphoria was alleviated by challenging the premise that biological sex was the source of the patient's problem.

Sadly, as "affirmative therapy" fever swept through his province in Canada, and conversion therapy was outlawed, the angry activist mob came beating down his door. Claiming that the aforementioned method he used was conversion therapy and making up false accusations that he humiliated his patients (which were later proven false) got him fired and his gender identity clinic shut down.[24] The activists' message is radical and clear: We don't care who you are, your experience level, or if you truly care for trans kids or not. Affirm these kids or lose your job and perhaps your license.

There's no question that people suffering from gender dysphoria are in an immense amount of mental anguish. Rates for anxiety, depression, and suicide ideation are alarmingly high, no matter what age.[25] Today's youth are plagued with more depression and mental disorders than ever before, especially adolescents who are vastly influenced by social media when it comes to things like eating disorders and gender dysphoria. All tweens and teens have to do is type in #pro-ana (pro-anorexia) or #pro-mia (pro-bulimia) to learn all the weight-loss tricks, while fooling your parents into thinking you've eaten, and to belong to part of a group, bonded by suffering. Or they can just punch in #trans to learn exactly what to say to the doctor so that they'll give them those gender changing hormones on the first visit. Influencers preach that dishonesty to doctors is completely fine if it helps move the transition along. One YouTube sensation suggests, "Get a story in your head, and as suggested keep the lie to a minimum. And only for stuff that can't be verified. Like how you were feeling but was too afraid to tell anyone including your family."[26] Trans influencers are telling them things like, "If you think you might be trans, you are."[27] Those who advocate affirming trans-identified children scare parents with the threat that any hesitation of assisting the child's gender transition can lead to damaging psychological affects and suicide. The research that they cite "does not align substantially with any robust data or studies in this area".[28] Unfortunately, the suicide scare tactic ignores an actual long-term study of transsexuals (the accepted term at the time) showing a rise in suicidality *after* sex reassignment surgery.[29] More relevant to today's gender-confused children, and more recently, Marcus Evans, a governor of the Tavistock and Portman Trust gender clinic in the UK, resigned after a report was leaked stating that rates of self-harm and suicidality did not decrease even after puberty suppression for adolescent girls.[30] Evans told the press that he feared the clinic was fast-tracking youths to transition to no good effect and in some cases to their harm. The lies and mis-facts are continually perpetuated by activist mobs, silencing any dissenters. Parents are scared that their kids are going to commit suicide if they don't immediately affirm them, no wonder switching genders has taken off like a virus.

While suicide fear eats away at panicked parents, their trans-identified kids are depressed and buying into the narrative that gender transition will suddenly make life amazing. Shockingly, there are children's hospitals in the US, pushing kids to gender reassignment surgery, and double mastectomies, as well as masculinizing and feminizing procedures, that will total upwards of one hundred and forty thousand dollars when the medical transition is complete. When the highly-complicated gender reassignment surgery is not done correctly, sex organs may become gangrenous, atrophy, and die, sentencing the malpractice victim to life with a colostomy bag strapped to their thigh, or worse—death caused by infection. Why are we pushing this on our children? How can we stand by as parents 'rights to get counseling and help for their child is literally stripped away? It's a truly terrifying cycle for all involved, and we should all care deeply about these families.

But here's the thing, people don't care how much you know until they know you care. For us to make a difference in this movement we must start by building relationships. If I don't do that, then I'm just another angry voice. When I saw a teenage boy dressed as a girl volunteering at our local library, I didn't want to judge him, think myself better than him in any way, or say something snarky to him like combat boots don't typically pair well with linen midi-length skirts.

My heart went out to him, I wanted to show him love and care about his future. If we're not willing to journey with them, then we might as well not even enter into the conversation, because there is a lot of pain there. There's pain in not knowing who you are. Even the most stable adolescents are always trying to carve out an identity. Am I a student, an athlete, a leader, a musician? Unfortunately, what we have failed to teach kids is the one identity that truly matters: You are a son or daughter of the King of Kings and the Lord of Lords. A child of God. After they believe that, everything else will fall into place. But in today's post-Christian world, we can't just say, "Here's Christ, take it, apply it, and go off on your way." If we have the opportunity to build a relationship with a trans-identifying person, we must encourage them to search for the truth. If we really believe God is truth, and if they're really searching for truth, guess what they're going to find. All the better if we can show them that we genuinely care for them and that they are loved. As one mega-church pastor rightly put it, "Our attitude should be: if you have good morals or no morals, I'm still going to love you. If you're clean and sober or strung out and addicted, I'm still going to love you. If you're gay or straight, republican or democrat, black or white, Muslim or Christian, Believer or Atheist, doesn't matter I'm still gonna love you. Jesus said, 'By this will all men know that you are my disciples, if you love one another'." [31] Only then will they listen and want that knowledge for themselves.

As for our own children, parents, we need to stop taking our kids to drag queen story hour in the hopes of teaching tolerance and start talking truth into our kids' lives early, because trusted teachers, social media stars, and the world in general, are certainly getting their indoctrination time with them. Everyone needs a basic teaching of the faith...that heteronormativism follows God's laws and the laws of nature, that sexual immorality is wrong no matter who it's with or what orifice you use. Pardon my curtness. Those are the truths that I will teach my children. Is that conversion therapy? I more like to call it "soul-guarding" or how about "innocence preserving", or "foundations-of-belief-building." Whatever you call it, I certainly have that right. Unfortunately, those who send their kids to school don't have that right, and have to worry if Child Protective Services will try to take their kid away, because home with mom and dad is no longer a "safe environment." Rather, safe to them is allowing self-diagnosed-trans-identifying biological males to use girls' bathrooms, which resulted in the sexual battery of two girls by the same transgender teen[32] on a government school campus. To them, 'safe' is administering hormones to a little girl, who may have never exhibited any gender dysphoria symptoms before in her life—just because she asked for it, and her friends are doing it too—hormones that stop brain development, block puberty and cause irreversible sterility. To them, it's safe to allow a thirteen-year-old to go ahead and cut off her completely healthy breasts.[33]

COMPREHENSIVE SEX-ED

It's enough to make one sick with sorrow. Yet, I haven't even told you about Comprehensive Sexual Education (CSE) which has made its way into so many schools in the US and around the world. It's rife with age-inappropriate pictures, instructions on getting to third base and beyond with suggested dialogue, like "Can I take your shirt off?" Anal sex is introduced to twelve-year-olds, and students are encouraged to use non-microwavable Saran Wrap as a prophylactic for oral sex.[34] As the late Zig Ziglar said in his book *Raising Positive Kids in a Negative World*, "Sex ed without moral instruction is sex permission." Which is exactly what 'Our Whole Lives' promulgates. This curriculum for 12-14-year-olds actually has a chapter entitled *Redefining*

Abstinence. It encourages readers to go ahead with 'mouth-vulva contact, mouth-penis contact, mouth-anus contact, fingering a partner's genitals, and touching a partner's nipples. There's even a chapter instructing on anal sex telling students "The sphincter muscles should be relaxed with a finger massage before penetration."[35]

Before CSE came along, sex-ed used to be a simple biology lesson that took one day, they separated the boys and the girls and explained the basic facts of reproduction. At least that's how they did it when I was in seventh grade. Perhaps you share the view of my doctor friend Tammy. Seeing too many young pregnant girls in her office (as young as thirteen years old) she's worried that parents aren't educating their children on sex. Somebody should. Why not the schools? But this has gone off the rails, instead of teaching about abstinence as the safest bet, STDs, and pregnancy, sex-ed is now meant to sexualize and push the kids to aggressively explore their sexuality. If you're like me, you're not only enraged to learn what they're teaching to young, impressionable minds, but you also wonder, *How did it get to this?*

The base of CSE comes from a few, sexually deranged men, that promulgated the ideas of sexualizing children, gender fluidity, and freeing society from moral constraints like monogamy and heterosexuality to give way to all sexual desires and deviations. Alfred Kinsey, Dr. John Money, and Hugh Heffner were three key players who laid the groundwork for the poison of CSE and gender ideology that is infecting our children, chipping away at families, and slowly destroying America.

One of the men that would change America forever and for the worse was Alfred Kinsey. He believed that sexuality is "not an appetite to be curbed," and published an errant study, "Sexual Behavior in the Human Male," in 1948. To him, literally, no sex act was off-limits, even asserting that, "pedophiles were misunderstood, and their punishments unjust" [36] and that "child rape benefits the victim." [37] He conducted experiments on babies as young as two months old that were blatant sexual abuse. Not only was his research horrific, but it was also fundamentally flawed. His sample sizes were too small, and his demographics were grossly skewed—mostly convicted felons in prison. He took his false information to lawmakers and was successful in loosening sex offender laws. Since his erroneous study hit the streets, sexual morality has been in a downward spiral.

Society greedily gobbled up his idea that humans are pansexual and that traditional morality which is upheld by Judeo-Christian values is destructive. Kinsey and his everything-goes sexual ideology was the linchpin in the paradigm shift of America from Judeo-Christian to the attitude that many hold today: If you are not accepting of all manners of sexual deviance, then you're a bigot.

Psychologist, Dr. John Money took the perversions of the Kinsey reports to repugnant levels, performing torturous experiments on children which resulted in pain, misery, and multiple suicides. [38] Like Kinsey, he was deeply troubled, referring to pedophilia as "a love affair between an age-discrepant couple." Incest was also fine with him, he said, "For a child to have a sexual experience with a relative, was not necessarily a problem." [39] Believing that children were born a blank slate and could be pushed into either gender, he experimented on children in an attempt to prove his radical theories. It was Money who popularized the term "gender identity" and founded the world's first gender-identity clinic at John Hopkins University in Baltimore in the US in 1966 (thirteen years later the clinic halted sex-change operations under the leadership of Paul McHugh who believed that "Hopkins was fundamentally cooperating with a mental illness.")

When Hugh Heffner, read Kinsey's work in 1948, he declared that he would be "Kinsey's pamphleteer" and launched his pornographic empire. Heffner made millions mainstreaming pornography and in 1964 provided seed money for the founding of the Sexuality Information and Education Council of the United States (SIECUS). This organization would make sure that Heffner always had customers. They changed sex-ed from informing about unwanted pregnancies and sexually transmitted diseases to a celebration of children as sexual beings. Breaking from traditional views, their goal was to teach children to explore and express their sexuality as this was a natural and healthy thing to do. Referencing Kinsey's egregiously false data, SIECUS founder, Dr. Mary Calderone told parents, "Children are sexual and think sexual thoughts and do sexual things. . . parents must accept and honor their child's erotic potential."[40]

EDUCATION NOT INDOCTRINATION

Considering the people who let loose these sexual ideologies, you must see the importance of protecting our children from them. Lots of parents are catching on proliferating no shortage of viral videos featuring irate moms at school board meetings reading the filth in the curriculum out loud to school board members. Some rays of hope pierce through the darkness as people fight against woke ideology indoctrination. Governor Ron DeSantis of Florida was the first to enact a Parents' Bill of Rights, (soon other states followed) which enshrined into law protections for the parents' role in their children's education. Parents are guaranteed the right to inspect the materials being used in their child's school, through curriculum transparency legislation and classroom instruction when it comes to "toxic racial ideologies" and the sexualization of children. It's against the law to teach "sexual orientation" and "gender identity" to children in third grade or younger, "or in a manner that is not age-appropriate or developmentally appropriate for students in accordance with state standards."

As DeSantis said, the fact that these laws had to be enacted shows how far the modern school system has moved from its core mission of education. The people who opposed this bill attached to it a misleading moniker, *The Don't Say Gay Bill*, (of course, it doesn't prohibit saying 'gay' and would've been more accurately called an "Anti-Grooming Bill.") Governor DeSantis said of them, "They support sexualizing kids in kindergarten. They support injecting woke gender ideology into second-grade classrooms. And so, what they're doing with these slogans and these narratives is they are trying to camouflage their true intentions."[41]

It's not only saddening but unfathomable that trusted adults are intentionally leading our children astray with errant, life-damaging philosophies. But I'm not finished. Another controversial ideology urges American youth to take on a victim mentality and that their success depends on their skin color because America is systemically racist.

CRITICAL RACE THEORY

So that you can understand Critical Race Theory (CRT), I'll first tell you about its origins, then its core beliefs. You can decide if CRT, which is another worldview, aligns with a Biblical perspective and if it's a belief system that you'd like instilled in your children by teachers and administrators. In 1923 in Frankfurt, Germany, the Frankfurt School was founded with the aim of developing Marxist studies, perpetuating Freudian psychology, and dismantling oppressive societal structures like the class system, the family, and Judeo-Christian values. In the next chapter, I'll tell you more about the Frankfurt School's move to America.

Today, if you send your child to a government school or even a private school for that matter, there's no way of escaping the Frankfurt School's terrible influence on our society. But for this chapter I want you to know that it's the place where Critical Theory (CT) was born. CT argues, as Marxism does, that social problems are influenced and created more by societal structures and cultural assumptions than by individual and psychological factors.[42] CT rejects concepts of rationality, objectivity, and universal truth and "seeks to liberate human beings from the circumstances that enslave them."[43]

CRT is a spin-off of CT. In 1989, founding critical race theorist Kimberle Crenshaw coined the term "intersectionality" by positing that gender, race, class, and other individual characteristics "intersect", therefore some people will feel more oppression than others. Marxism framed human existence through the lens of "Oppressor" and "Oppressed," (the rich, bourgeoisie versus the poor, proletariat), and the main ideas of CRT are born of this post-modern, Marxist, atheistic worldview. CRT's goal is to liberate people of color from the racism that oppresses them.

While you may have heard the buzzwords surrounding it, such as *systemic racism* and *white privilege,* you may still be confused as to what CRT actually is. Author Jannique Stewart asserts, "As Christians, it is crucial that we know if the ideas behind CRT are biblical, and what degree of common ground Christians might find with those who embrace CRT."

Whether one is for CRT or against it, we can all agree that it's evil to treat someone differently because of their skin color. We should call racism to light and stamp it out wherever we find it. Those who embrace CRT frame it as a way to make everyone aware of racism and to defeat discrimination in its many forms, but as we look deeper into CRT, we will find that it provides no solution, and just like other CTs, fails to provide rational standards by which it can show itself superior to other theories of knowledge and practice. The core tenets of CRT actually contradict our beliefs as Christians. Furthermore, as it's being taught, people are accepting its *theory* as factual and don't even question the truth of its claims. This is dangerous, especially when CRT is an ideology that informs movements aimed at social activism, social justice, and racial justice, and is being pushed onto our children all across the country under the euphemisms of Culturally Responsive Teaching, Diversity, Equity, and Inclusion programs (DEI), or Social and Emotional Learning (SEL).

There are four core beliefs to CRT:

1. CRT asserts that the most important thing that determines our identity is skin color, which divides us into the 'Oppressor' and the 'Oppressed Victim'.
2. It also asserts that racism is permanent and always present (exposing whiteness, white supremacy, and colorblindness).
3. CRT trades objective truth for subjective opinions and feelings.
4. CRT requires the acceptance and liberation of ALL oppressed groups.[44]

First of all, claiming that skin color is the most important thing that identifies us, as CRT does, is unbiblical. We are made in the image and likeness of God,[45] and this is where we find our identity and dignity. Plus, if we must be assigned to either the oppressor or the oppressed, then where do mercy and forgiveness come in? As, Stewart points out, "CRT expects whites to 'repent and atone' for the actions of their ancestors, but does not acknowledge any avenues for legitimate reconciliation between the Oppressors and the Oppressed. CRT's 'justice' is not the same as biblical justice, which forbids excluding according to group status. Biblical justice requires that we 'not show partiality to the poor nor give preference to the great,' and that we consider everyone fairly (Leviticus 19:15). According to CRT, justice is only for the Oppressed. Biblical justice is for both the victim and the accused (Micah 6:8, Exodus 23:1-3)."[46]

Moreover, if we are to judge by outward appearances who is racist, according to skin color nonetheless, that is itself racist. As it says in 1 Samuel, "The Lord does not look at the things people look at. People look at the outward appearance, but the Lord looks at the heart." If we agree with the teachings of CRT, then we must make superficial judgements—not only on individuals, but on entire people groups—not based on character, but outward appearance alone.

Do you believe that we can make a blanket statement inclusive of all people of a particular race? It would be categorically wrong to say, "All Black people are lazy." But According to Robin DiAngelo, author of *White Fragility,* it's completely acceptable to say whiteness is inherently racist. She says, "White people raised in Western society are conditioned into a white supremacist worldview because it is the bedrock of our society and its institutions...Entering the conversation with this understanding is freeing because it allows us to focus on how-rather than if—our racism is manifest."[47] Doubling down on the premise that all white people are racist, author Ijeoma Oluo wrote, "If you are white in a white supremacist society, you ARE racist. If you are male in a patriarchy, you ARE sexist. If you are able-bodied, you ARE ableist. If you are anything above poverty in a capitalist society, you ARE a classist. You can sometimes be all of these things at once."[48]

Another flaw of CRT is that it trades objective truth for subjective opinions and feelings. Belonging to a disadvantaged minority group gives one special access to truth and moral credibility. CRT asserts that "lived experience" is necessary to understand racism. [49] The only people able to discern what is racist are those who have been victims of racism. Olou writes, "It is about race—if a person of color thinks it is about race...We are, each and every one of us, a collection of our lived experiences...And our experiences are valid."[50] The assumption that darker skin color gives a person credibility is just as bad as giving credibility to a person because they have light skin. It means that with regard to things such as police shootings and accusations of racism, there is no need to pursue truth because what is true has already been decided based on skin color.[51]

Because CRT requires the acceptance and liberation of ALL oppressed groups, those who teach it say that we must dismiss a natural and biblical view of sex and gender as part of being antiracist.[52] Ibram X. Kendi wrote, "We must accept the premise that the other majority, White based-'isms' and 'itys' (racism, heteronormativism, Christianity)-are the result of oppressor-based systems, and they must be dismantled simultaneously." He continues, "To be truly antiracist is to be feminist. To be truly feminist is to be antiracist ...(recently adding, 'to be antiracist is to be pro-choice'.) We cannot be antiracist if we are homophobic or transphobic...To be queer antiracist is to understand the privileges of my cisgender, of my masculinity, of my heterosexuality, of their intersections."

Even if we wanted to go along with CRT, it doesn't even begin to cover all the groups that face discrimination. Since CRT only focuses on race, gender and class, it's mitigating the impact of discrimination due to other categories such as disabilities, health, native language, ethnic origin, education, age, marital status, and the presence or absence of dependent children.[53] As author Noelle Mering succinctly puts it, "An ideology built on reminding, reemphasizing, compounding, and comparing a woefully incomplete list of grievances ends up being a broad and perverse form of injustice in the name of justice resolution."[54]

This injustice is exemplified by the fact that today white liberals think that blacks and Latinos are actually *worse* off than they think *themselves*. White liberals are now *less likely* than African Americans to say that black people should be able to get ahead without any special help.[55] Mandatory race training seminars in the workforce are driving the belief further by teaching concepts like "work before play", and a "can-do attitude", even being on time, are rooted in oppressive white male culture and are devastating to women and people of color.[56] For them, whiteness is defined by hard work, a good attitude, and time management, life skills that they think are unrealistic for Blacks.

Even more ironic, the same proponents of this woke ideology will actually strip Black people of their blackness if they don't agree with them, or vote for them. President Joe Biden told Black voters if they were having difficulty choosing between Trump and himself, then "You ain't black." Nikole Hannah-Jones editor of *The 1619 Project* which aims to reframe American history to when the first slave ship landed, tweeted "There is a difference between being politically black and being racially black. I am not defending anyone but we all know this and should stop pretending that we don't."

No matter whom they voted for, or whether they fit Hannah-Jones' definition of "politically black", 70% of blacks polled don't think that they need special favors to succeed.[57] As one fed-up Black woman Quisha King, of *The Quisha King Show*, pointed out, "Black people in America are the most successful [Black people] in the world. If you can't succeed here in America, then there's probably nowhere you can go." America has more Black billionaires than any other country in the entire world. Please quit listening to the lie that America is still a racist nation, it is actually the most racially diverse and racially tolerant nation in the world. Orlando Patterson, a liberal sociologist from Harvard University actually set out to prove how racist America is, but this is what he found, "America is now the least racist, white majority society in the world. America has a better record of legal protections for minorities than any other society, White or Black. America offers more opportunities to a greater number of Blacks than any other society including all of those in Africa."[58]

America has come a long way since dismantling the wretched institution of slavery and the inhumane Jim Crow era. But I know that discrimination still exists. When you compare Black people to whites in America today, Blacks are less likely to get a call back on a job application—especially if they have a Black-sounding name. They also have more pregnancy complications and maternal mortality and are more likely to have contact with the police and the criminal justice system.

These disparities are concerning to me as an American, and as the mother of a bi-racial daughter. However, it does not follow that these are the reasons for the wage gap or other imbalances that people point to as systemic racism. Don't individual life choices have something to do with it? What about the real pandemic of fatherlessness? Sadly, today 71% of Black births are out of wedlock, compared to 53% of Latinos, 27% of whites, and 10% of Asians.[59] Congressman and former president of the NAACP, Kweisi Mfume asks, "Between the presence of racism and the absence of Black fathers, which poses the greater threat to the Black community?"[60]

Instead of teaching our kids to take a victim mentality, and hate the greatest nation in the world that literally affords them more freedom and opportunities of any other country on the planet, we need to hold a quick session of truth school. Have you heard of the "Success Sequence"? It's a series of sequential life events and for those who adhere to it, 97-98% will escape poverty no matter their race. Here it is, The Success Sequence:

1. Graduate from high school (at least).
2. Get a full-time job.
3. Get married before having children.[61]

BREAKING DOWN BARRIERS

World-renowned neurosurgeon Dr. Ben Carson was the first person to separate craniopagus conjoined twins (twins joined at the head) with the survival of both patients. His list of accomplishments includes performing the first successful neurosurgical procedure on a fetus inside the womb, developing new methods to treat brain-stem tumors, and revitalizing hemispherectomy techniques for controlling seizures.

He grew up poor, fatherless, amongst racial tension, and has often been on the receiving end of blatant racism. His mother had less than a third-grade education and was illiterate for many of her parenting years, but she was the wisest person Carson ever knew. And her wisdom said, no, you better not even come at me with that victimhood mess. In his book, *Created Equal* Carson argues against CRT and warns every Black person to never buy into the victim mentality. Through his voracious reading about successful people, he realized, "...color or race had much less to do with success than hard work, vision, and determination. Yes, there were some people who perhaps had a steeper mountain to climb in order to achieve success, but that simply made them stronger and more capable of scaling the next mountain. With that realization, I stopped listening to people who claimed that the system was rigged against the success of Black people. What does in fact increase the chances of failure is a defeatist attitude associated with victimization."[62]

Listen, I'm no race scholar. But I know that for the individual, racism stems from the beliefs our parents handed down, personal experience, and just plain ignorance of other cultures. However, after researching what race scholars had to say through CRT, it negatively impacted my behavior toward people that have more layers of oppression than myself. Now, instead of being lovingly outgoing toward all people of color, I find myself hesitant to compliment the black woman sitting at the table next to me on her beautiful dreadlocks. I wonder, does she hate me because I'm a white oppressor? Am I even allowed to compliment Type 4 hair that coils since I have Type 1 straight hair? When the ridiculous thought crossed my mind, I took it captive and got up my courage to compliment her anyway. Kind of sad that I had to muster the courage to talk to another human being, but that's what looking through the lens of skin color does. This self-screening before speaking to another person is actually a regression from my cultural development through an adolescence that was free from the prejudicial ideology of CRT.

When I was twelve, my family moved from a tiny town in the rural Mid-West where we had three Black people in my entire school which included all the grades, K-12. We landed in a suburb of Orlando, Florida and my new middle school was a melting pot of ethnicities. My new best friend was a Filipina. I was amazed that many kids spoke a different language at home and English was their second, or that their parents didn't speak English at all. I found the diversity an exciting new world to explore. As an avid basketball player, most of my teammates were Black girls, and we clicked. Their sense of humor, way of dressing, and smack-talking on the court fascinated me. As we deepened friendships through the bond of sports, I imitated them and we learned from each other. They accepted me, despite my whiteness. I became fluent in Ebonics and was a font of adolescent wisdom when they asked me, "Maeve, why do y'all white people, fill in the blank...dress a certain way, not season your food, talk back to your parents." I'll never forget when I learned that for a black girl, a perm is the exact opposite of what it was for a white girl. When I left the salon after a perm in the 1980s, I looked like a frizzy-curled poodle. When my teammate, Idosha left the salon, her formerly kinky hair would be bone-straight! I had to clarify to my friends that I was not rich, far from it, we were on government food stamps and my parents lived paycheck to paycheck. But because of the cultural barriers, every one of my Black friends thought we were wealthy just because we were white. We learned from each other, laughed a lot, and never felt as though we were filling the roles of oppressed or oppressor.

Through high school, my identity as the token white girl around all my Black friends blossomed and I was culturally appropriating before it was [un]cool. Not only did I don hip-hop clothes, rock the air Jordans, and hang in the 'hood, but I did it with cornrows in my blonde hair. Here's what was so attractive and enveloping about that identity: they accepted me and I accepted them. Walls of prejudice came down on both sides. Black Mamas and Grandmas were so loving to me, treating me as their own, and feeding me plates of soul food piled high with collard greens, baked mac-and-cheese, and fried chicken. Glory be, Mmmmm-mm, Southern soul food is some of the best cooking on the planet! I'm still grateful to Auntie 'Nette who taught me how to cook fried chicken her way. I often wonder would these friendships have happened if CRT had poisoned our minds.

I share my past and personal details to illustrate how concerned I am for the future. For our young Americans who sit at a desk listening to a trusted teacher, like the third graders in a Cupertino, California elementary school were forced to deconstruct their racial and sexual identities, and then rank themselves according to their "power and privilege". Thusly, the eight-year-olds were separated into categories of oppressors and oppressed. Or the students under the California Department of Education who had to take an "ethnic studies" curriculum that calls for the "decolonization" of American society, and includes chants to the Aztec God of human sacrifice. It's about stopping the nonsense of the Seattle, Washington School District that told white teachers that they are guilty of "spirit murder" against black children and must "bankrupt [their] privilege in acknowledgment of [their] thieved inheritance." It's about calling out the nonsense that reaches parents, like when the Arizona Department of Education created an "equity" toolkit claiming that babies show the first signs of racism at three months old and that white children become full racists— "strongly biased in favor of whiteness"-by age five.[63]

C'MON PEOPLE. LET'S USE OUR BRAINS.

Instead of proliferating any of the above damaging ideologies, CRT, gender ideology, or the complete sexualization of children, we would be wise to heed the advice of Dr. Carson as he explains the remarkable human brain and its "massive intellectual potential." Using this brain in our heads is how our ancestors survived among savage beasts when all they had as weapons were rocks and the ability to reason. This brain is also what gives us the ability to recognize and respect each other. If you compare a human brain to a dog's brain, we find that the dog's brain has a more developed mid-brain, the part that allows a being to react— also known as fight or flight—which is why animals react much faster than humans. Humans have much larger frontal lobes than dogs, which is where rational thought processes happen. This means that we are smarter than animals and can use those lobes to analyze the content of one's character.[64] Why would we waste that skill and teach our kids to merely use their brains and react to skin color as animals do?

Then there is the fascinating phenomenon of brain plasticity in small children. Those that suffer from incurable seizures, may need to have half of the brain surgically removed, an operation known as a cerebral hemispherectomy. This sounds dramatic and life-altering to lose half of your brain! But young brains have so much plasticity that the remaining side of the brain can be retrained and recruited to take over functions that were lost when the other part of the brain was removed. Isn't that fascinating, a child with half a brain, can have a near-normal functioning life?! If you have been a parent for even as little as a couple of years, you've already marveled at how amazing that sponge-like brain works taking in the information we feed them. How important it must be—since there are actual neuroanatomical reasons that young people are so accepting and vulnerable to what we teach them,—that we are teaching them the right things. We should be fighting with everything in us to make sure it's objective truth and 100 percent correct.

Before you tell yourself, 'Yeah, that's all terrible stuff—gender ideology, CSE, and CRT, but it's not happening in my area.' Let me warn you that it is seething everywhere, you could be one election away, one rogue teacher, one drag queen story-time away from it being presented to your kids no matter where you live. Depending on your state's laws protecting parents' rights, you may have little recourse to protect your child from the aforementioned lies and the who-knows-what, even crazier stuff coming down the pipes. Have you heard of "furries"? These are animals that are trapped in a human body. Yes, it's a thing, and schools in Michigan, Utah, and Iowa have all had to debunk myths that litter boxes are provided in bathrooms for students who identify as cats.[65] You can't make this stuff up. You can go to school board meetings with a group of other angry parents.

Kudos to those who do, and keep up the good work! But unfortunately, as we've seen in some cases, it might make no difference at all. The absolute and effective difference you can make to change what your child is being taught is to go snatch them out of government school right now and bring them home to be taught by the one to two people on this entire planet that love and care for them more than anyone else. You. Can. Do. It.

Key Idea:
Educators are injecting harmful ideologies into young minds sexualizing children, promoting hatred for America, and sowing division through race, and parents can be powerless to stop it.

> *"He alone who owns the children owns the future." — Adolf Hitler*

Action Item:
Teach your children that immutable characteristics have nothing to do with someone's character. Demonstrate how to treat everyone as an individual created by a loving Father in the image and likeness of God. Don't accept, believe or joke about racial stereotypes which are perpetuated through society. Also, the next time your child tries to play the victim, blaming someone else for their problems, read this poem by Mayme White Miller, which Dr. Carson's wise mother would recite to him:

If things go bad for you,
And make you a bit ashamed,
Often you will find out that
You have yourself to blame

Swiftly we ran to mischief
And then the bad luck came
Why do we fault others
We have ourselves to blame

Whatever happens to us,
Here are the words we say,
"Had it not been for so and so,
Things wouldn't have gone that way"

And if you are short of friends
I'll tell you what to do
Make an examination,
You'll find the faults in you.

You're the captain of your ship,
So agree with the same
If you travel downward,
You have yourself to blame.

LIE #6:

Private or Christian Schools are Just as Good as Homeschooling, If Not Better.

"The most necessary task of civilization is to teach people how to think. It should be the primary purpose of our schools. The mind of a child is naturally active, it develops through exercise. Give a child plenty of exercise, for body and brain. The trouble with our way of educating is that it does not give elasticity to the mind. It casts the brain into a mold. It insists that the child must accept. It does not encourage original thought or reasoning, and it lays more stress on memory than observation." -Thomas A. Edison. Inventor, homeschool graduate.

"No pupils are greater than their teacher; but all pupils, when they have completed their training, will be like their teacher." Luke 6:40

FIRST, LET'S ACKNOWLEDGE THE reasons that parents see private and Christian schools as a good option. Perhaps they think that the teachers are more qualified to offer a solid education than themselves. Or, that a Christian school will do just as good a job at imbuing faith and a Biblical worldview as any parent could. They might feel like there'll be fewer behavior problems than those in government schools. Deep down they hope their child will become associated with a peer group that is driven to succeed by family legacies and parent pressure that will establish and build up his maturation and drive. Helicopter parents that hover over every detail of their child's education, urging him to pursue advanced classes and extra-curricular activities, see private schools as a cornucopia of opportunities that'll spruce up that college resume.

Unfortunately, the general population has been duped when it comes to most of today's private institutions. Usually, a Christian school merely mirrors government schools in many ways (allow me to draw a comparison at the high school level):

- Structure—students have around six classes a day on a bell schedule, and see as many teachers with copious amounts of wasted time, and hours of homework each night.
- Grouping—Academic classes are grouped by age and have 16-20[1] students per class on average (comparatively government schools have an average of 24 students per class).
- Teaching methods—Students sit at desks, listen to lectures, and take notes, with very limited time for hands-on learning or off-campus learning.
- Learning requirements—Students get a limited choice of courses to take for graduation with limited consideration for their own interests. (Inversely, as a homeschool parent catering an individualized education for my children, I have the freedom to choose exactly what they'll read, write, and study for any and all of their classes. I create and name the courses accordingly, whether it's English One, Geography, U.S. History, or any other class).

Parents end up paying big tuition, but with several students to accommodate in each classroom their kids still don't receive individualized attention. Children are zapped of their love of discovery as they are force-fed the same state requirements as government school students. It makes sense that the lower the student-to-teacher ratio, the more individualized attention and tutelage students receive. But even the most hoity-toity private schools can't boast the low ratio that the biggest homeschool families can.

Obviously, there are behavioral problems at every school, even the smallest homeschool, population one, will have to focus on teaching solid character to bypass bad behavior. However, another sweeping generalization persists that private education will have a positive impact on our children's social development and behavior. A study from the University of York found that a private school may actually damage students' social and emotional development. Yes, private school students are less likely to have behavioral problems than government school students but are still 15% more likely to be bullied, 24% more likely to take risks and are younger when they have their first alcoholic drink[2].

I will concur that there are some benefits that private and Christian institutions provide over government schools. They teach the kids about Jesus, and faith, and give them a chance to worship at school. My Catholic parish has a Pre-K thru eighth-grade school and I know that those kids that attend are truly learning about Jesus and the history of their faith. I asked my friend's eleven-year-old daughter about the *Immaculate Conception* and this little faith-filled child explained it to me perfectly! This is a concept that is very confusing for adults—even Catholic adults! Every December eighth, sitting in the pew before the start of the mass to celebrate the feast of the Immaculate Conception, I ask my husband, a Catholic since birth—or "cradle Catholic" as we call them, "What are we celebrating today? He attempts an answer, "Uhhhhh, when Mary got taken up to Heaven?"

"No."

"Oh, it's the wedding feast at Cana?"

"Nope."

"The miraculous conception of Jesus in Mary's womb by the Holy Spirit?"

"No, honey." I literally tell you this every year! It is the conception of Mary in the womb of her mother, St. Anne, *without the blemish of original sin.*"

"Ohhhh yeahhhhh," he concedes as he fails his quiz yet another year.

Kudos to *all the schools* with God in the curriculum that center on Jesus' teachings. America needs more of them and I pray that their enrollment grows. Unfortunately, that is not what's happening. Catholic schools are in a steady decline. From 2010-2020, nearly one in five catholic schools have been boarded up— the number of students declining by 439,581.[3] You'll start to understand why after I tell you about the problems that my family ran into when our eldest attended a Catholic high school.

I bought into the fallacy of Christian-schools-can-be-just-as-good-as-homeschooling during a transitional time in our family when we decided that a private Christian high school was my child's best option. During the six months that she attended, the things she personally witnessed, I can scarcely write without blushing. From kids fornicating on picnic tables outside the homecoming dance to rampant drug use. From sexual harassment among students—including the sharing of nude pictures on social media, to an inappropriate teacher-student relationship leading to the termination of a teacher. The issues ran the gamut of things from which parents hope to protect their kids.

One novel that my daughter was *required* to read in tenth grade had filthy language, racial slurs, and adult scenes. We petitioned parents and even wrote a letter to the bishop of the diocese to try to remove the inappropriate book as required reading. When we met with the principal, he told us that he supported his teachers' choices and granted them autonomy when choosing their materials. Something that I could've easily protected her from under my own [school] roof, became a glaring example of ungodly curriculum surreptitiously slithering its way onto a Christian school campus and into my daughter's life. If you're someone who is thinking, "Oh, that's no big deal, that's the norm with high school culture." I'd say, you've been hardened by the world's values. Desensitized. Now, you think you can't guard your daughter's innocence and purity. Sexual impurity is evil and relentless in pursuing our adolescents. We must be hyper-vigilant in protecting them. Like a Belgian Malinois attack dog, who locks his jaws on the trainer in the bite suit refusing to let go until the bad guy is suppressed, we must fight against it in all of its destructive forms, especially when it's presented innocuously by a teacher as required reading.

Fortunately, we went back to homeschooling that child. And our letters must've gotten through to the Bishop, and action was taken because the following year, that school had a new principal. Still, you can see how one teacher can open your child's mind to things that you'd not want in there at all.

As parents, we also want to protect children's developing minds from the anxiety and stress that today's youngsters are experiencing in record numbers. Anxiety caused by meritocracy, which bases a person's worth on ability and talent, is rampant in private and Christian schools and is having a horrible effect on students' mental health. The drive for private school students to achieve and keep themselves in the upper percentile is causing anxiety at rates three times that of their peers throughout the country. In a Silicon Valley high school, 54% of students displayed moderate to severe symptoms of depression, and an astonishing eight out of ten showed moderate to severe symptoms of anxiety [4]. Their parents are pushing for uppers to study with or downers so the child can sleep. Bouncing around until they hit upon the right doctor that'll prescribe drugs and diagnose the child thus securing an untimed SAT test, they carve out yet another advantage for their dear one. These infractions seem like a minor over-stepping of boundaries compared to Hollywood big-names bribing for perfect SAT scores and positions on athletic teams of sports their children didn't even play. Like something straight off the pseudo-script of the reality show *Real Housewives* they paid hundreds of millions of dollars and went as far as photoshopping their kids' heads onto other kids' bodies for phony team pictures to get them into choice colleges.

YOU'RE ENOUGH

Another falsehood that parents have gobbled up is that we aren't smart enough, educated enough, or have enough "classroom" experience to give our own child his best educational journey. Just because someone has a college degree, or a few years of experience in a classroom does not mean that they're an expert to whom you should blindly yield the rearing of your child. No one knows your baby—or what's best for him as well as you do! Studies have proven that it doesn't matter if you *even have a high school education*, you are still the best person to educate your child, and your child will fare much better than those being taught in institutions that require college degrees and teaching certifications of their instructors. Truly, "A parent's educational background has no substantive effect on their children's homeschool academic performance. Home-educated students' test scores remain between the 80-90th percentile whether their mother has a college degree or did not complete high school. Public school students were only in the 50th percentile."[5]

A POOR MODEL

Also, while we are on the subject of same-grade private schools—copycats of the government institution, it's a good time to dive a little deeper into where the American education model came from and the men who influenced it. In the late

18th century, Prussia, which is modern-day Germany, was one of the first countries to introduce free, same-grade, state-led education. After being defeated by Napoleon because the Prussian soldiers didn't follow command, they came up with a way to instill loyalty to the Crown and to train young men for the military and the bureaucracy. As German philosopher Johann Gottlieb Fichte, a key influence on the Prussian system, said, "The schools must fashion the person, and fashion him in such a way that he simply cannot will otherwise than what you wish him to will."[6] Fichte also made some speeches touting German superiority that were Anti-Semitic. Which made his philosophy and educational system deeply influential in the rise of the Third Reich. For real, he's referred to as the "Spiritual Father of Modern Neo-Nazism". He prophesied, "Education should aim at destroying free will so that after pupils are thus schooled, they will be incapable throughout the rest of their lives of thinking or acting otherwise than as their school masters would have wished." Fichte continues, "When this technique has been perfected, every government that has been in charge of education for more than one generation will be able to control its subjects securely without the need of armies or policemen."[7]

By dumbing kids down, killing the imagination, and removing any self-agency, this system worked splendidly for the basic training of minions. Citizens who can't or don't think critically are so much easier to govern than highly read, educated citizens who do. They wanted none of those thinking types. Instead, the goal was to reduce everyone to the same level of standard citizenry, thus squelching dissidence and individuality. Behavior modification techniques influenced students' habits and beliefs, like the bell system, for example, that would teach future factory workers to promptly start their day of monotonous work. It was successful for the Prussians in its design to get the students to do whatever the state commanded of them. It's been successful for social theorists indoctrinating America's youth for the last 8 or 9 decades, but I'll get to that in a moment. This begs the question, why would America take on an education model created by the "Spiritual Father of Modern Neo-Nazism"? A model which is the antithesis of homeschooling, might I add— not meant to inspire the love of learning or the flourishing of young minds. They did it, not for the good of the individual but for the good of the government. They did it for power and money.

Before I get to the men driven by money, I'll mention the influencer who was driven by government power. Horace Mann, also known as the Father of American Public Education was an American educator, who served on the US House of Representatives, and was the inaugural Head of the Board of Education in Massachusetts in 1837. He visited Prussia in 1843 to see for himself how their education system worked. Back then, access for all to free education was a pioneering idea, I cannot fault him there. But Mann, who grew up in Massachusetts during tense times between Catholics and Protestants figured that sending kids to the same small classroom could be a means of blurring the lines of religious differences, and as well, the class system, creating a more tolerant, civilized society.[8] He campaigned for the system in America, his home state of Massachusetts being the first to install it, along with compulsory attendance laws. Spreading from there it took about 50 years to implement throughout the United States. Homeschooling was the norm back then, and many parents opposed the compulsory laws. In some instances, the National Guard was called to force compliance.[9] Mann, however, recognized that snatching children out of the loving influence of their home life would be key for indoctrination, promoting the concept of the children belonging to the state when it came to education.

John D. Rockefeller, who also visited Prussia to see this well-working machine first-hand, provided the money and influenced the expansion of the Prussian system in America. Rockefeller must've been giddy when he saw the success they were having, imagining the droves of drones that the education system would be pumping out for his factories. Donating $180 million toward the implementation of the General Education Board (GEB), Rockefeller said, "I don't want a nation of thinkers, I want a nation of workers."[10]

A prominent member of the GEB and business advisor to Rockefeller, Frederick T. Gates, said himself," We shall not try to make these people or any of their children into philosophers or men of learning or of science. We are not to raise up among them authors, orators, poets, or men of letters. We shall not search for embryo great artists, painters, musicians. Nor will we cherish even the humbler ambition to raise up from among them lawyers, doctors, preachers, statesmen, of whom we now have ample supply."[11]

BAD INFLUENCES

Couple that depressing model with the influence that the Frankfurt School and its members had on educators in America and we have the woke mess of schools that is ripping America apart today—I already told you about government schools that have gone off the rails in adopting woke agendas, and please don't fool yourself into believing that it's not seeping into private and Christian institutions as well. The Manhattan Institute reports that 92% of young people who attended private schools were exposed to woke ideologies like "white privilege", "systemic racism" and that gender is a choice unrelated to biological sex. That's the same amount of exposure reported by those who attended government schools.[12] It's no wonder when you have rogues like Laura Delvecchio, assistant superintendent of the Plainfield Community School Corporation saying, "We stay under the radar. And we like to keep it that way," speaking of quietly slipping teachings on racial equity—including the "white privilege walk"—into school curriculum. [13] Other teachers bragged on hidden cameras about how they still teach the content from CRT and SEL, they just leave off the labels, so parents aren't privy and therefore cannot ask them questions or raise any concerns.

John Dewey's atheistic, Humanist influence on our modern education system didn't stop with compulsory attendance laws or the institution of the Prussian model. He also facilitated the move of the Frankfurt School from Germany to New York's Columbia University in 1935. "Bringing with it the dramatic convergence of Marxist philosophy, Freudian psychology, rank perversion and all manner of lurid ideas and practices introduced for the destruction and dismantling of Western culture by way of the destruction and dismantling of the family." [14] The guiding principle of the Frankfurt School, Critical Theory (CT)‹ is pervasive on college campuses today. The precursor to CRT, critical theory turns educators into activists, shifting the purpose of education from the goal of knowledge to the goal of change. Dewey taught philosophy of education at the teacher's college at Columbia University and by 1950 a whopping one-third of the nation's principals and superintendents of large school districts in the country had been trained there. [15] They returned to their districts and spread his philosophy throughout the nation. The insidious ideologies coming out of the Frankfurt School can be implicated in the sexual revolution and the rampant fatherlessness in our nation.

The mess of fellow Frankfurter Wilhelm Reich's childhood gives a glimpse into the perversion that he would incite through the sexual revolution. His mother was engaged in an extramarital affair for as long as he could remember. In his teens, he exposed the affair to his cold-hearted and abusive father. Later, his mother committed suicide because of the fallout. His tormented father attempted to do the same.

From childhood, Reich was consumed with sexual desires and deeds, including sexual encounters with maids, and sexual fixations with animals. A Communist with fervor for Marx's writings, he was a perfect fit for the Frankfurt School. His book, *Sexual Revolution,* which earned him the title of The Father of Sexual Revolution, propounded that it's only through the complete liberation of the libido that we can shed those pesky traditional, Judeo-Christian morals. Morality was always repressive, politically repressive even. Sexual freedom through meaningless sex, the birth control pill, and abortion would work to change society by freeing women for sex and chipping away at the family. For it is in that family that children's innocence and the notion of family is preserved. He believed that children should be encouraged to explore their sexual desires from an early age, and what better vehicle to get them to do that than mandated pre-pubescent sexual education? The sooner that kids are exposed to sex, especially when away from the moral guidance of their parents, the sooner they would want to act it out for themselves.

Today it's well-known in our Post-Christian world that many people despise God and conservative values. However, it is a bit baffling as to why these members of the Frankfurt school wanted to destroy the family. Why would anyone advocate for fatherless households? It's just evil. They shrewdly foresaw that Western culture was resistant to upheaval because of the authoritarianism imposed through the patriarchal family and belief in God.

Life is fulfilling when you serve God and welcome suffering. The very tenets of Christianity teach that to endure suffering brings you closer to God, building character, and bringing holiness. Because of this, Karl Marx deemed religion the "opiate of the masses". The members of the Frankfurt School, therefore, focused on weakening these two pillars of society—family, and faith in God, so that when they crumbled, all of society would too. If they could make people turn from God, and tear down the family unit, then misery would prevail until all people would revolt.

Have you been outside lately? Have you caught even one news headline across your home screen? Because if you have, you'd probably agree with me when I say, *Their strategy is working*. Today, one in four children in America lives in a fatherless home. In Mississippi, where it's the worst, that number is actually well over one-third. The absence of the father is to blame for many of the intractable social ailments affecting children, a detriment to a healthy childhood, and to the health of our nation. The presence of a father reduces the risk of emotional and behavioral problems, injury, obesity, poor grades in school, incarceration as a juvenile, alcohol and substance abuse, criminal activity, and suicide. Girls without fathers are seven times more likely to become pregnant as a teen and more likely to perpetuate the cycle by having babies with absentee fathers. Literally, an active father is so influential, his presence makes a difference even when his child is still in utero, low birth weight and infant mortality rates go down.[16]

The indoctrination system of schools—both government and private, that is rampant in our culture is having a raging success in subverting the father as the head of the family, weakening families, and turning people away from God. Christianity is hemorrhaging young people, Campus Renewal out of Austin Texas estimates that 60 to 80% of students leave their faith pretty much *as soon as* they get to college.[17] Can we really take the aforementioned system and throw in a Bible class and chapel once a week, and expect it to drive home the beliefs and values of our faith the way loving parents who build an education around these values could? If you believe, as I do, that the answer to that question is a resounding *No*, then read on. In the next chapter, we will talk about things that parents can do to strengthen their children's faith and that of the whole family.

Key Point:
Private and Christian schools have some of the same shortcomings as government schools and will be nowhere near as effective or influential as a parent teaching the faith.

Home is where the truth is:
Not sending your child to an educational institution can reap huge spiritual benefits. Let's not only consider the eighteen years in your care but also eternity. Millennials who were homeschooled are less likely to leave the faith than individuals who attended private or public schools. [1] Statistically, homeschooled young adults were six times as likely to be believers and seven times as likely to be stronger in their Christian beliefs as Millennials attending private schools.[1]

Action Item:
If your child attends a private school, think about all the money that you'll save on tuition when instead you're homeschooling. With your family's input, plan an educational trip with that money. If homeschooling is not in your immediate future, then get involved at the school (if you aren't already). Find out their policy about teaching progressive ideas like racial theories and gender ideology. Make a request and appointment to preview the curriculum they use for sex-ed.

LIE #7:

It's The Youth Pastor or Catechist's Job To Teach My Child The Faith.

"What is nobler than to rule minds or to mold the character of the young?"—St. John Chrysostom

"We will not hide these truths from our children; we will tell the next generation about the glorious deeds of the Lord, about his power and his mighty wonders. For he issued his laws to Jacob; he gave his instructions to Israel. He commanded our ancestors to teach them to their children, so the next generation might know them—even the children not yet born—and they in turn will teach their own children. So each generation should set its hope anew on God, not forgetting his glorious miracles and obeying his commands."
Psalm 78:4-7

O NE DAY, WHEN THIS life is over, we will all stand before God for judgment. I imagine there will be a review of the love we poured out, and what we did for His kingdom while we were on Earth. For posterity's sake, the most important of these: did you teach your children His truths? Precious parents, lean in as I tell you, it's *our* job and no one else's. Sure, it's great to have pastors, theology teachers, and youth leaders in the lives of our children, but the Christian home is the place where children receive the first proclamation of the faith. For this reason, the family home is rightly called the "domestic church", a community of grace and prayer, a school of human virtues and Christian charity.[1]

It's not only our responsibility, but our *privilege* to evangelize our kids and we must do it from the youngest, most tender, sponge-like age when they soak up everything we teach and without any doubt-they simply accept it. We should be the ones to teach them to pray, it's our job to familiarize them with God's teaching through reading Sacred Scripture, and we should be their biggest guide in helping them find their vocation from God. As a homeschooling household, you will find a vested joy in the development of their God-directed passions while teaching them the tenets of the faith.

Driving home from one "passion pursuit," a field trip to the local serpentarium, I had to laugh out loud as I read the huge decal blazoned across the rear glass of an old teal Honda Civic. Only eight letters, yet it chronicled a lifetime: *Mama Tried*. As a former renegade to good parents, I instantly related to my traffic chum. Also, having an adult progeny that could very well put that on her own car gave me a double chuckle.

To imbue the faith, my parents' efforts were dauntless and persistent. Mass attendance was a must every single Sunday, a high fever or scratchy throat was literally the only thing that got you out of it. (Believe me, I tried many times to skip.) They lived righteous, upright lives, serving others and showing us true examples of the Christian walk.

One trip antiquing with my parents as a child brought us to an old-time vending machine chock full of modern candy bars. I talked Dad into getting me one of these sweetmeats, as he pushed coins into the slot, I squealed in sheer joy as my *Three Musketeers* slid down the rust-encrusted ramp into the collecting bin. While happily playing with knobs on the relic, I realized that due to a glitch in the mechanics, it would spit out candy bars without putting more money in. My eyes bulged at the chocolate jackpot that I had just hit. As soon as

I reached to turn the knob again my Dad quickly shoed my hand away forbidding me to make it rain candy bars for all my siblings.

"No Maeve, you only paid for one. You may only take one or it's stealing," said he.

He straight-up made me strand the free candy bar in the machine, left as a testimony of honesty. Writing about it now, I still feel the pang of that life lesson. I can however find some respite in imagining the next little kid that came along and the elation that free shiny silver candy bar must've brought unto him.

This lesson in uprightness did stick because as an adult I try to live by the same honesty policy. When that small candle in the bottom of my TJ Maxx cart doesn't get rung up, I trudge across the sweltering parking lot, go back inside, and pay for it.

"Thanks for coming back," says the smiling cashier "Most people don't."

But that's just grown-up Maeve. Childhood Maeve still had quite a drifting journey ahead. My parents didn't realize that they were planting me, a tiny Christian seedling, out in persistent drought conditions, the harsh sun beating down on me, weeds choking me out in the hegemony of government school. Despite my parents' steadfastness, every day on government school campus eroded their efforts. The odds were horrible: classmates, peer pressure, and secular theories chipped away a little each day at all that mom and dad instilled in me. In a place where God is banned and irrelevant, and the truth is subjective, it was easy to get swept away in behaviors that were completely normal to most of my peers.

At my school, it was normal to lie to get ahead, or out of trouble. Cheating off of someone else was common and seized at every opportunity. I was the poster child for ditching my parents' values and trying to do whatever I could to fit in with my friends. (Remember the Prussian school model, that quickly transfers loyalty from family to friends?) I wasn't morally strong enough to do the right thing when twenty-five other kids my age were doing the wrong thing.

Maybe your kid is strong enough to make the right choice every time, I know there are some out there. I can remember them from my childhood. The "goodie-goodies" we dubbed them and taunted them every time they tried to stand up for what was right or simply refuse to do something wrong, or worse; cast light on our dark dealings. Is not the most common government school proverb: "Snitches get stitches?"

In a government school setting, around hundreds of peers...faith, God, and Jesus were all white noise for me and most of my counterparts.

Our little faith seedlings will grow much better in the protection of a greenhouse, where they get the proper nourishment and exposure. At a certain maturity level, (a level that the gardener will recognize) it's time to leave the greenhouse. The plant is healthier, stronger, and able to stand on its own in pretty much any condition.

The high school and young adult years proved impossible for me to stand on any moral convictions. You could've lumped me in with the 33% of young adults today that were raised in a Christian home and attended government school who engaged in cohabitating and fornication. (This is compared to only 9% of homeschooled individuals). [2] My story doesn't have a bad ending. I did personify the story of the prodigal son. After a life of partying which lead to horrible decisions, I left the lowermost dredges of the pig fields behind and returned to the Lord Jesus and the faith of my childhood. The emotional baggage collected along my prodigal path didn't shed immediately. Even though I can say that my path shaped who I am today, blah, blah. I wish I never went through it all, because some regrets never fully go away. To this day, when I'm trying to shut out the bad memories, I often wonder, what if I had been homeschooled? What if I had a cool youth pastor at my church who shared with me the fulfilling power of Jesus Christ over a stack of pizzas at youth group?

Youth groups can be an important tool in tilling the fertile soil of your child's heart. Meeting up with a bunch of age mates to play hilarious, team-building games is a fun and sociable way to introduce teens to Jesus, especially when there's food there! (Some of the best advice I ever got: NEVER have a Bible study without food.) I am so grateful for the wonderful youth pastors, and youth leaders that dedicate their time to the difficult, yet rewarding ministry to tweens, teens, and college kids. Unfortunately, we are bleeding out faith-filled youth in this country. It's called the "Youth exodus" and the statistics are both sad and scary. Much research is being done to find out why Generation X and Millennials are leaving the faith of their childhood, in droves larger than even Moses himself could corral. Of the 18–29-year-olds that were raised in church, at least 64% leave the faith.[3] A Lifeway study has the number of those who left the church in their college years, going on to declare themselves atheists, agnostics, or "none" (no religious affiliation) at 70%, and they're not coming back either. So don't tell yourself the lie, "Oh, everyone rebels and comes back to the church once they have kids of their own." That might've been the case with the Baby Boomers, but it drastically slowed with Gen. X, who are raising kids in a post-Christian world. Of the church drop-outs, only about 50% eventually return. Shockingly, only 9% of Generation Z and Millennials attend church.[4]

You might be thinking, well, those kids surely never went to Sunday school or Vacation Bible School, or maybe they didn't have a youth group where they could get a relatable message. But Ken Ham, founder of *Answers in Genesis* commissioned America's Research Group to dig deeper into the reason for the youth exodus. What their research found is astonishing. The study revealed that Sunday school was actually detrimental to spiritual health. Kids who grew up in a Sunday school environment were more likely to have a secular worldview than those who didn't.[5] *Wait, what?! How does that happen?*

As Hillary Morgan Ferrer points out in her book *Mama Bear Apologetics,* "Surprisingly enough, coloring pictures of animals in a boat and acting out "stories" on a felt board doesn't actually teach kids that what you are saying is *true.* It turns out, they believe exactly what we tell them: that these are Bible *stories.*"[6]

We must teach our brood how to view the world through a Biblical lens from a very early age and even more so in the middle to high school years. Train them in how to defend the truth and become disciples. Youth groups focus on entertaining the kids, and rightly so, what kid is going to invite their friend to come along and pray the rosary for an hour and a half? Winning (and retaining) kids requires pizza, lots of laughing, and of course Christ. Of the small amount of time they are at youth group, a large chunk of that will be spent playing Floor-Is-Lava and 'Heads Up!'

Gifted youth pastors know that it has to be fun to retain attendance and have youngsters with which to share the Gospel. Even though I'm not a youth pastor and my church didn't even have a youth group when I was growing up, I too know how important it is to teach the faith in an exciting way. Coming up in the Catholic church in the '80s, all we had was 'CCD', the most boring catechetical training ever inflicted on youth. I still don't know what the letters, CCD stand for, but it was widely used in the Catholic Church and still is. Gah! What a bore. As we sat there staring at a boring ol' handout, while the catechist droned on, I remember counting Styrofoam ceiling tiles in the agony of disinterested disgust! And yes, I too promptly left the church as soon as I could drive myself to mass. "By Mom and Dad, I'm taking the car to 12:00

mass." (Yeah right! More like, "I'm going to the nearest friend's house for exactly one hour.")

So yes, youth leaders we need you! Please bring on all the games and keep it fun! Unfortunately, it's hard to teach enduring discipleship in the remaining half-hour. As Lifeway's Ed Stetzer succinctly puts it, "Too many youth groups are holding tanks with pizza. There's no life transformation taking place. People are looking for a faith that can change them and be part of changing the world."[7] After all, your youth group leader, no matter how funny, relatable, and on-fire-for-the-Lord he is, cannot do in two hours a week what takes a lifetime of saturation.

When you look at how corrosive the culture is especially through the government school system, it's no wonder the 'nones' (those with no religious affiliation) are trending younger and younger. Some studies indicate as much as 46% have spiritually checked out as early as middle school, just cute little pew-warmers because their parents take them. However, your kids are your disciples, and with the help of the Holy Spirit (And Youth Pastor Kyle), you can teach them the faith.

Disciple comes from the Latin *discipulus* pupil, and from *discere* to learn. And wow, do they have a lot to learn if we want them to have a fighting chance. Unfortunately, it's not like two generations ago, when you merely had to know God created you, and the saving power of the Gospel. As Christianity becomes less socially accepted, and the youth exodus continues, we parents with faith and wisdom need to contend as if we were on a battlefield, fighting for their lives, nay fighting for eternity! We must never grow weary of the training and be relentless in pursuing their souls for Christ. Today they need worldview training—with what lens will they view their decisions? What are they going to say to the first person who tries to "save" them out of Catholicism or disprove Christianity? With Atheism, Moral Relativism,

Marxism, New Age Mysticism, and even Progressive Christianity, to name only a handful of the One-True-God detractors, we've got our work cut out for us, parents.

"Oh, that's your truth, but it's not my truth." With Relativism so rampant in our culture, what response would a young person have for that, if they haven't been taught that God is the source of truth, therefore truth is not a matter of individual opinion? If something is true in God's mind, then it's true regardless of whether we accept it or not. We must teach them that everything is relative to God's moral law and to recognize the cultural mendacities like, "Live your truth" (isn't that what Hitler was doing? *Living his truth.*) And, "Follow your heart," worst advice ever! Your heart will betray you, honey.

Relativism is self-defeating. For one, it demands that everyone is tolerant. But how tolerant are moral relativists to the intolerant? You Bigot, you homophobe, you transphobe, you're canceled. If a moral relativist says, "All truth is subjective," simply ask, "Is *that* truth subjective?" Let's try to get them to engage in logical reasoning. As they tout, "It's wrong to judge other people's truths," even the most *laissez-fair* weather relativist will have trouble saying that it's OK to torture helpless animals or to sell people as sex slaves. We all know right from wrong, it is "written in our hearts".[8]

As our children are bombarded with the false doctrine of Relativism at the lunch table, they need only walk to the science building to hear some secular, science-loving, scholarly type throw out this doubt-inflicting statement: "How can you believe those stories from the Bible? Science has disproven them?" If not armed with the truth, this question—which is a complete lie from the pit of Hell, has the potential to completely shut down a young Christian. But the facts are that science actually *proves* the accuracy of the Bible.

Let's take a look at the soft tissue that has been found in multiple dinosaur bones. Even a supposedly 180-million-year-old fossil of an extinct marine creature called an ichthyosaur contained blubber, residue, and skin that was still flexible![9] We observe in a lab the rapid breakdown of soft tissue. Even in the most ideal conditions, completely protected from moisture and elements it certainly cannot last hundreds of millions of years. These findings support the young Earth theory that comes from counting the generations from Adam to Jesus.

Speaking of Adam, does your child know that through the study of human DNA scientists found that all humans came from the same set of parents? (The report comes out of Rockefeller University and the University of Basel, Switzerland, published in the journal of Human Evolution). Even though the scientists who did the study don't believe in an 'Adam and Eve', and still tout Darwinian evolution, we believers know that finding confirms what Genesis tells us of our origin story.

The global flood can be proven by fossils of sea life found on the tops of mountains like the fossilized shellfish found in the Himalayas.[10] More scientific evidence of the worldwide flood is revealed by sediment layers carried rapidly across great distances, like the Tapeats Sandstone of the Grand Canyon which can be traced across the entire United States, up into Canada, and even across the Atlantic Ocean to England. These rapidly deposited rock layers had to be eroded from distant sources and carried long expanses by fast-moving water over a short period of time. What could've done that besides Noah's cataclysmic flood?

I've only mentioned a modicum of the scientific evidence that supports the truth of God's Word found in scripture. As your child's teacher, you can take fascinating science to archeologically deep levels, gently brushing away fragments of doubt, to uncover perfectly preserved truths. Then your child, who can be sure of the accuracy of God's word, will be better suited to defend it when the need arises. *Answers in*

Genesis has a plethora of this kind of information that you can find online. Or I highly recommend taking a trip to *The Ark Encounter* and *Creation Museum*.

Save yourself thousands of dollars and forgo an expensive Disney vacation and keep your kids safe from its woke agenda, which includes barring their staff from using gendered greetings, and using animated shows to groom children. One show geared toward preschoolers called *Dino Ranch* attempts to conjure sympathy for two male T-Rexes that wanted to be fathers together.

"These dino daddies want eggs of their own. They want a family," say the heroes of the show. "Aww, they'd be great dads."

Now, there's an interesting angle on how the dinosaurs went extinct.

Blatantly, the show is using its platform to normalize a behavior that is an abomination to the Lord.[11] Instead of spending your hard-earned money at a company that seeks to groom young minds, take your family to the Creation Museum and Ark Encounter—theme parks that teach and support the science and history of our faith. I guarantee you that their jaws will hit the floor when they lay eyes upon the life-sized Ark, they'll soak up the truth as they see that the story of Noah's flood isn't some cutesy children's story to decorate a child's nursery, but the reality of God's judgment and wrath poured out on a fallen world that has forgotten about him. (A timely and necessary message for today's world, don't you think?)

"Oh yeah, well, how'd Noah keep the Polar bears cold on the ark?"

This is an example of a fallacy meant to mock God and make your kid feel like a dummy for believing the story of Noah's Ark. When the question is turned back on the sarcastic inquisitor, they may be the ones who feel silly. First of all, a polar bear doesn't need to be cold to survive. For another, scientists agree that all bear species are derived from the same kind and are simply varying expressions of a particular kind. For example, coyotes, wolves, dingoes, and domestic dogs can generally interbreed. Thus, they can be lumped into the same kind. Certain traits that help them to adapt to their habitat, for polar bears, thick coats of hollow-hair-follicles to keep them warm in the frigid arctic tundra, will make their species' survival successful—Polar bears developed *since* the time of the flood. Therefore, Noah didn't even have polar bears on the Ark, instead he had one pair of bears from which the other eight species adapted.

"You believe gay people are going to hell, what loving God would send someone to hell just for loving another human? Why do Christians hate gay people?"

Oh, how our culture likes to disprove God with this moral dilemma, while making us feel guilty for holding to the truth of God's word, right!? No! We don't hate gay people. Sadly, there are some very hateful people who claim to be Christian yet treat homosexuals hatefully. And I would apologize on behalf of all Christians to anyone that has been treated wrongly because of their sexuality. Unfortunately, there are not many on either side of this argument that know what the Catechism of the Catholic Church says about how we should treat homosexuals which is: "The number of men and women who have deep-seated homosexual tendencies is not negligible. This inclination which is objectively disordered constitutes for most of them a trial. They must be accepted with respect, compassion and sensitivity. Every sign of unjust discrimination in their regard should be avoided. These persons are called to fulfill God's will in their lives, and if they are Christians, to unite the sacrifice of the Lord's cross and the difficulties they may encounter from their condition."[12] Does that sound hateful?

These are just a few of the fallacies that are going to beleaguer our children when they profess the Christian faith.

Even if you're not a creation science expert or a certified catechist there are some simple steps you can take to impact your children. For the following advice, I tapped into the wisdom of Rick Grinstead. Mr. Rick, as he is affectionately called by youth, has 26 years of experience in youth ministry and is currently director of Youth and Young Adult ministry at the Knoxville Cathedral of the Most Sacred Heart of Jesus. Formerly the youth pastor at my parish, I was blessed to know him and have my teenager go through his youth program. Truly a gifted minister, relationships are key for him. No matter the age of the child, he can in mere moments bond with them, kneeling down to their level, he asks them about themselves, and with a *high-five, low-five, you're too slow*, they instantly feel the acceptance for which all kids are searching. His slight sarcasm and quick wit engage the teen demographic, his sermons hit them where they are.

When Grinstead came to our parish, he was the first person in its 150-year history to take the youth group on a mission trip! Hyping *Alive in You* youth conferences with engaging and dynamic keynote addresses in the summer, fall would find him and his team of high schoolers putting on weekend retreats in which hundreds of kids would get to know Jesus through sharing testimonies, praying over one another, performing powerful skits and eating trays and trays of lasagna. His wife, Stephanie always helped in the kitchen to feed the hordes of high schoolers, even when she was about to birth their fifth, sixth, seventh, or eighth child.

The kids that came through Grinstead's program loved him and learned about Christ through that thriving relationship. They felt the unmistakable message: come as you are and be loved. This couldn't've been more blatantly illustrated by Jesse, a 16-year-old fella that you might've been scared to pass by on a dark street corner. Bedecked with grungy clothes, a pocket chain, and a pointy pink mohawk that stood a foot above his head, he humbly led his peers in the prayers of the Rosary each week.

Grinstead's advice to parents is that we have to get this idea out of our heads that we are our kids' friends, or that they even have to like us all the time for us to be good parents. Being a loving parent means calling them out on things that are harmful or not right *because* we love them. They might not like us in that moment, but we have a lot more wisdom than them. If we acknowledge that truth as a foundation for our parenting and do four specific things, then we can equip our kids to get through the doubts, the valleys, the famines, and the crises of faith.

FOUR NECESSARY THINGS IN THE RAISING OF GODLY KIDS.

"Number one is we have to pray with them daily. It's every day," said Grinstead. "My family likes nighttime prayer. (Making sure of course to pray before meals, which is great, but I don't count that.) It has to be a dedicated time to just pray together. The second thing is you have to read scripture. I don't even care if it's just sharing a bible verse every day. Listen to Father Michael Schmitz's Bible in a year, whatever it is, Bible every day." Rick continues, "And then the third thing, which I think is as important as the first two in the formation of the child is every single day the parent must tell the child they love them. My personal tip is three times a day, but you've got to say I love you to your children every single day."

The fourth thing we can do to influence their faith is to take them to church every single Sunday. Yes, even when we're on vacation or have a soccer tournament. Even though they may bemoan the boredom, the importance of making church the first priority cannot be overstated. (If they are anything like I was as a young adult, they will thank you for it in adulthood.) Those four things are going to sustain the hard years and make you the progenitor of faith and a trusted source for answers to tough questions.

Instead of going to Google for life's great mysteries, wouldn't you rather be their first trusted source? Many parents don't realize what kind of an impact we can have on our children. There's a distortion in society that has us believing that the more people we get our kids in front of the better, more well-rounded they'll be in all aspects of life. This simply is not true. You are key. Whether you are a hardcore Jesus Freak living the Christian walk or a parent who never talks to their kids about religion, you are going to influence them, one way or another. In your child's faith journey, you matter most. 67% of Millennials surveyed said that it was their mother or father, or a combination of both parents that gave them the most spiritual guidance in their life.[13]

Grinstead can tell within the first five minutes of talking to a kid which way their parents have influenced their spirituality—whether for the good or the bad. Those who are formed by their parents stand apart and stand up for what they believe a lot more strongly than the ones with parents who are more whimsical in what they view as acceptable or not. There are always exceptions and conversion stories of course, but if you want a child that has a strong faith, then you as a parent must demonstrate it, you must guide them towards it.

Now, on the flip side of that, If you want them to have a faith that's going to flounder in high school, college or beyond, then just be accepting of everything. If you want them to join the youth exodus then have this attitude: "What's right for some people is right, and then what's acceptable for others is OK for those people, regardless of what the Bible says." That's the way to breed some weak little Christians. The message of what's right or wrong is already very confusing because it varies from state to state, between social media platforms, and from school to school. We have the opportunity to be a firm anchor for them in a tumultuous sea of ambiguity.

I've heard some parents talk flippantly about this role, "Ah, they'll be in college in a couple of years anyway, what's the use?" What? No! We are not just having kids to graduate them and get them out of the house. I'm guilty of doing the math to figure out how old I'll be when we are finally empty-nesters--and don't ask—let's just say "past retirement age." But we only get one chance at raising them which will be over in the blink of an eye. Our role for those 18 years is to create disciples who will then create disciples. They should leave our house on a mission, on fire, and ready to make disciples in the world. It doesn't matter if I have helped them get straight As, a full college scholarship, and a sweet ride to cruise campus. If they are not leaving my home ready to go make other disciples, then I've failed miserably.

The duty is ours, but the results are the Holy Spirit's. With his guidance, and the powerful family bond that you'll share God will continually amaze you. When you are willing to follow while entrusting your family's faith journey to him, he will certainly lead an epic adventure. Faith-teaching moments will be popping up constantly.

When traveling, we make it a point to visit the local parish for Sunday mass and especially any Basilicas in the area. These little jaunts, in which we make worshipping a priority have constantly imbued us with faith and holy history. We've worshipped in countless breathtaking edifices and beheld a great deal of iconic art and architecture without having to travel to Europe to see some of the Greats.

In Cincinnati's Basilica *St. Peter in Chains*, we stumbled upon an exact replica of what some call the greatest sculpture ever created, Michelangelo's *Pietà*. When bombs were flying over Italy during World War II, this was cast from a mold made from the original in case it became a casualty of war. Here we stood close enough to see every fold of Mary's robe and take in the emotion on her face. We thanked God for the chance to see such a work of art and for the WWII history lesson that accompanied it.

Walking in the footsteps of saints and explorers who went before us is the most effective of history lessons when teaching the faith, or anything for that matter. Try as the government institutions might, you can't separate history from Christ. As my *Connecting With History* curriculum rightly puts it, *history is "His story."*

This was exactly the case when five Spanish galleons made landfall in what is now the oldest city in America, St. Augustine, Florida. Spanish explorer Don Pedro Menéndez de Avilés made it his duty to claim *La Florida* for Spain and spread Christianity to the indigenous peoples.

A 500-foot cross towers above the deep inlet, marking the site where Father Francisco López de Mendoza Grajales celebrated the first mass in the new world. Centuries later, when my family explored St. Augustine, my kids frolicked on the same "Sacred Acre" as it's now referred, under juniper trees that danced like ribbons in the breeze.

Almost as memorable, the visual aids that the Lord provides through archeologists and museum curators are major added bonuses. The kids marveled at Menéndez's stubby little coffin which looked like a child's, the average height of Spaniards being around five feet tall in his day. We gawked at ancient buckles, broken pottery, and barbarous weaponry with which you would not want to get killed.

On the same site as the first Mass in America, the Spanish settlement started a devotion to Our Lady of La Leche (Mary nursing the infant Jesus). And 450 years later, there in a chapel pew, I nursed my son, as I gazed upon a resplendent statue of Mary nursing baby Jesus. In a gracious moment like this, a parent can scarcely do more than thank the Lord and pray for more of them. Moments when parenting suddenly becomes weightless because we are living, learning, deepening, and passing on our faith all at once.

Key Point:

Parents are the greatest influence on their children. With that knowledge, we can rise to the blessed calling of teaching our children—not only what to believe, but why we believe it, therefore giving them the tools to defend their own doubts and their faith when challenged by peers. We must pray with them, read scripture to them, tell them we love them, and take them to church regularly.

Home Is Where the Truth Is:

In the U.S. currently around 3.3% of kids are homeschooled. 8% of the men in Catholic Seminary were homeschooled.[1]

Action Item:

Start digging into resources that can help you teach your children the faith. Sites like Answersingenesis.org, books like *Mama Bear Apologetics* by Hilary Morgan Ferrer, and tools like Friendly Defenders Catholic Flash Cards will all help implement the faith no matter what your current wisdom levels are.

LIE #8:

Homeschoolers Are Weirdos.

"Normal? What is normal? That's just a setting on your washer." —Heidi St. John, Author, and host of Off The Bench Podcast

"But now, O Lord, you are our Father; we are the clay, and you are our potter; we are all the work of your hand." Isaiah 64:8

A s I write this, I am interrupted by my tween asking me to safety-pin her ancient-Mesopotamian robe, a ripped-in-half sheet, bedecked with fabric marker stars, wrapped around her slender frame and thrown over her shoulder. A queen's headdress adorns her head, fashioned from poster board and tempura paint. Our history study of ancient culture sparked her imagination into live-action role-playing as the ancient Sumerian queen. Indeed, all of the kids— even my boys, are on an imaginative quest, wearing robes and playing the part of Gilgamesh's contemporaries.

I think back to my ninth-grade English in a huge government school and remember shuddering at the teacher's mention of togas for a class play. No way was I going to drop my cool factor one iota of a percent and let any of my public schoolmates see me try to embrace any culture that wasn't pop. Fitting in, being mainstream was the only thing that mattered to me, to the demise of my imaginative self-expression.

For some people, when they hear the word homeschool, their mind automatically conjures a stereotype. Perhaps something like Laura Ingalls Wilder milking the goats in a long prairie skirt, or an awkward kid dressed in business-casual attire with his golf shirt buttoned all the way up, pants jacked-up almost as high, homeschoolers are just weird. But you don't have to walk very far down the sidewalk of a government high school to see all kinds of people who don't fit a "normal" mold. You'll see kids way into their teen years wearing Hello Kitty beanies, you've got "band nerds" as they were derogatorily referred to in my high school, Anime aficionados, Emo kids, all different types of self-expression. So actually, what is weird? Who decides? The popular kids at school? Mainstream, pop culture? Even sadly, parents that want their kids to fit in? Let's remove all those from the eccentric equation, (as pop culture should be...need I remind you of sagging britches, The Macarena, and the mullet which has surprisingly made its second comeback.)

Then who does? God, that's who! Each individual is fearfully and wonderfully made with just that—individuality! Self-expression without the fear of judgment is how a child will gain confidence, forget about pleasing the crowd, and become the best version of themselves.

Now, if you are a parent thinking about homeschooling and you believe the lie that homeschoolers are weird, ask yourself this: Am I weird? While you are introspecting in this fashion, can you recall blurting something out that made you say, *Wow, I've turned into my mom.* The statement that made me say it was, "We can't have anything nice, thanks to you kids!" Another trait I definitely inherited from my Mom is Misophonia (which is being triggered by certain noises such as smacking, slurping, or the super-annoying voices of cartoon characters like Gonzo from the Muppet Babies cartoon of the 80s.) And even though fourteen-year-old Maeve was adamant that she would never employ *any* of her parents' parenting methods, fast-forward thirty years and it seems as though I've stolen their playbook entirely.

Remember what I told you in the last chapter about how much influence you have? Let's have some pattern recognition here. It doesn't really matter if someone attends school or doesn't attend school. Likely, they're going to have some of the same personality traits, mannerisms, and beliefs as the people who raised them. Consider how much you turned out like the parents who raised you, whether for the good or the bad. This one will really fall on you, Mom and Dad.

Along this same 'weird' thread, I've had multiple parents tell me that they just want to expose their kids to real-world stuff so that their children will know how to react, or won't be shocked when social bumps and bruises occur. That first time someone snatches the ball out of their hands. Getting publicly dissed, and laughed at by the crowd. Friends backstabbing. Broken hearts. It's all bound to happen. So why not throw them to the wolves while they're but five years old, surely they'll eventually fight their way to the top of the pecking order, right? Can these parents really have thought it all the way through? They are refusing to keep their own child in an environment where they are constantly thriving (home), to instead send them out to get harassed, bullied, and basically just have lots of sucky days. All for the simple skill of learning how to react to these skirmishes?

No matter who you are, or where you rank on the popularity spectrum, the wisdom of Mike Tyson applies to you. "Everybody has a plan until they get punched in the mouth." With the myriad problems in government schools, trying to fit in with the crowd, and peer loyalty over familial loyalty, I will choose to give my kids less practice reacting to the proverbial punch in the mouth and more practice using the genuine personality with which God created them.

Yes, I will admit that my children were older than kindergarten age when they got their first experience with jerks. My son was nine when we sent him to his first soccer day camp. He came home with stories of a kid continually talking smack about his goalie skills. Now, I must tell you that smack-talking in the sporting arena is actually a life skill that we Jemisons hold in high regard. My husband is a living legend, you don't want to battle against him, because depending on your 'dissibility', which is your capacity to be dissed—you could get straight-up roasted. We've had bouts around the dinner table, drilling our kids on witty comebacks. "C'mon honey, just find a weakness and hone in on it," we tell them. "Saying anything is better than saying nothing," urges Hubs. "Deescalate with humor!" We worked those dissing muscles for when it was time to bust them out in the real world. We aren't aiming to hurt anyone's feelings, but kids need the verbiage to easily deflect that which the bully hoped would deflate them. When it came to the soccer brat, we did what any good parents would do, we gave him some one-liners to trash-talk back at the kid. Then had him practice them a couple of times for delivery's sake, and sent him back with the confidence to defend himself. Which he did.

My "sheltered" homeschooled son had an advantage over all the other kids out there who get these types of mental beatings on a daily basis. He saw behavior from a peer that he didn't want to accept as normal. He trusted my husband and me enough to come to us for advice to solve it. Because we as his parents are his first teachers, main mentors, and life coaches we know him best and easily crafted a solution in a clever comeback that shut the other kid down. He stopped picking on my boy, gave him some respect, and even complimented him on a blocked goal the following day.

This was a trifle situation on the soccer field. On campuses where children get bullied constantly day in and day out it's a much bigger problem. They may try to ignore the bullies, and try going to the authorities, but the antagonizing remains relentless. I saw it when I was a high school teacher and I remember it from when I was in school. Today, one in five kids reports being bullied, the most common reasons being physical appearance, race/ethnicity, gender, disability, religion, and sexual orientation. [1] Less than half of them report it to an adult.

This can turn much more vicious and sadistic leaving devastated families and innocent victims in its wake. Since 1982, there have been 126 mass school shootings (at the time of this book's publication), The 20-21 school year had the highest amount since data collection began, 93 school shootings with casualties,[2] and 2022 broke the record for the most school shootings in over four decades.[3]

Since there is no shortage of marginalized, emotionally disturbed, angry young people in America, this count is most likely going to continue to climb. Although there is not a specific psychological profile that'll predict if someone will turn into a deranged psychopath releasing their anger on classrooms of innocent people, there are some things that most school shooters have in common, such as profound feelings of rejection and a history of having been bullied. Many shooters also display a fascination with guns and a preoccupation with violence.[4]

I'll never forget the day of the tragic Sandy Hook shootings. Halfway across the country secure under my own roof I knew my children were safe. My stomach churned as I watched the terror the parents felt as they waited outside the school for their child, hoping to see their precious, innocent baby come running into their arms. My close friend, Laura, who sent her kids to a private Christian school was watching it unfold and called me with tears in her eyes, her voice quavering, "I just can't believe how evil this is, it could happen anywhere. I'm going to homeschool my kids," Laura decided that day.

Your kids will never be as safe as they are in your home. With their trusted parent as a teacher, and siblings as classmates, in a 'safe learning environment'. One where kids are free to give the wrong answer without snickers from 25 other kids. They are free to express themselves through their wildest imagination without a peer looking down their nose at them, making fun of them, or worse attaching a nickname to their unorthodox personality.

Now, let me be clear, I am not suggesting that their own housemates will never give them dirty looks or scoff and roll their eyes at wrong answers. I battle this all the time, especially in the older, all-knowing teenagers. But as a parent, you can discipline that kind of junk behavior and teach the character of tolerance and understanding.

As you regulate the bad behavior of the ridiculers, it's just as important to teach those on the receiving end to be resilient. We aren't trying to raise a bunch of snowflakes. There are going to be many traumas in childhood, whether its "little t" trauma like falling down in front of the whole class and them laughing at you, not making a sports team, or skirmishes with playmates, to "big T" trauma, like the loss of a loved one, being dumped by the love of their life, and not getting into the college of their dreams. Resiliency is learning from negative experiences and coming out of the valley more mature and wiser than when you walked in its shadows. It's the opposite of fragility which prizes playing it safe over the risk of failure. Resilient people look at problems as opportunities for growth. They live life unafraid to try new things and grow through the learning process, instead of sitting out—safely on the sidelines.

Dr. Kathy Koch, founder of *Celebrate Kids* and author of many books teaching parents how to raise thriving kids, has influenced thousands of students, parents and teachers through speaking engagements in over 25 countries. Her book, *Resilient Kids, Raising Them to Embrace Life With Confidence* is a treasure trove of tips and tricks parents can use to teach their kids to bounce back, I highly recommend that you read it to dive deep into resilient coaching but in the interest of getting you some tools right now, ahead are some of her nuggets of wisdom.

One of the wisest and most effective things that we should employ as parents is an intentional connection through ongoing conversations. Healthy connections mean strong bonds between you and your children, this empowers children to turn to you for help in becoming resilient. It can be hard to get a child to talk about their hurts and fears. All parents have been on the receiving end of grunts, silence, and shoulder shrugs when trying to dig deeper into our kids' psyche— or even when asking something as simple as *What do you want for dinner?*. Kids are more likely to open up when they don't think that you are listening to judge them, but instead listening to understand them. Don't dismiss their pain, acknowledge it.

After my son allowed his little brother to play with a cherished Grave Digger monster truck, he became irate after realizing li'l bro had lost it. When my elder son came to me in tears, I was tempted to say something like, "Oh honey, he didn't mean to lose it, he's only four years old." Or "It's just a toy truck you have dozens of them. It'll turn up soon." Instead, I did what Dr. Koch suggested and named his pain. "You must be angry that he didn't take care of your toy," I acknowledged. "You were kind to him, and he was irresponsible, and that doesn't feel good, does it?" He melted into my warm hug, and I realized that was what he needed to get past the disappointment.

Another great tip in these bonding conversations is to make leading statements instead of follow-up questions. Follow-up questions like *"What happened next?"*, *"Why'd they make fun of you?"*, Or *"What did you do after that?"* can shift the conversation down a different avenue that the young mind wasn't ready to think about. We should avoid those especially since our tone of voice can betray us revealing judgment, anger, fear, or disappointment. We might not even realize it until it's too late, but kids are adept to pick up on these tones. Instead, with a leading tone of voice, you could say, *"Keep sharing," "Help me understand,"* or *"I have time...go on."*

Be careful when listening, and "wear your parent face" to hide emotional responses. While a child is sharing their feelings, they're more likely to keep talking when parents are emotionally neutral for the time being. If you show anger, fear, aggravation, or disappointment they might clam up or even change the story to try to keep you placated.

When you have the golden moment when your child is confiding in you as the safe place to share their hurt, what an inopportune time for your phone to go off. Leave the phone behind. Silence it and let them know you've done so. This will make your child feel important, which lays the groundwork for more heartfelt conversations. We've all had enough experience in this tech-obsessed world to know that we don't want to share in intimate conversations with someone who is always checking their phone. We especially don't want to start a difficult conversation if we think there's a chance we'll have to start all over because of a phone alert.

We parents are key in the resiliency process. Yes, teachers, mentors, and coaches can help too, but this job is mainly ours. "When you teach them how to bounce back, make healthy decisions, and develop mature character, they can be competent. Now you are their coach," Koch says, "By being a voice of truth, their dictionary, safe healing place, a source of hope, and their coach, you provide profound support and give them inner resources."[5]

Our children's success is top on our life's wish-list, but we shouldn't provide too much support. This is a difficult one for me and I'm sure for a lot of other control-freak-child-bubble-wrapping homeschool moms. Struggling is good for our children, so we need to step back and let them work through hard things without jumping in the minute they start whining and doubting themselves. There are some not-so-good outcomes if we do our best helicopter imitation over everything they do: They'll be dependent, which isn't the same as trusting you. It can actually make young people angry because they may start to see you as interfering. [6] Quit hovering. It sends several wrong messages like, *I'm incapable, My parents don't think I can do anything right, I can't make a mistake or mom will be mad.* That is a fragile child's self-talk. We can rescue them when they need help, but not before they work through the challenge on their own. We want their inner voice to say things like *My parents believe I can do this, Dad can help me get better at this, It's ok to fail if I learn from it and don't give up.*

The next time you're tempted to jump in and save your child from a hardship stop and ask yourself, "Has my character been changed for the better from overcoming challenges?" Haven't you grown when you were stretched beyond your comfort zone? When children are faced with hard tasks it forces them to discover those strengths, abilities, and passions that might've otherwise laid dormant. They'll get that good taste of diligence, perseverance, and problem-solving. When they work those resiliency muscles they'll charge into new things because failure won't be so scary.

One father's optimism toward failure impacted his daughter greatly. Sara Blakely The founder of Spanx Shapewear, was named the world's youngest, self-made female billionaire by Forbes Magazine and one of TIME's 100 Most Influential People. She said, "Growing up [my father] would actually encourage me to fail. I would come home from school and he would say to my brother and me, 'So, what'd you guys fail at this week?' And if I didn't have something he would actually be disappointed. But if I came home like Dad, Dad! I tried out for this thing and I was horrible," then he would say, 'Yeah!' And slap me a high five."[7] She didn't realize it at the time, but he was just changing her definition of failure. Her definition of failure became not about the outcome, but about *not trying*.

I'm stealing that! What a wonderful way to show our kids that we are proud of them for trying hard things, for struggling through hardships, and for having the courage to keep trying, because failure isn't final unless you give up.

The next time you are tempted to judge a homeschooler as weird because they don't fit your idea of normal, instead ask yourself, is this kid comfortable being himself? Is he resilient to others' judgment? To the detriment of society, I would suggest that the following are anomalies in the general population:

- School-aged kids who are not interested in auditioning for others' approval.
- School-aged kids who are not afraid to try new things because they are resilient and know how to process pain, fear, and regret in a healthy way— by learning from it.
- School-aged kids who trust their parents for advice and mentoring because the parents are fully present in all aspects of their children's lives.
- Parents engaging in intentional ongoing conversations to keep an emotional connection, and to help their children deal with doubt, depression, and questions in real time.

Well, if those things are weird, then sign my kids and me up! I say, "Kids get dressed in your business-casual attire, we're going out into the world (while all of your government school counterparts are stuck in a classroom) to try new things and fail at them. Again, and again!"

Key Point:

Individuality should be celebrated and nurtured. Letting our children develop their God-given personality without judgment and scorn from a mainstream peer group is much healthier for them than trying to fit into a 'normal' mold throughout their adolescence. We also must let our kids struggle through challenges so that they lose the fear of failure and learn the powers of perseverance, diligence, and problem-solving.

> *"Trying new things and not being afraid to fail along the way are more important than what you learn in school."* ~ Sara Blakely, Spanxx inventor

Action Item:

Reflect on your own character qualities that you hope to pass on to your children. Realize that you are imbuing them with all that goodness. Feel good about yourself as a parent. Also, consider your foibles that you don't want to see in your kids when they grow up. Pray for help in overcoming them.

Visit CelebrateKids.com, browse through the plethora of wonderful parenting advice, put Dr. Kathy Koch's books on your reading list, follow her on Instagram @celebratekidsinc, and check out her podcast.

LIE #9:

They'll Miss All of Their Government School Friends.

"Be courteous to all, but intimate with few, and let those few be well tried before you give them your confidence." — George Washington

"The righteous choose their friends carefully, but the way of the wicked leads them astray."
Proverbs 14:7

A CUTE, LITTLE, WISPY-soft head bobs in the picture window of a red brick home perched on a hilltop in Suburbia. The panoramic view of the street below boosts his adrenaline as he awaits his beloved brother. Although there's only a couple of years difference, hero status is well-established, and watching his hero arrive home from school every day sets his little heart atwitter. Finally, he hears the squeaky brakes of the big yellow bus, and off slogs a tired third-grader after another long day cooped up in a room of 30 age-mates. His backpack carries an empty lunchbox and a heavy homework folder. He's frazzled, hungry, and cranky because of a bully's snarky comment about something as trivial as the socks he chose that day. "Bubba!" The little one yells as he wraps his big brother in a waist-high bear hug. But all Bubba can muster is a dismissive pat on his back as his backpack slides down his arm, landing with a thud. All he wants is to get as far away as possible, to the nearest video game or glowing screen to decompress. The teacher got his most energized hours, which are far behind him now. Home life gets the worst of him because time at home is simply a place to sleep, change clothes, and charge a device. Mom has been reduced to a list-checker. Did you do your homework? Did you turn in your assignment? Time for bed. Time to wake up. Quick the bus'll be here! Go! And the little stranger in his own home is gone again on a never-ending cycle.

Let me invite you to a new routine, one that allows you to be enchanted with your children, to encourage them, to form them, to know them. Your precious darlings are sons and daughters of the King, therefore he put the family in place so that parents could delight in their children, as He delights in us. So that parents can intimately know their children, as He intimately knows us.

Some parents were willing to go to jail to cling to that kind of relationship with their li'l folks, refusing to send them off daily only to have them come home as strangers. Back in the mid-1980s, Zan Tyler was threatened with jail time by the State Superintendent of Education if she didn't obey the compulsory attendance laws in South Carolina. Although she was scared and all alone— the Tylers didn't know one family in the entire world that was homeschooling—she fought and lobbied for what she knew was best for her children. Her battle was arduous, with many trips to the state capitol over eight years. Her enemies told her, *You'll never win this.* Despite her battle fatigue, she refused to accept the first offer lawmakers offered. Because they tried to attach stipulations to the homeschool bill requiring parents to have a four-year college degree and to use state-mandated curriculum. Even though there were times when she wanted to quit, she persevered and ultimately helped write the homeschool law that South Carolina adopted and is still using today. That is, any parent with a GED or high school diploma can educate their kids using whatever curriculum and methods they deem best for their family.

Now that her kids are grown, she gets joy from inspiring homeschool families on their journey. In her book, *7 Tools for Cultivating Your Child's Potential*, Tyler says, "God ordained the family to be a powerful, life-shaping force in the lives of our children...it should be a vibrant center of education, industry, service, and worship. God created the family to be a place bursting with activity and conversation while simultaneously providing peace and refuge. The family was chosen by God to energetically and effectively nourish and cultivate human potential."

God wants *you* to be the main influence in your child's life, and your home to be a place where you serve, work, study and just chillax together. Homeschooling allows that freedom. When you don't have to wake up at 6 AM and drop them off at three different schools (just imagine the time you'll get back from parent-pick-up lines alone!), you have time to study your kids, give them emotional support, and deal with bad character issues in real-time. When there's no clock to rush against, meaningful conversations ensue naturally. A slow pace and the Holy Spirit are the two main ingredients for the sharing of teachable moments, deep questions, and real-life stories.

When they aren't pulled hither and tither with extracurricular activities you get the best of them, and their siblings get the best of them. Instead of people who annoy them, younger siblings become playmates. (There will still be times when they vex one another, of course that won't completely disappear.) One of the most beautiful and enjoyable things about our homeschool journey is the ever-ripening bond of our family. Moments that cultivate our family culture and help us to know one another deeply come to us as little treasures along the path of life. For instance, in one of our read-alouds, an awkward protagonist tripped over a piece of firewood, embarrassing himself in front of his crush. I recounted the story of their dad's flirting skills (or lack thereof) back in our early days. Ordering a John Wayne Burger at least once a week, and always requesting to be seated in my section at the BBQ joint where I waited tables, one compliment that dang man gave me went something like, "Your hair looks really good today, usually it looks like you just got out of the shower and came to work like that." Now, would I have ever been able to dis on Mat's flirting skills with an analogous and historical family story if we hadn't read that book together? Yeah probably...but talk about the perfect segue.

Parents to children and sibling to sibling, the relationships forged in a homeschool deepen over the years especially when there are not countless peers vying for their attention. When the Prussian school model isn't able to turn kids 'loyalty away from their families, that bond is strengthened through *dependence on* and *time with* one another. These are bonds that will last a lifetime and since we are raising parents for our grandchildren, we'd better take it seriously. If you take your children out of school, it will probably only be a couple of weeks until you see your family becoming more united in love.

There's another change you may start to see in your kids when you bring them home. This amazing skill that I'm about to tell you about gets sucked out of them by the original Prussian school model, (that I told you about in chapter six) which forcibly keeps kids together — whether they like each other or not —throughout their school years. Homeschool children have uncanny confidence and a sharp knack for discerning when a friend isn't right for them. From around the age of seven or eight, all of my kids have edited kids off the playdate list, and for valid reasons. There was an extremely hyper friend who refused to listen to house rules and would constantly horseplay as soon as I was out of the room. My son saw the disobedience and disrespect and wanted nothing to do with him. Then there was the playmate who constantly used a rude tone of voice and peppered in "G-Bombs" (using the Lord's name in vain). The dishonor of herself and The Lord was too much for my daughter. She pulled me aside later telling me why she didn't want to play with that peer. When they did that, I always honored it.

This channel of communication always leaves me a little awe-struck and proud. Thinking back, that was a skill I can remember possessing as a sassy six-year-old, but as a government school student, that skill eroded over the years until I happily palled around with parents'-worst-nightmares when it came to bad influencers. Indoctrinated with a yearning to fit in with the popular crowd, their character was of no importance. I couldn't have cared less if they were good friend material, or even if they were nice to me. I just wanted to be accepted. What mattered was status: were they a jock, super pretty, or top of the high school pecking order? This lack of discernment on my part led to low self-esteem and a regrettable bad-boy phase that I'd very well like to forget. This skill—expunging toxic people and false connections is one that I want my children to hone as sharp as a razor. Can you imagine all the drama and deadbeats they'll disassociate with over the course of their social life, how much heartache from which they'll save themselves?

Since it's common for young people, especially teens to have relationship-based beliefs[1], we must be very selective and careful about whom we allow our children to hang out with. As the old adage goes: "Show me your friends and I'll show you your future." If your kids are hanging around with people who don't believe in God, or don't believe in the saving sacrifice of Jesus Christ, or do believe that gender is completely fluid, you shouldn't be surprised if they begin to question what you've taught them. It may only take one influential peer to turn your youngster's belief system on its head, completely rejecting teachings with which they previously agreed.

During adolescence, healthy teens usually look for ways to separate from their families and define themselves as individuals.[2] Therefore, it is highly beneficial to help them find healthy role models. We must be on high alert, seeking out other adults and proper mentors who will support us in our efforts. If these people are closer in age to our children, they may be able to better relate to their temptations and struggles than we could. Don't limit your standards of "proper role models" to the ones that your kids can physically hang out with. You must be present in your child's life and intentional in knowing the social media influencers they're following, the shows they are binge-watching, and the songs they're playing on repeat. All of these will also have a major influence on beliefs.

I took my eldest child out of government school in sixth grade, at the beginning of a blossoming social life. When I tell you that my first born is a social butterfly, I mean that she scored the highest possible score for a social extravert on the personality test, literally the quintessence of someone who loves to be around people. Pulling her out mid-year, I readily admit that I was worried about her missing her friends.

Looking back on it now, she says that she really didn't miss those sixth graders that she was used to seeing in her classrooms, lunchroom, and school hallways. "I realized that they weren't really my friends and I only considered them friends because I was with them every day," she said. It's worth stating that she does still have her best friend whom she met in kindergarten even though that friend stayed the government school route. If two kids truly have a bond, it'll prevail over the years through different seasons of life, school changes, and even relocations.

Friends outside the home are important, I'm not saying to hole up and make your kids stare at each other all day every day. There are some friends you hope your kids never meet: pimps, street gangs, cartels, or gang recruiters. You might think that I am being a bit sensational here, but according to Joseph Travers, founder of *Saved in America,* a group of ex-law enforcement officers, and Navy Seals that search for missing victims of human trafficking, there is something very dangerous happening on middle and high school campuses.

A 16-year-old Southern California high school girl walks into the living room where her mom sits watching TV. "Hey mom, can I ride my bike to Janey's house? I'm done with my homework."

"Ok, hon stay on the main road, don't take the back roads. Be home before dark."

When she doesn't come home, Travers's team of retired special operators and social networking investigators, don't have to dig very far to figure out what's happened. They quickly find in her social media, that to which she was blind. With low self-esteem and naïveté, she was a prime target for grooming from gang recruiters. Pouring it on thick with compliments, double-tapping to 'like' every post, they know that all they have to do is get her alone, offer her drugs and they'll have something to sell over and over again—her.

Since 2008, when the borders were opened, the sex trafficking industry has sky-rocketed. This is because the trafficking of drugs is directly connected to the trafficking of humans. At any time in the U.S., there are 100,000 enslaved individuals being trafficked.[3]

You might have a flash of the Liam Neisen movie *Taken* where a naive girl travels to a different country and gets snatched by an evil drug lord. And think, "I would never let my teen travel to a dangerous place alone, therefore it can't happen to my child." But here's the scary truth: According to Travers, there is at least one recruiter in every high school and middle school in San Diego. Knowing this information, he says that public schools are where traffickers find most of their victims.

These scum lurk in public schools, using cell phones and social media to groom young girls with low self-esteem or who are emotionally vulnerable. Unfortunately, a little flattery and flirting can be all it takes to win the girls over. Coercion quickly escalates with drugs, verbal and physical abuse. Sex traffickers' drugs of choice are alcohol, cocaine, sedatives, marijuana, and especially heroin because of its highly addictive nature. When addiction sets in, they'll do whatever it takes to keep access to the drugs. Running away from home, they sell their bodies for drugs.

Travers gives all the glory to God for the fact that he has reunited over 260 lost children with their parents. Is it any surprise that he suggests one of the things you can do to protect your child is to homeschool them or at the very least send them to a private school? Also, he suggests parenting them by knowing exactly who their friends are, monitoring what they are doing on social media, and being familiar with what interests them. "The most important thing is, a parent needs to know a child's cell phone. These little computers we have in our hands at our disposal, kids are getting them younger and younger," Travers warns. "The parent should know as much about the cell phone as they possibly can. That's how the traffickers communicate with the child."[4]

Although, *Saved In America* has had great success in reuniting families, the trauma that these young girls go through cannot be undone. Sadly, many sex-trafficking victims are found dead, or never heard from again.

We only get one shot at raising our kids. Educating them at home is not for the lazy parent or the parent that wants someone else to raise their kids for them. Rather, it's for the parent that wants to delight in their child with limitless perseverance, influence them, and teach them a Biblical worldview. When those 18 years fly by and it's your turn to stand in the picture window, waiting for them to come home, do you think you will say to yourself, "Man, I wish I would've had less time with them, why didn't I just send them to school every day?"

Key Point:

God designed the family to be a source of influence, support, camaraderie, and refuge. Not only will relationships in a homeschool household strengthen when kids are no longer sent away to learn among peers every day, but kids will be kept safe from the pimps and gang recruiters that lurk in middle and high schools looking for victims.

Home Is Where the Truth Is:

Kids who attend school spend at least 25,000 hours away from their parents from ages 5-18. Factoring in bus rides and extracurricular activities pushes that number to nearly 30,000 hours.

Action Item:

This one is two-fold and both are of immense importance. If you don't already, check your child's phone and social media. Know with whom they are communicating and what they're talking about. Also, pray for the continued success of the life-saving team *Saved in America* and the complete eradication of child sex-trafficking. Go to savedinamerica.org to learn more, donate or volunteer with this essential organization.

LIE #10:

You Should Teach According to the Government Benchmarks Instead of Igniting Their Passions and Tailoring Their Education.

"A freeman ought not to be a slave in the acquisition of knowledge of any kind. Bodily exercise, when compulsory, does no harm to the body; but knowledge which is acquired under compulsion obtains no hold on the mind. Do not use compulsion, but let early education be a sort of amusement; you will then be better able to find out the natural bent." —Plato

"Do not be conformed to this world, but be transformed by the renewal of your mind, that by testing you may discern what is the will of God, what is good and acceptable and perfect."—
Romans 12:2

THE HARDEST PART ABOUT HOMESCHOOLING is *making the decision* to homeschool. Shoot. Before, all you had to do was decide what district to live in for the best schools and everyone else did all the work. Now, it's too dangerous to send your kids to school, too serious to turn a blind eye and deaf ear to the sexualization of children, and to the woke agenda with which progressive Edu-crats, Administrators, and some teachers are willfully poisoning the minds of our youth. Condemning our kids to the conveyor belt of the mass education system, stuffing them with facts while removing family loyalty and their ability to think for themselves is not what we want for our family or our nation.

However, once you come to the decision to homeschool, you will yearn for guidance as you realize "I'm supposed to do what...I'm supposed to homeschool who?!" For real, any parent who removes their children from government or private school languishes in the fear that they won't be up to the monstrous undertaking and they might ruin their progeny.

But just you wait, once you get over the hump of that difficult decision, it's not long until the glories of homeschooling start thriving in your life. It'll be as though the Lord is chasing you down the street, beating you over the head with blessings! A whole new world opens up, with lots of time for family bonding, growth as a parent, and the joy of leading your child as she seeks out her passions! To pave the way for this paradigm shift, one of the first things that I want you to do is to divorce yourself from everything that brings to mind government, institutional, or private schools: Hard desks, force-fed facts, strict schedules, eight-hour school days, large course loads, standardized tests, and especially state standards or benchmarks. We are going to gleefully throw those out the window never to be oppressed by them again. Firstly, let's learn from a talented teacher who's in the government school trenches and has been for the last 31 years.

It's the first week of high school for Don Franklin's[1] freshman English students and they are about to witness something they've never seen before.

Seemingly unprovoked, Mr. Franklin suddenly grabs his behemoth hardcover Webster's Dictionary with both hands, raises it high above his head, and slams it to the ground. It hits the classroom floor loudly, shocking all 30 students whose eyes are as big as fried eggs. He forcefully swings his hand flipping a hard plastic, metal-framed chair, sending it clattering loudly as it bounced across the floor. He then winds back like a professional baseball pitcher, hurling an eraser across the room where it bounces off the shiny cinderblock wall as he bellows in his angriest teacher voice, "I'm not going to take this anymore!"

Franklin is not in the midst of a mental breakdown; he's teaching his newcomers the classic "show don't tell" writing precept. After the pandemonium calms down, he'll ask students to put strong verbs and concrete nouns to his hissy fit. He just demonstrated how to turn the sentence, *'The teacher was angry.'* into visuals that these budding writers will never forget.

In his spare time, he writes fiction novels or editorials criticizing Florida's standardized testing, and the politicization of education. His classroom lessons come to life creating lovers of writing. His school had to add a third creative writing class to the curriculum because his students hungered for more after completing their first two years in Creative Writing 1 and 2 with him.

Wouldn't it be great if we all had even *one* teacher like Franklin? One who teaches with passion and vigor, constantly rejuvenating his lessons and activities. He scoffs at the deluge of headaches coming down the pipeline from the secretary of Education and other Edu-crats, like new benchmarks every few years, requirements of standardized testing, and the required dull lesson plans.

Alas, Superhero teachers like Franklin are few and far between. Despite his greatness, he is not only annoyed but would be stifled by benchmarks, if he let them. Benchmarks or state standards are listed categories of things that kids should know by the time they are done with that school year. A set of guidelines in that regard doesn't sound so bad at first, but the arbitrary ways that they derive and evolve are the bane of veteran teachers' existence and are driving new teachers away from the profession in a mass exodus. They are instated as a way to measure student aptitude, but they have blind spots and don't cover everything. If forced facts zap the joy

148

out of learning, state standards are like Uncle Ned when his ill-aimed bellyflop from the trampoline into the above-ground pool crushes the wall, draining all possibility of fun instantly into the ground. They're boring to teach and even duller to learn, especially in a checklist style, inapplicable to anything about which the student is passionate. They're always changing too! In the last 30 years Floridians have had five different sets: the *Sunshine State Standards*, *Sunshine State Standards 2.0*, *Common Core*, *Florida Standards*, and *Best Standards*.

"Every time there's new standards, they act as though it's the be all and end all, as though they are sacred objects. And you're not supposed to have any ideas about what you're teaching," said Franklin. "Standards sort of prevent teachers from thinking about what they're teaching in any kind of deep way, most of what goes on [with standards], doesn't actually promote thinking." Franklin continues, "Some of the standards aren't that good, aren't that engaging. It's like, if I were a kid, I wouldn't want to do this."

The pressures to adhere to benchmarks can be maddening for everyone involved, unwitting parents, teachers who don't need them, and students who couldn't care less about them. Retired Teacher-of-the-Year and tutor extraordinaire, Kathy Alford's[2] phone rang one afternoon.

"I got your number from my neighbor, Angela. She told me you're the best tutor in town and you helped her daughter tremendously, I hope you can help mine," the mother says in a tremulous voice. Alford can hear the anxiety in her voice as she continues. "My child is behind. She is having trouble with reading; can you help her?"

"Ok, how old is she?" Alford asks.

"Four."

What? You're breaking up? Four? At that age kids should be playing games and barely even thinking about letters. In Alford's forty years of experience teaching and tutoring, she knows that it's very rarely a child can read by the age of four. But these poor parents felt so much pressure from *Pre-K*, that they were ready to hire a tutor at $40 an hour to get their child up to the standards. Lots of kids can read by the age of six. But it's certainly not *all* kids. Of the ones that do learn at six-years-old, many struggle with proficiency and comprehension. Some kids can't learn to read until eight or nine, or even later. So what?

I hope that my experience can save you, my dear reader, from the years of self-doubt and imposter syndrome that I felt as a homeschool mom when my kid couldn't read by age six. Years ago, as I vacillated on the decision to home-educate, I had this one *huge* fear: Would I, a high school journalism teacher, be able to teach my kids to read? It would be my worst nightmare to toil and teach my own child a concept that wouldn't sink in. What would my husband think of me? Failure taunted me as I prayed about taking the step into the homeschool world. My complete compliance to benchmarks did not help, for I thought certainly my child must be able to read by age four...five at the latest.

I'd like to tell you, "That was a ridiculous fear! Of course, I taught my kids to read. How silly to think it would be a hard task!" But unfortunately, I cannot. The reality is that my nightmare has come true *twice*. And I still have one to go that's not at reading age yet! Gahhhh!

My second eldest has never stepped foot into school or had any teachers other than myself. Save, one year at a co-op when she was about six years old. Through all the reading games, practice, lessons, and videos this child could barely sound out three-letter words at seven years old. Which caused me to utter many four-letter words as I pulled my hair out trying to get her to read. "You *just* read that word in the sentence prior." I would say through strained patience and perceivable frustration. I cringe to think back to how I must've made her feel when I grew angry because she couldn't get it and I didn't know how to make her.

Thankfully there were a couple of wise homeschool moms in my life that spoke the truth to me, that I'm about to speak to you.

"She'll get it when she's ready."

"She will read."

"Everyone doesn't read at five years old."

"My child didn't read until she was eight, and now she's a voracious reader."

"It's just going to click one day, then watch, you'll be amazed at how quickly she's reading chapter books and soaring above grade level."

You know what? They were spot on!

What was good for my child, at the age of seven and eight was to back off and not put so much pressure that it turned into a hate of reading. There was no magic bullet, it was a long process of trying lots of different reading strategies. Something that did help greatly when the timing was right for her was a set of books called Pathway Readers, which came out in 1975. Still in print, these books shine front and center at many reading booths at homeschool convention expos. The key to these books 'success for my emerging reader was that they repeated the same words over and over, telling a story with just a few words. Same principle as the Dick and Jane books of yesteryear, but with richer, lengthier stories. About ponies nonetheless! It gave her the confidence that she could read. Even if some of the words were sight words that she had actually memorized instead of decoded.

When it finally did click for her, she was reading chapter books in a matter of a few weeks. Now, she is a bibliophile to the nth degree. She's read every book on our shelves a couple of times, is always listening to audiobooks and pleads for a trip to the library on a weekly basis. I can barely keep her in books!

When we as parents help our kids to develop an enjoyment for the subject—and not just literacy, but any subject, we are laying the groundwork for joy and engagement, then we will be able to teach them anything.

"We spend time measuring kids when we should be investing in kids. Instead of worrying so much about standards when they're little just read to them. Like crazy," Franklin urges. "I was reading my kids chapter books from the time they were four, we would read a chapter a night. Sometimes we'd read six chapters in a night if they were really into the book and we were near the end. With the younger kids, I would just make it all play. There's this whole idea that you have to be rigorous and the most rigorous stuff, I think is the most like play."

Investing in kids means going back to what I've explained about passion driven learning and fanning the flames of their interests. In turn, your child will develop lifelong learning skills because they are searching out what they want to learn. Think of the fun that you'll have as you take them to forts, museums, and battlefields to incite in them a love of history. There's fresh air and vitamin D beckoning you to explore nature to develop their curiosity about science. Keep your brain young by playing brain teasers, puzzles, and card games with your little ones. This will entice in them an interest in math and problem-solving.

Although this is relatively new to me, as a former government school teacher and even as a homeschool mom who has admittedly forced my children to learn some useless facts here and there, it's not new knowledge. Ancient Greek Philosopher Plato said 2,500 years ago, "A freeman ought not to be a slave in the acquisition of knowledge of any kind. Bodily exercise, when compulsory, does no harm to the body; but knowledge which is acquired under compulsion obtains no hold on the mind. Do not use compulsion, but let early education be a sort of amusement; you will then be better able to find out the natural bent."[3]

Finding your child's bent is the same as helping them find the path to which God has called them. He has a plan for your child that no one else on the planet will be able to fulfill. Where benchmarks bend them just for the sake of bending, their infatuations dot the path toward a purposeful life of serving Him and loving others. Put the fun back in parenting and use your children's interests as waypoints in an adventure catered unequivocally to them.

Key Point:
The sooner you stop worrying about what your child should know related to what age they are, the less stressed and worried you will be as their primary educator. Contrive their education depending on their interests and passions, they'll learn voraciously due to the joy of discovery. Engagement and enjoyment come first and then you can teach them anything!

Home is Where The Truth Is:
You may've heard the legend of the brilliance of our nation's third president, Thomas Jefferson, a perpetual student who spoke many languages, practiced the violin for three hours a day, and whose knowledge spanned many subjects. Under the tutelage of George Wythe—America's first law professor, Jefferson quickly became one of the country's greatest leaders and thinkers.

Best-selling author, Oliver DeMille studied Jefferson's education to model it for the masses. In his book, A Thomas Jefferson Education: Teaching a Generation of Leaders for the Twenty-First Century, he lays out the "Seven Keys of Great Teaching". Graciously, they don't include a single government benchmark, but instead prescribe: "Classics, not Textbooks; Mentors, not Professors; Inspire, not Require; Structure Time, not Content; Quality, not Conformity; Simplicity, not Complexity; and You, not Them."[1]

Action Item:
Using your child's interest or hobby as the starting point, find books and activities to help them learn more about it. Dig into the history, prominent figures, even the numbers. Find tips to becoming better at whatever it is. Research places to visit related to the hobby. Invest in your child. Teach their heart.

LIE #11:

I work, Therefore I Can't Homeschool.

"I have so much extra time, I think I'll homeschool." —*No One, Ever.*

"He who trusts in his riches will fall,
But the righteous will flourish like the green leaf."
—*Proverbs 11:28*

RING....RING...RING.
-Hello?
-Yes, Hi. We are calling all of the student's parents. You're going to have to come and pick your child up from school. It seems that we've found carcinogens in the school. Prolonged exposure to these poisons will kill all imagination, creativity, and critical thinking skills. Unfortunately, at this time, the best prognosis we can provide—If your child does survive, is that they will most likely suffer a spiritual death.
-I'll be there in ten minutes!

What parent wouldn't immediately drop everything if we got that warning call? Evidence and research which I have conveyed thus far have been stacking up over the years proving how destructive the mass school system is to children. We only need to open our eyes to our nation's political climate and the woke agenda being forced upon our kids to understand how complicit that system is to the destruction of conservative values, like belief in God and objective truth. An environment rife for indoctrination, it casts an effective dark spell over its prisoners, shifting their loyalties so that a child quits wondering "How can I please my parents?" And instead does whatever it takes to fit in with peers.

Are time and money the major obstacles keeping you from getting your child out of that environment and taking the homeschool plunge? You and your spouse both have to work, so when and how would you ever find time to educate your children? You'd run into a burning building to save them, so why drop them off daily to get slowly poisoned? Whether you want to, need to or have to work, you don't have to succumb to the sub-standard education of the masses. You can still homeschool your children and keep your job.

Squashing homeschool misconceptions is my goal because the benefits for your entire family are irrefutable. But allow me to be clear, I'm not trying to vilify teachers, administrators, and campus advisers who love their jobs and love the kids that have been entrusted to their care, and are simply trying to educate them, not brainwash them. At a local art show, I chatted with an artist who was in his fifties about the impact his high school swim coach made on him.

"Coach was always so positive. He would have an inspirational quote on the board every day. He really changed my entire outlook on life from a pessimist to an optimist, and I was able to tell him that many decades later," he recounted.

Teachers can make a memorable impact on kids' lives and set them on a path that they might've never found on their own. We will certainly never have enough good teachers, and I appreciate all the gifted teachers that mentored me when I was a new teacher. Unfortunately, the government system is so poorly designed, and on top of that, infested with activist groups that have politicized education. We need to get our children out of there no matter what.

Being ignorant of the dark underbelly of mass education, of course, I didn't always feel that way. I recently heard the mother of a six-week-old echo my exact sentiment when I had an infant. "I cannot stay home with my baby all day every day. I need to have a career, something for myself. I seriously don't know how stay-at-home moms do it!"

Putting our kids in school was the necessary step to having a life outside the home. (Even as I write this, as a stay-at-home mom, 23 years later, I have a five-year-old who has completely ignored my office door sign that says *"Mommy's writing, please come back later."* Climbing on my shoulders, wedging himself between my spine and my swivel chair, he creates a distraction by waving pens and a Scripto gooseneck lighter in front of my eyes in hopes that I'll turn my attention to him if even for a brief second. At times like this, I *still* relate to that old feeling of wanting time to myself.) Just because I have kids doesn't mean that I don't have hopes, dreams, goals, and things to accomplish. Every mom should. I don't fault anyone for wanting to pursue their passions whether it earns them money or not. It's valuable for your children to see you working toward a goal, chasing a dream.

However, that feeling of wanting my own career outside the home waned with every new baby. A few years into my high school teaching career, I had my second child. The campus provided a daycare so that all the 14–18-year-olds that got pregnant during their high school career could continue to get their free education with their kids safely in the nursery. Teachers could also take advantage of the on-campus childcare, which I did. Located directly below my classroom, during lunch I could swiftly bound down the stairs and be climbing on the mats with her in two minutes flat. However, it just wasn't enough time with those cute little pigtails and chubby cheeks. Something in me started to change. I wanted to be home with her, to have the full hand in raising her. By the birth of my third child a couple of years later, that was it. I put in for a year-long leave of absence, but even as I filled out the paperwork, I knew that I'd never be back. I never again wanted to work outside the home, leaving them in childcare all day. I wasn't even thinking about homeschooling at the time. It was simply an evolved feeling after ten years of motherhood. I went from not really knowing how to entertain a baby all day, to knowing what was in their best interest, leaning into motherhood full tilt, and embracing every stage of development.

Of all my seasons of parenthood, none have been more rewarding than being home with my kids all day every day, teaching them, witnessing their joy of discovery, seeing their interests grow into passions, and being the first person they turn to when they have a question. Recently as I shared my vision for this book with my daughters, I told them the same. I seriously got choked up when I tried to convey how meaningful homeschooling them has been, truly my life's greatest joy (well, being Mat's wife is just as awesome, but definitely top two). I hope and have been praying that every reader gets to experience the bonding, adventurous calling of home education.

No parent should have to let their child be raised and educated by someone else if they don't want it that way. Kudos to the parents doing the hard things to not let anything stand in the way of giving their child a well-rounded, faith-filled education based on that child's interests and passions. They won't be deterred by the workload, nor by the possibility of poverty, and if they need to, they'll spread themselves thin for the sake of their children. While lots of families that home educate have given up a dual income because only one parent works, there are still options for families where both parents have to *or want to* work. Let me reassure you that it can be done with both parents working; over a third of homeschool families are already doing it! That's hundreds of thousands of families. Single parents, you can do it too! 14% of homeschool families are in a single-parent situation—in which that parent works. [1] You must be wondering, what are the secrets to juggling a job while educating your children? Well, it's not going to be easy and pain-free. But ahead, I will explain some helpful tools to get your hard-workin' self on the homeschool bandwagon.

I've already made the point in previous chapters we are not going for the factory-mold-government school recipe of force-feeding them different subjects for eight hours a day and checking off all the benchmarks. (You can review chapters three, four, and ten for solid research to this point.) Throw the rigid schedule, stacks of textbooks, and hours of homework out of the equation. Your kids are going to be working a fraction of the time and getting a better education. For the elementary years, a couple of hours a day is more than ample time. When they get older, you'll have children who are intrinsically motivated to learn about their passions and can work for hours *if needed.*

FAMILY CALENDAR

"If it's not on the schedule book, it's not happening." Dr. Chrysalis Wright bluntly stated from the podium, then paused for dramatic effect. This mother of six has homeschooled her children while working for over ten years. Dr. Wright is a developmental psychologist who coaches parents and families toward life balance, time management, discipline, instruction, and proper media use and monitoring. My pen was practically smoking as I jotted down all she had to say in her lecture for working parents who homeschool. Families must have one principal calendar—whether digital or paper in which *everything* gets logged. Every music lesson, co-op day, doctor appointment, tutoring, soccer practice, social event, facial and nail appointment goes in. And just as important, don't forget your rest days, leave some white space in there, moms and dads.

"But Mom, tonight's the skating rink holiday bash that I wanted to go to with Caitlyn," implores your daughter, who forgot to log it into the calendar.

"Sorry, honey. It's not on the calendar; we didn't plan for it," you'll say with as much empathy as you can muster. I know it sounds harsh, but it will probably only take one time missing a desired event to cement the importance of planning ahead. The calendar teaches time management, team cohesiveness, and prioritization while enabling you to have a plan for each day. This makes it easier to tag team your spouse, Grands, or whoever comprises your support system.

Tag teaming. Does that term take you back to the nineties? Wrestling icon, "Nature Boy" Rick Flair bounces off the wrestling ring ropes, his bleach-blonde head whips back rhythmically with every elbow he absorbs to the face. Beaten bloody, he is just inches away from tagging his partner Triple H's hand. If...he...could...just...reach... it. Ding! Suddenly his partner rushes in and relieves the tired, sweaty, bloody Nature Boy who goes crawling out of the ring on his hands and knees. Triple H is fresh, pumped, ready to scrap! "I'm gonna kick that math lesson's ass!" Oh oops, what are we talking about here? Oh yeah, you need someone to help you. This analogy is going to be just a little too real on the worst homeschool days. Who's your tag team partner? It might be a spouse to check their planner or teach one subject. A grandparent to go over math with them or take them to the park. I tag team with my elder four children to play with the youngest. Their checklist on a daily basis includes reading with him and playing with him, which on a great day, can add up to about two hours for me to focus on other tasks even if it is broken up into twenty-minute increments. That is still a big relief. Just like those helpful dinners that neighbors cooked and dropped off after you (or your wife) gave birth, the smallest gesture of help will be huge in bearing the daily to-dos.

There will assuredly be stretches when you have to take a wider look than a daily plan, and intervals when you need the kids' education to go on cruise control (And sometimes that'll be because you're in survival mode, which is ok too.). "There are times when I have to tell my family, 'I won't be available for two weeks," said Dr. Wright. "This is why you have to work toward fostering their independence."

Find their currency so that they can work without you hovering over them. Whether it's passion-driven learning, or a checklist to complete before they get screen time. Help them develop intrinsic motivation by giving them some autonomy. Give them a voice as to what they want to learn. For example, teens who love sports or who become obsessed with fitness gains can use their time practicing toward high school credit. When our skinny little 14-year-old suddenly wants to bulk up, 60 hours of weightlifting can go down on transcripts.

Checklists that are blocked off incrementally by time are a great way to give kids control while keeping them on track. For example, one hour of math, one hour of Biology, thirty minutes of listening to an Audiobook lets kids work at their own pace without the added stress and pressure of having to complete a whole chapter or entire math lesson. They chose the order of tasks. Remember, it's just as important to put the proper recreational time on the checklist. One doctor suggests 20 minutes of recess for every 40 minutes of instructional time. Checklists are especially helpful for kids who are disorganized, lack focus, or need help planning, prioritizing, and initiating tasks, but anyone can enjoy the benefits.

Another time saver and strategy to keep them working when you're not around is grouping kids that are close in age on the same subject. If they are only one or two years apart, most subjects lend themselves to teaching across the age gap. I've taught my kids grouped together through unit studies but also individual subjects like grammar, writing, physical education, science, poetry, history, and Español.

Also, speaking of grouping together, make it a priority to plug into a homeschool community. If there are days that both parents have to work, and kids are too young to stay home alone, there may be a homeschool family nearby with which they can learn. I have a friend, trained in Montessori education, who seeks out other families to come over and learn with her children on a regular basis because she knows it is so beneficial to have multiple ages learning together. One of the major tenets of the Montessori philosophy, age mixing has been greatly studied. It reduces competitiveness, provides opportunities for kids to learn from one another, and fosters creativity and bonding. Younger children have someone closer to their size than the adults in their lives to observe, learn from, and emulate. Older children practice nurturing and leading and can obtain a deeper understanding when verbally explaining a concept to a kid who's a bit behind them in understanding.[2]

There's another convenience to lighten your load. Audiobooks are not only one of the best tools for imbuing your child with the love of reading, a robust vocabulary, and a command of language, but they are also efficient as a time saver and teacher's assistant. All genres are available on audio, even textbooks. Glorious audiobooks, we have so much to thank you for! Now car rides become a way to get science work done as you play the textbook audio. We've found the 15-minute drive to the park is the perfect instructional block for us as we listen to historical biographies, our Spanish pronunciation guide, and skip-count together.

Hopefully, when you arrive at the park, there's nobody but a handful of two-year-olds toddling around shadowed by their grandparents, and your kids can enjoy the indulgence of having free reign of the entire place, unfettered by hordes of misbehaving kids. This brings us to another perk of homeschooling: year-round school. Not only can you spread the learning evenly throughout the year, but you can take breaks whenever you want! Wisely doing school work while the rest of the world's kids are on summer break, jamming up parks, playgrounds, swimming holes, and field trip venues. My kids have had it all to themselves: giant springs in which to swim, private audiences for the venom extraction at the serpentarium, science centers, museums, forts, and marine parks that were practical ghost towns before we walked in. We're so spoiled, that when we pull up to a field trip destination and see a big yellow school bus parked, there will be a disappointed and collective, *'Ahhhh man!'* from the backseat. Field trips are just not quite as fun with fifty other rambunctious kids present, especially when they just got out of their cinderblock holding cells. And wow, do we feel sorry for the teacher yelling every five minutes, "STUDENTS, YOU ARE AT A LEVEL ZERO RIGHT NOW! NO TALKING!!"

Homeschool veteran Nancy Nelson wanted to keep her children out of that kind of classroom and provide a better education than the minimum standard that government school provides. Homeschooling was a priority for her and her spouse, and yet she has worked the entire time that she's been homeschooling—twenty-one years and counting! Nelson has worked for a book publisher, tutored at a local learning center and done all kinds of different things working on site or remotely. Even though she had her self-doubts, and every day might have looked a little different, her family thrived.

"I doubted myself and doubted myself for years of homeschooling. 'Oh, is she ever going to be prepared for the world?' Well, my daughter is a straight-A college student—

and we didn't do every subject every single day. But she learned how to read, she learned how to write, she learned how to reason and she could do some math. When she went to college, she took an intermediate algebra class before her algebra 1 class, and she did just fine," said Nelson.

For Nelson, time blocking was her best friend. Instead of doing all the subjects all the days, she worked from 7 to 9 AM, then set aside 9 AM to noon to teach and guide the kids' schooling. Whatever they got done in that amount of time was the entirety of school for them that day. If you're gasping right now, thinking, *How can three hours of school be sufficient?*, then you may be a little bit brainwashed by the government system, I was too. Experienced homeschool parents agree since we don't have wasted time in the halls or in the classroom waiting for 25 other kids to finish an assignment before moving on, a handful of focused hours is plenty of time.

Another misconception that I want you to steer clear of as you grow as a homeschool parent, please try to keep in mind that your kids 'achievement is not a reflection of you. When you engage in small talk with a homeschool Mama, and all of a sudden, she's talking about how her kids learn at the Chautauqua Institute, speak Latin, and are rounding out their Russian IV credit, you aren't going to celebrate that, but flee from her and try not to get stuck in a conversation her ever again. What good is it to listen to a braggart? And please, stay humble if your kids are prodigies. Another of the innumerable perks that keep stacking up in the homeschool corner is the honoring of individuality. What works for one family or a child's achievements should have no bearing on anyone else. We'll keep everyone's burden a bit lighter by not getting caught up in parental validation through our progeny's performance.

As you start to believe that you can do this homeschool thang while working, there might be a side of you that would like to stop working so that you can focus on it full-time—or at least make your own schedule and work when *you* want. Looking back on the Covid pandemic we can find a couple of silver linings. Lots of parents' eyes were opened to what their kids were being taught, followed by a realization of home education being a viable option, and they stuck with it, bringing thousands of kids home to bloom and rediscover that there is actually so much joy in discovery.

Also, companies that would've never considered allowing their employees to work remotely suddenly had to—and continue to do so. Entrepreneurialism reached an all-time high in July 2020, affording people the flexibility to be their own boss.[3] Now, an explosion of people working for apps like DoorDash, Uber, and Lyft, and personal grocery shoppers provide opportunities to add to the family's bottom line. Through the direct sales business model, I had a side hustle helping women discover their fashion sense as a clothing stylist. I got dressed up, conversed with adults, and forged friendships while earning money—all things that the daily homeschool routine didn't provide. If your budget says that you absolutely must work, maybe one of these options will provide the oomph it needs.

Most likely, you've already thought about all that you'll save on childcare, tuition, school clothes, and gas from not running them to and fro every day. But have you considered the intangible savings you'll be enjoying, like not sitting in the parent pick-up line for two hours a day, freedom from the rigid school calendar with complete control over your family's schedule, protecting your child from conflicting worldviews, honing their creativity and passion for learning, and being the number one influencer in their life. You'll be surprised at how many organic and meaningful conversations spring up between you and your kids. When your role as parent includes teacher, they naturally tend to ask *you* everything they want to know. Having open channels of meaningful conversations is not only important in raising resilient kids, as I explained earlier, but conversations can be the best teaching tools! Life is full of opportunities to teach them through sharing anecdotes and family history, which is poignant and memorably drives home a point. Facts and figures serve a purpose, but information is more easily retained when it's relatable, like a personal story told by a loved one. Conversations are *teaching moments* that help children develop critical thinking skills by considering your wisdom and perspective. You really can't put a price on these conversations.

One such spontaneous chat with my son started flowing as we walked around a campground in north Florida, observing license plates. A plethora of New York and other northern plates led to an explanation of the economies of big cities like New York, which led to American history on the influx of immigrants to New York, then to weather and the equatorial tropical regions. We touched on the draw of California's topography and ocean temperatures, as well as Hawaii's. He kept asking questions, I kept expounding knowledge, and we kept walking together under the pine trees in the soft, cool breeze. Many times, these conversations are ampler than the best curriculum, and create moments that a textbook never could.

Speaking of textbooks, there are some very fancy boxed curriculum sets, that appear to be great tools for the homeschool family. These can be a hefty investment, anywhere from a couple hundred bucks to a thousand or more. If you can't afford something like that, please don't let it dissuade you from homeschooling. As a matter of fact, if you're on a tight budget, do everything you can to avoid it. You don't need it!

As a new homeschool family, it sounds so appealing to have something that tells you exactly what to do and when to do it. It all looks so perfect and shiny sprawled out at the curriculum fair. Like the sirens that called to Odysseus, that 90-day-money-back guarantee will sound foolproof. But stuff your ears with wax and tie yourself to your mobile book cart and keep moving. You must consider the human factor. It might not resonate with your kids or with you. You'll still feel obligated to stick with it because it was a big investment. It'll suck the fun out of learning faster than a homemade balloon-powered car loses momentum. Hammering a wedge of anxiety between you and your kids as it gathers dust, it'll taunt you from high on its shelf, 'You dropped nearly a thousand dollars on me; you better use me.' Instead of developing a facial tick and hearing other voices in your head, it might be better never to bring it home.

There are lots of affordable and free alternatives. Unit studies are both fun and affordable or *free* if you pull your own together. Use the library for an unending supply of books. Remember that community into which you are getting plugged? Even an online group will be a big help, you'll find curriculum swaps and people purging books and supplies that they've outgrown. With social media groups, you'll stay abreast to free community events, local lectures, and 'homeschool days' at learning centers and museums.

We recently attended a lecture at our library entitled *The Timucua of North East Florida*. Our speaker, Felipe De Paula, a Florida history expert was vastly knowledgeable about the indigenous peoples of Florida thousands of years ago. Although the subject might not sound exciting to everyone, my family shares an affinity for Florida history, especially the natives who built dugout canoes and lived here back before bug spray and air conditioning. We learned all about archeological gold mines—shell middens—the dumps of distant past where villagers tossed garbage and oyster shells. One of the biggest shell middens in Florida was only an hour's drive and it had a boardwalk for hiking to the top.

In the same talk, he told us about a future free astronomy night at a lighthouse that would have the biggest telescope in the area. Of course, we loaded up the minivan and made the hour's drive. The kids had to pull up a step-stool to look into the telescopes as local Aeronautical University students lined them up to see Venus, craters on the moon, the gas giant Jupiter, and four of its 64 moons.

For some bonus wisdom, we climbed 203 steps to the top of the burgundy brick Ponce Inlet Lighthouse. That special evening they gave visitors access to the lens deck, which is usually closed to the public. An expert dressed in a lighthouse keeper's uniform from the days of yore taught us about the rotating lens made from prisms of glass. Standing close enough to touch it, we had to shield our eyes each time the light rotated by our faces. Riding home from the astronomy event, my kids were pumped about what they had seen. We talked about space and the planets for most of the ride home. These events were not only immersive, physical, and dynamic, but they were free.

Free is always good! Especially when one out of every five families that educates at home is living at poverty level—interestingly, that statistic is the exact same for those who attend government schools. Many families have prioritized providing their children the best possible education over comfort and status, doing without many luxuries and living on one income. It's so inspiring!

I will admit that I'm no expert on saving and budgeting. Although I did put myself through college as a single mom with the assistance of a Pell Grant, student loans, and a great cart-girl gig, it's been a while since I struggled to make ends meet. Thanks be to God for pairing me with a savvy businessman and saver.

I was fresh out of college working as a waitress at the local barbecue joint when a handsome, sun-kissed Filipino man bedecked in business attire came in for a John Wayne Burger. His weekly lunch outings in which he'd request my section led to a beautiful relationship. I started my teaching career, we got married and

built up to a comfortable living wage as a team. Anyway—he's the money expert with 23 years of experience helping people invest and save for retirement. I asked him what steps a family should take to get expenses down or to be able to get by on one income.

Ask yourself, are you living outside your means? What can you trim from your budget? What discretionary expenses are you willing to forego?

With the average American $96,371 in debt [4] , it's important to take a look at your expenses and try not to spend like the average American.

It's recommended to have about three to six months of savings to fall back on in case someone loses their job or gets sick and can't work. Also, have a conversation about the willingness to go back to work if that becomes necessary.

Consolidate your debt and pay it down. It doesn't matter how much money you make if you're up to your eyeballs in debt because that never goes away if you're only paying minimum payments every month. Do not buy it if you don't have the cash and have to use your credit card. And you don't have to buy it just because it's on sale! (Ask me how many times I've heard that one...but he's right.)

The bottom line is this: it isn't about the bottom line. I know you have to survive, but you really can't put a price on being with your kids while they are still young. Please don't outsource the teaching of your faith, your family traditions, and how to be good humans. You're the absolute most capable person to build your child up a firm foundation for a lifetime of following their passions. This eighteen-year contract pays a priceless salary. The sacrifices are worth it! Your only regret will be if you don't try it.

Key Point:
It is possible to educate at home while working outside the home. If you do give up an income, the benefits for your children and your entire family, will far outweigh the material sacrifices. Plus, your kids' youth is like the blink of an eye, don't squander those years sending them away, if you don't absolutely have to.

"So, content people may not have the best of everything, but they make the best of everything. That is who you want your children to be." – Dave Ramsey

Action item:
More great wisdom from personal finance guru Dave Ramsey, "A budget is telling your money where to go instead of wondering where it went." Download the budget and expense managing app Mint. With all your accounts and expenses in one place, you'll find the motivation to pay off debt and cut spending, especially when you see how much you're spending in each category.

LIE #12:

You're Not Doing Enough.

"Comparison is the thief of joy."
—Theodore Roosevelt

"Am I saying this now to win the approval of people or God? Am I trying to please people? If I were still trying to please people, I would not be Christ's servant." Galatians 1:10

I F YOU ASK ANY homeschool parent about this lie, they will affirm that they have felt this way at some point on their journey. It's a close relative to the lie that seeps into our psyche, "I'm going to ruin my kid." I remember bouncing this belief off of my dear friend Sherry, a veteran homeschool mom who had already graduated three kids. She sighed, bowing her head in acknowledgment; yes, she had felt the same way as a homeschool newb. Now that her kids were grown, she absolutely knew that homeschooling was the best decision she ever made. However, this lie can get a little whack-a-mole-y because it is so easy to look around and compare what you're doing with your kids to the homework load of your girlfriend's private school pupil. Oh, Sally is doing a trifold board project on inventors of the nineteenth century...could my child produce something like that? Your mind quickly condemns you. It's science fair time in government schools? "Quickly! Grab the baking soda and vinegar. We are making a volcano right now!"

Even if you don't succumb to those levels, comparing yourself to others is never a healthy habit. You'll either end up feeling insufficient because you don't measure up or haughty because you're doing it better. Neither of these attitudes is what God wants for his sons and daughters. Do you remember what he told us through the prophet Jeremiah? For I know the plans I have for you," declares the Lord, "plans to prosper you and not to harm you, plans to give you hope and a future." Focus on his plan for you because when we try to imitate what's working for someone else, it won't be long before we are doing too much. Burn-out quickly sets in, mental energy gets zapped, and you'll be counting the days until your next vacation, Oh, and perhaps worst of all, your bones start to rot. "A heart at peace gives life to the body, but envy rots the bones."[1]

One afternoon, my dad did me the huge favor of taking all the kids to the park and out for ice cream so that I could get three hours of quiet time and rest. As an added bonus, when the kids got home, they were tuckered out, happy, obedient, little sugar-filled specimens. Elation covered them all; they had met a wonderful family at the park. But wait it gets better: A homeschool family! The Clarke family had four kids that ranged the exact ages of each of my kids! Not only did they have those two cornerstones in common, but these kids loved to run and play just like mine. Each kid's doppelgänger rivaled them in athletic prowess, so the more they chased around, the more they vibed off of one another's energy. It was kismet!

With each passing park meeting, our families grew a little closer, and we were just pinching ourselves that our families found each other. Since then, they've become some of our best friends and we've spent many Easter, Thanksgivings, and Super Bowls together.

Now, the reason I am telling you about this wonderful family—that is a blessing in our lives, is because if I played the comparison game, I could've sent myself into a slight depression after Mrs. Clarke invited us over one day for "Math Monday". Ok, this lady already has it together better than I do. She has a nifty little moniker for each day of the week with their homeschool schedule. Math Monday, Tech Tuesday, Wisdom Wednesday, Can't remember what Thursday was, but she had one! And that "th" diphthong is hard to find fitting alliteration. I was tempted to compare my schedule and the fact that some days I don't even know what we are going to work on, let alone match it with the letters of the days. Some days we don't even start school until 1 PM, or the whole of our school day is one math lesson (that the kids do online and I have not a hand in) and quiet reading time.

Her whiteboard posted schedule was one thing, but just wait until I tell you about her home! In every cubby, on every shelf space, even in the defunct fireplace they had learning apparatuses! I'm not talking about calculators and flashcards, my friends, these were Montessori manipulatives! For those of you who don't know, which I didn't have a clear idea either at the time, the Montessori mantra is: "The mind and the hands engaged in purposeful work." There are so many products that look like a game to be played amongst students, or alone, that are actually learning tools. It's a great concept, these kids are tactilely learning at the rate of their own joy of discovery. Mrs. Clarke had turned her modest three-bedroom home into a literal Montessori school for her kids. Remember the unused fireplace? It had a curtain over it that when pulled back revealed a trove of Legos. I'm talking 10 one-gallon freezer bags full of them. And girl, these Legos were separated by color! Her organization was on point! She had turned the bedrooms into learning rooms! It was wall-to-wall shelves and nooks full of learning tools, giant three-ring binders that mapped out everything one needed to know about this method of learning, and rolled-up floor mats. No beds, no furniture at all really, save a couch and dining room table.

When she stood in front of a curtained doorway, and said, "This space is off limits, this is where we sleep." I hope she didn't see my jaw hit her shiny, clutter-free wood floor. This is where *we* sleep? This mother is so devoted to her kids' schooling, not only did she earn a master's degree in Montessori education for the sole purpose of teaching her own children, but also has them all sleep in the room with her and her husband so that they can use the bedrooms for learning spaces! Let me just say, the day that I move any of my children into my own bedroom, go ahead and cart me off to the looney bin because that's where my mind already done went.

My point is this: that all seems amazing, but that's not my wheelhouse. Never will be. I'm a more spontaneous teacher, who plans in pencil because even when I do plan, half the time I go off on the many side roads, rabbit holes, or nature walks that come up when educating my brood. At the end of the day my classroom looks like a Tasmanian devil spun through it getting out every multi-piece toy we owned and flinging them to the far corners of the room. We do pick-up and reorganize every few days. But geez, perseverating over the ways that I'm not like Mrs. Clarke would diminish my self-worth, which leads to resentment and that doesn't help me one bit.

What does help me is to focus on what I'm good at and how the Lord has gifted me when it comes to mothering, nurturing and teaching. Remember how I said I'm more spontaneous? Well, spontaneity leads to fun and laughter. God has revealed to me that if I'm bored and slogging through it, then so are they. And that's the government school recipe right there. Don't want none of that! God has also gifted me with a knack for interior decor that rivals some Better Homes and Gardens spreads. During the long homeschool day, our beautiful home is a place from which we derive energy and peace. Personally curated with lamps, artwork, and textiles that spark joy, it's an extension of my personality. I would literally be rocking in a corner, hugging myself to cling to my last shred of sanity if I had to trade all my throw pillows and shelf coral for math manipulatives.

When I start to lose focus, I pray for God's guidance. I discovered a wonderfully succinct prayer through a *Walking With Purpose* Bible study by Lisa Brenninkmeyer, helpful when applied to my life: *"Lord help me get done what's on your to-do list and not mine today."* It's so freeing to pray those words and let God take control of my day as he guides me. I listen through promptings that fall on my heart. My kids' enthusiasm, or my frustration level let me know whether I'm going in the right direction, or if it's time to call "dumpster fire" on this assignment and regroup. That's how I know that I'm doing enough.

It's easy to buy into the lie that homeschooling just isn't enough when you look at a government school schedule. With class changes every hour, they see seven teachers and study as many different subjects. You're only one person and probably not an expert on any one subject. But take into account the amount of wasted time in a day of institutional learning, from parent drop-off, class changes, disciplinary problems, sitting quietly waiting for others to finish their work, and general classroom distractions. Let's not even think about when the teacher is out...if there's a substitute you can usually chalk up that day as a complete waste. In my district, it's common practice to send whole classes of kids to sit in the gym, while one administrator watches over hundreds of kids, because of substitute shortages.

Speaking of shortages and distractions, do you know the phone frustrations that these poor teachers put up with? If they fight the ubiquitous phones at all, it's certainly an uphill battle. In some schools, they're not allowed to take away phones from students because it's their "personal property." If a teacher is lenient about phones, the kids will be texting and scrolling as she's instructing. If the rule is to keep your phones in your backpack or pockets, then students are constantly asking for a bathroom pass to go respond to a text, that's if they aren't sneaky enough to just have it in their lap hidden by the desk and blind text. Yes, kids are such whizzes at texting that they need not even glance at the screen to fire off a quick one. Parents are part of the problem. A friend of mine that teaches high school art often has students ask, "Can I just respond to this text from my Mom real quick?"

Exposure to unacceptable content on other students' phones became frequent and was just one of the myriad reasons that I knew it was time to remove my eldest from sixth grade at a government middle school (grades 6-8). She had attended government school since Pre-K and we dealt with bullying through social ostracism, and although I didn't know it at the time, I can look back and see that her loyalty quickly switched to her peer group instead of her family. But she got to experience a gender-specific all-girls classroom for a couple of years and she flourished academically. Middle school however, had a deluge of new problems. My girl is social, smart as a whiz, and loquacious. When she completed her work in 10 minutes, she sat bored for the remainder of class. That is until her self-control sapped, boredom overtook her, and she gave in to chatting with her nearest neighbor. *Disruptive. Too much talking.* The daily little slips of paper tattled on her. At this time, I had already been praying about homeschooling for months. Finally, the Lord made it clear, that the best thing for her—and our entire family was to bring her home to learn.

It was January, exactly halfway through the year when we pulled her out of middle school. She would finish the last half of the school year with her exact same class load online. This child finished the second half of the school year, 18 weeks (720 hours to be exact) in the comfort of our living room in a mere six weeks! If you didn't instantly do the math in your head, that is 12 weeks of wasted time! Family bonding activities became more frequent, we had more hobbies in which to dabble, more passions to explore, 480 hours more to go on field trips, or to sit in a pile of pillows and get lost in a book. The point is, well, there are two points. 1: So much time is wasted in school institutions. And 2: No matter what you are doing as a family, homeschooling forms your child in deeper ways than the school system will *ever* be capable of.

Don't stick to the idea of educating with a herd mentality as government schools do. Divorce yourself from the one-size-fits-all framework and pressures of the arbitrary state standards, set by who knows who, which drive veteran teachers bed-bug crazy and greatly shorten the shelf-life of new teachers. Attending school every day, memorizing force-fed facts and regurgitating them for the test, (and later forgetting said facts) may give the appearance of education, but it certainly doesn't ensure that your child is actually learning or flourishing.

When you think about educating your child, listen to what New York teacher John Taylor Gatto had to say about it, for he knew what it meant to make learning come alive. He taught rich kids and poor kids, but in the latter part of his teaching career he taught predominantly poor 8th graders in Spanish Harlem. His classroom experience spanned nearly 30 years and he received teacher of the year accolades multiple times. In 1991 after winning New York State Teacher of the Year, he resigned the next day with a letter in *The Wall Street Journal,* saying he didn't want to "hurt kids to make a living".[2] He went on to author multiple books calling for education reform. In Dumbing Us Down: The Hidden Curriculum of Compulsory Schooling, Gatto writes, "Whatever an education is, it should make you a unique individual, not a conformist; it should furnish you with an original spirit with which to tackle the big challenges; it should allow you to find values which will be your roadmap through life; it should make you spiritually rich, a person who loves whatever you are doing, wherever you are, whomever you are with; it should teach you what is important, how to live and how to die."[3]

Is your child's education making them spiritually rich? Parents, let's never forget that we are blessed to be in the position to help our children find the talents and interests that they'll use to glorify God in their lives.

While you don't have to look far for examples of spiritual malnourishment, stories of spiritual richness transcend the decades, like that of Olympic gold medalist Eric "The Flying Scot" Liddell. For him, holding fast to the Lord's command of honoring the Sabbath was more important than Olympic glory. In 1924, he bowed out of the 100-meter sprint, his best event because it was on Sunday. He would go on to win bronze in the 200-meter and gold in the 400-meter, an exciting neck-and-neck sprint around the track as depicted in the 1981 film *Chariots of Fire*.

"I believe God made me for a purpose, but he also made me fast! And when I run, I feel his pleasure," said Liddell.

How will *your child* feel God's pleasure? You get to help them figure it out! As you educate them at home, you'll be guiding them to Christ's purpose for their life.

Is there any calling more substantial?

Honey, you are doing more than enough.

Key Idea:
Having your child home, learning with you, and developing their talents and passion have so many benefits that you should never think you aren't doing enough. Ever.

Home is Where the Truth Is:
It's freeing to understand that you *are* doing enough for your child and that homeschooling is the best thing for her. For posterity's sake, think about this: 82% of grown-up millennial homeschoolers plan to use homeschooling for at least part of their children's education.[1] You are raising your grandkids' parents, think of the generational benefits for your offspring if you decide to or are already homeschooling.

Action Item:
On social media, mute or unfollow anyone to whom you compare yourself with. Even more effective, do a complete social media fast for an allotted period of time.

LIE #13:

I Don't Have
The Organizational Skills.

"Unlike art, the making of home does not stay done. Every morning, every evening the mess awaits us. The messy, hungry beautiful world, wanting and needing our touch."—Rebecca McClanahan

"Cast all your anxieties on him, because he cares for you." 1 Peter 5:7

W E'VE ALL SEEN the memes:
Please excuse our messy house, we are making memories.

Or:

The room was clean yesterday; sorry you missed it.

And:

It's messy. People live here. Get over it.

The one that resonates with me the most:

It's either me or my home, it seems both of us can't look good at the same time.

Have we bought into the lie that says good moms have sticky floors, messy kitchens, laundry piles, dirty ovens, and happy kids? Yes, all good Moms have those things at some point on a pretty regular basis. But can we please be as crystal clear as my glass table top after a good Windexing and realize that clutter sucks our joy, zaps our motivation, and overwhelms us to the point of shut-down. Read: "Mommy needs a nap, my sweeties. Please be nice to each other, play on the other side of the house, and DON'T wake me up."

Listen, there are some days when I want to lean into this lie. The whole house is a cluttered wreck, I've got two appointments to get to, and I cannot even muster the willpower to open the three-ring binder teacher's guide to see what we are supposed to be reading today. Disorganized days are energy-sucking and mentally defeating, so it's much better for us to find little ways of optimizing the keeping of home, records, and schedules.

Let's look at the specific areas of life that you feel too unorganized to allow your kiddos the chance to discover and learn at their own pace, led by their own passionate pursuits under the supervision of the one who loves them the most. Is it housekeeping? Schedule keeping? Record keeping? A little bit of all three? Whew, that can create the perfect storm. After reading this chapter you can cut yourself some slack on the expectations of how organized you really need to be while getting some ideas to shipshape your life.

Don't get it twisted. I am not an uber-organized, OCD-type who never has a disheveled home. Heck, right now to even get inside the garage door you will have to trip over 4 pairs of flip-flops, kicked off in the staggered footsteps of the wearer who didn't pause for one nano-second when disembarking from them. At the side of my bed, is my bra and t-shirt pile that I wore for the last week, which I will pull from when I get dressed the next day if it's not too stained or stinky. (#lesslaundry) And yes, no matter how tidy it starts out in the morning, our homeschool room will look like a tornado swept through it sparing nothing and intermingling toy cars, wayward railroad tracks, counting bears, and dried-out markers, with a peppering of dingy, balled-up socks.

As I walk through my cluttered home, each out-of-place item jumps out and grabs me, like a parasitic flea pouncing on his next victim. I might not notice the first few hours or even a whole day of a messy house. I can try to ignore it, but the negative juju just keeps building until my whole home is pressing down on me and instead of getting out the math lesson, I give up on getting anything accomplished—not even straightening up.

Flashbacks of my childhood home where both parents worked full-time and four kids had free destructive reign come to mind. Understandably, it was a complete disaster most days and straightened up perhaps every few Sundays. The bathroom I shared with my brothers (who took years to finally get that aim right), rivaled some truck stops with that odor that just slaps you in the face the minute you walk in. We splattered and spit toothpaste until the mirror was speckled. I often awoke to my Mom's frustrated grumbling about the sink full of dirty dishes from dinner the night before. I remember being so embarrassed when a friend sat down at my dining table and literally drew blood on her forearm scraping it on a glob of dried-up Cocoa Pebbles spot-welded to the table.

Thank God for my high-school best friend and her family who taught me what a clean house looked and felt like. This Italian family from New York was meticulously clean. They did things like dry the shower out with a big fluffy towel after every single use to stop soap scum and mildew. Before leaving the house, they would vacuum themselves out the door so they didn't leave footprints in the carpet. I'm not talking about dirt from your shoe footprints...oh Gosh, if you even dared enter Mrs. G's home with your shoes on, you'd better duck and run because she would throw something at your head as she yelled, "GET OUT OF HE' WICH YA' SHOES ON!" No, they left vacuum tracks in the carpet all the way to the tile. Glorious, symmetrical, inverted triangles which formed plush rectangular waves where the vacuum had sucked all the carpet fibers backward, then a little discoloration as the vacuum propelled forward moving them in the opposite direction. I will admit it was a sleek sight to leave *and* when arriving home it greeted you as a base layer of orderly *feng shui*. (And boy, it sure did make it hard to skip school and go to her house. You had to be a stealthy, jumping, teen ninja to sneak out at night.) This was back in the early 90s, wall-to-wall carpet's heyday. If you came up in the Berber era, or with wood floors, and cannot picture what I'm talking about, search Google images for "vacuum tracks in the carpet" and you'll see some fierce ones and even find a tutorial if you're so inspired.

Well, the innumerable Saturday mornings that I spent with them after a sleep-over, basketball games, beach days, and all the fun I enjoyed with them over the years; we *cleaned*. Windexed *every* surface, even the house plants' leaves! This family was so renowned for their cleanliness that my friend and I would get cleaning gigs from their neighbors. To be taught how to clean by this family was a blessing that morphed as I did from my teen years into an adult. My cleaning skills grew as my young family did. Knowing life in both a clean house and a messy house gave me perspective on the calm or chaos that ensued respectively.

The good feeling of walking through a clean home is physically palpable! It calms, energizes, and helps you focus. And while I don't suggest that we go to the extremes aforementioned, we do have to declutter and clean toothpaste globs out of the sink, and stains out of toilets once every week or two. And our kids do too! It's a form of self-care and self-respect. Cleaning chores can teach your kids responsibility, initiative, tidiness, organizational skills, orderliness, and diligence. Even toddlers can help unload the dishwasher or spray the glass cleaner while you wipe down surfaces. Around my house, there is no chore that a child cannot do.

I mean, you do realize that you have a clean-up crew, depending on how many kids you have and how old they are, right? Anyone can be taught to clean and the standards thereof. When they don't have a constricting government school schedule, that opens up the opportunity for children to have more cleaning responsibilities.

Give yourself and your little work crew some grace here, because most of us can use some expert advice in keeping a tidy, clutter-free home. In the book that set off a closet-purging revolution and pushed Goodwill donation bays to landslide proportions, *The Life-Changing Magic of Tidying Up,* author Marie Kondo suggests getting rid of whatever doesn't bring you joy. Take an item, any item in your hand, and ask yourself, "Does this bring me joy?" If you do not literally feel a joyful energy emanating from it, donate it.

I purged my entire home, (well except for my husband's closet, he wouldn't allow me to worm my way in there,) getting rid of whatever didn't bring me joy. I donated 18 lawn-waste-sized garbage bags, six of which came from my closet alone! My clothes were folded, my junk drawers organized, even the kids' areas got a systemized thrashing. It's a great feeling.

Unfortunately, nothing is forever. It may only take one pile of laundry or a couple of days of living but all of these spaces are going to end up disheveled. I am here to tell you that putting things back where they live once every day or two is good for the homeschool soul. And you're not the only one that's going to do it, you're going to employ that slew of students to help you. And by employ, I simply mean forcing them to do it. A small allowance is nice if you can afford it, but not absolutely necessary if you can't. If you even commit to five minutes every day (times *x* number of kids), it'll make a *huge* difference, ten minutes and your house could be so clean it'll look like Disney on Ice.

One of my favorite tools for promoting clean-house longevity is declaring "no-toy-zones". Let's say we decluttered to acceptable levels on Wednesday and are having guests Friday for dinner. Well, guess what is not coming into the living room, front room, dining room, or kitchen? That's right, *toysssssss*. I highly recommend you stand in an area of your home and ceremoniously flail your arms to indicate and incite your first no-toy-zone. Give them a deadline so they know how long to keep the toys exiled and enjoy two to three days of blessed tidiness in that zone.

I know that there are some people who could not care less about junk piles stacked in corners or three-year-old Cheerio crumbs in the highchair, and they might even skip this chapter. "Cleaning just isn't my forte," they say, "I don't really care that much." But adding fractions might not be your thing either, does that mean that you're not going to make your kid learn how to do it? And who knows, it *might* be one of your kids' forte! I have one that *loves* to organize and declutter. She often tells *me*, "Mommy it's time to do a little decluttering." Her siblings relay their own nightmarish tales of how she makes them clean when she's left in charge to babysit.

"She makes us declutter, says my eleven-year-old as she looks up at me with watery eyes, "Mommy, it's horrible."

Maybe none of your kids will like chores, but that doesn't mean that you shouldn't make them do them. There are a lot of kids that don't have chores. Even though 82% of us had to do chores growing up, only 28% of us make our own kids do chores.[1] That's roughly three out of four families whose kids don't have to do any chores.[2]

If you don't make your kids join in the housework, you're not only missing out on free child labor, but you're actually hurting your kids' character and development. While the numbers vary on how many kids actually do help around the houses of America, there is no contradictory information from experts about the advantages of assigning them chores. Chores teach kids how to function on their own, and life skills that they are going to have to learn anyway—at some point. It makes them feel like a part of the team, strengthens family bonds, teaches them responsibility, and that they have to work for things. One study followed two groups of people over 75 years, Harvard grads and non-Harvard grads who grew up poor in the inner city of Boston. Researchers hoped to find what psychosocial variables and processes from early life can help determine a person's later health and well-being. They found that those who were given chores ended up being more independent, better able to work in collaborative groups, and better able to understand that doing hard work means you're a valuable member of a community.[3]

This brings me to another great point: consequences. Every poor choice has one. Being unkind to your family members gets toxic *really quick* in a homeschool. So, when you are whack-a-moling the same behavioral problems over and over put them on a consequence chart. Some examples are:

Infraction	Consequence
Saying mean things	Say something nice about them.
Leaving your dirty clothes on the floor	Organize your drawers.
Antagonizing	Clean a toilet.
Not putting my garlic press in the correct compartment.	Organize the utensil drawer
Not doing the chore up to standards	Redo it up to standards and $0.25 docking of allowance
Being bossy	Organize pantry shelves

I'm sure you get the idea. The more cleaning and organizing consequences you apply, the better. One amazing homeschool mom and author thought of a great consequence for her child: dusting one-by-one the hundreds of leaves on the fake house plant that stood 5 feet tall!

Besides making the kids clean the kitchen, do their own laundry, and declutter every couple of days, we have a rotating chore chart that serves us well. Your weekly chore might be to water the house plants, vacuum Mama's minivan, or sweep all the lizard poo from the front porch. And if there is any living-breathing document, it's certainly our charts. In the spring we add weeding flowerbeds. When I'm digging for the blender, I realize cabinets need to be next on the consequence chart. Have you checked the baseboards lately? Those things collect grime like my minivan grill collects bugs driving over a body of water on a steamy Florida evening. I challenge you, Moms and Dads, to get creative with what'll work for your home. The next time you are frustrated by a mess that's been there too long, make a mental note, or do a note on your phone so you won't forget. I have a running *Consequences* note on my phone. You'll be proud of yourself for starting the eradication of the mess, and it's fun to find those niche things that make your home more comfortable, livable, and easy to learn in. It's never too late. The sooner you instill in those little ones how cleaning is a team effort, organizational skills are awesome, and clutter is not your friend, the less chaotic your home will be *and remain*. And guess what else, you won't be sending someone off to college who's a scourge of a roommate and doesn't know how to operate a washing machine.

SCHOOL RECORDS

Even if you send your kids to school right now, there is still some level of expectation that you have to keep up with their grades, whether it's checking grades online, or checking their homework and progress reports. So, you're already farther along than you think. When it comes to record keeping, we can take a cue from the government school system with a couple of gems they rely on: three-ring binders and student planners. Use one three-ring binder per student per year in the elementary years, and as rigor increases, you'll get the rhythm of how many to use, perhaps one per subject. I file mine in a closet and keep them for a couple of years past their completion. In my state, which has low regulation, that's the extent of my record-keeping. I submit a homeschool evaluation from a certified teacher once a year, to our district school board. While requirements may differ between evaluators, ours interviews my children. She asks them what they've been working on this year and writes the evaluation based on that.

There are other options for the once-a-year evaluation, like standardized tests, student assessment tests or an evaluation by a state-licensed psychologist or school psychologist; or "any other valid measurement tool as mutually agreed upon."

Some states have more requirements so I encourage you to go online to a wonderful resource for families, Homeschool Legal Defense Association, HSLDA.org to research specifically for your state. In more highly regulated states, on top of the aforementioned evaluations, requirements may be to teach certain subjects, (you know all the staples: reading, writing, arithmetic, geography, US History, even music and Physical Education depending on where you are), teach at least 180 days, and maintain a portfolio with student work samples and a log made "contemporaneously with instruction." Now, this might sound scary at first, but let's unpack it a little.

There are no specific requirements for how often the required subjects must be taught or at what grade levels so you'll enjoy autonomy and flexibility. And as far as how many days or hours you instruct, pshhhh, every single day in a homeschool setting there are teachable moments and a life of learning. Your walks aren't simply a stroll outside, they are observation of nature, bird watching, and plant species identification. Baking cookies with your sweetie is a lesson in following directions, multiplying fractions, and kitchen safety. Don't think for one minute that you have to be standing in front of a whiteboard for 1,000 hours a year, while your student sits in a hard plastic chair doing worksheets the whole time!

As for the contemporaneous log, have your kids keep a reading list in their planner to help you. Your library can be a huge help as well by providing an itemized checkout list for the entire year.

Official college transcripts can be daunting, even the mere word *transcript* is intimidating. This one piece of paper, accompanied by their college admissions test score, has the potential to get them into the college of their dreams or not. It should tell the story of your child's homeschool journey, and there are many ways to correctly make one. One expert homeschool mom and transcript writer says, "Do you know what makes them 'official'?"

When you type the word "official" at the top.

If your child is high school age and college-bound, you will need to write their transcripts or hire a professional. Even if you do outsource, you will have to compile everything they've done toward high school credit, so keep track chronologically. As they finish each credit or class add it to the document that you've saved on your computer, or add it to the app on your phone. The app Modify Edu, allows you to keep track of classes and hours on your phone. Your student has access as well to add portfolios, assignments, and any other record-keeping. The app is new, so I can't vouch for how well it works, yet. However, I do know that the idea of keeping transcript records on your phone, and the ability for your child to help with the process will appeal to many parents.

As homeschool parents, we have autonomy and freedom over our kids' education. The same goes for the transcripts that we will produce for them. We can use a template, make our own, or use an umbrella school. We get to decide the names of the classes, we decide if we want to weight the grades like an honors class, what grading scale to use, and whether we want to include test scores like the SAT or ACT. When the time comes for you to start thinking about them, one little Google search for "homeschool transcripts" will serve up so many helpful articles that will quickly make your heart palpitations dissipate.

College may not be the definite path for your child. As a former public-school teacher, who had hundreds of students come through my classroom every year, I'm going to tell you it's definitely not the right path for every 16-18 year old. There are trade schools, 2-year programs, sheer passion-driven learning, interning and apprenticeships that can lead a person to their right career without spending hundreds of thousands of dollars at faith-flaying, liberal-agenda indoctrination camps, er-uh I mean, college. But I digress. For college transcripts, each college has different requirements, so it is important to first check the college to which your student wants to apply.

SCHEDULES:

As far as an "organized schedule" goes, I would love to place a nice little sidebar here of my schedule and tell you how easily we adhere to it every single day. It might look something like this:

8:00-8:30 a.m.	Family devotion/breakfast
8:30-9:00 a.m.	Morning chores/personal care
9:00-10:00 a.m.	Group Read aloud
10:00-11:00 a.m.	History
11:00-12:00 p.m.	Lunch/recess
12:00-2:00 p.m.	Individual work
2:00-3:00 p.m.	Math
3:00-4:00 p.m.	Create, Read, Play
4:00-5:00 p.m.	Dinner
5:00-6:30 p.m.	Sports Practice
6:30-7:30 p.m.	Family Read aloud
7:30-8:30 p.m.	Get ready for bed/ put littles to bed, read in bed

Honestly, even as I wrote that schedule which we have followed at times, I rolled my eyes recalling how nugatory it was for us. You just don't have to schedule every hour of the day in a home learning environment. We had more happy days scheduled in chunks like this:

7:00-9:00 a.m.	Morning stuff like breakfast, devotion, chores, instrument practice, and outside time.
9:00-1:00 p.m.	Unit studies, read-aloud, individual work.
1:00-4:00 p.m.	Doctor appointments, errands, imaginative play
4:00-8:30 p.m.	Dinner, family bonding, bedtime

I learned this chunking trick from Kim Sorgen at Unconsumed Ministries, If your morning gets side-tracked due to an appointment, or a snake on the front porch that you must relocate, just flip-flop the morning chunk with the afternoon.

Let's continue to broaden those schedule constraints to something that took my homeschool game to the next level. Look at your weekly calendar and block off at least three consecutive days to be home. No appointments, no play-dates, no errands...just school. Calm and peace ensue when I don't have to do my hair or make-up, be somewhere at a certain time, or even load the kids in the car *at all*. The kids enjoy so much more free time, imaginative play, *and* focused learning without the schedule pressures for those three or four days. I do have to warn you, you will be feeling a little *loca-en-la-cabeza* at the end of these days. So make sure that there's a lot of self-care peppered in; anything you do to give your brain calm enjoyment. I really lean into quiet reading time each of these days for all of us, bust out a puzzle or craft, lavender essential oils, and definitely have chocolate on hand...because I'm going to need them. Ultimately, the hardest part of this schedule is blocking off the white space on the calendar. You must intentionally guard them, especially when you are booking your next hair appointment and your stylist's only availability lies smack in the cool morning of consecutive homeschool day #2. Be strong Mama, keep those days clear.

I'm not saying to only do three days of school a week, but there have been plenty of those kinds of weeks for us, and that's ok. However, on a lofty-goals week for those other weekdays we still get some school in, and outings as well. For example, finishing a three-day home stint begs for a half-day trip to the library, visiting Grampy and Nana, or hiking at a nature preserve. As you immerse in this homeschooling adventure, leaning into the role as teacher, you'll find those teachable moments in everything you do, everywhere you go.

Key Point:
With your whole family home and learning, it can be hard to keep the home organized. When you do teach your offspring a system of cleaning and organization, getting your house from trashed to tranquil in ten minutes can become a way of life.

The homeschooling records which you must keep depend on your state, but even in most highly regulated states it's not a mountain of paperwork. Yes, you're responsible for your child's high school transcripts, but if the thought of that is such a stressor that it's actually discouraging you from homeschooling you can just as easily outsource it.

"Where there is order, there is also harmony; where there is harmony, there is also correct timing; where there is correct timing,
there is also advantage." —St. Irenaeus

Action Item:
If you're not already giving your kids chores, start now. Start simple, and first model how to do the chore, highlighting the standards that you expect. They watch, you do it, then you do it together, and finally, you watch them do it. Once they are doing the chore on their own, they should know that you will inspect the work area to make sure they've met the standards. When my kids, say "I'm ready for you to inspect, Mom!" I usually, say, "Ok, go ahead and inspect your own work first, then I'll be in there." Invariably, they'll find something to fix, and it keeps me from making three to four trips to the chore site.

Also, visit the very handy website HSLDA.org to see what your state requirements are for homeschool record-keeping.

LIE #14:

Other Family Members' Opinions Actually Matter In This Decision.

"Nothing would be done at all, if a man waited until he could do it so well that no one could find fault with it."—St. John Henry Newman

"I could have no greater joy than to hear that my children are following the truth." 3 John 1:4

I KNOW THAT YOU are a dedicated parent, open-minded and hungry for truth, willing to do whatever it takes to protect and rear your child through a healthy education. In any childrearing endeavor, it does take a village. Parents do better when they have a support system of close friends and trusted relatives they can depend on when life happens. There will undoubtedly be many moments when family members step in to babysit, keep the kids distracted, and pour their loving affection into your babies. These people will help to form your child, give you rest, and hopefully a couple of overnight babysits every quarter so you and the spouse can have some one-on-one time sitting by a pool sipping on a Margarita without worrying that a little person could drown. Unfortunately, some of those old-fashioned relatives with their prying questions have bought into every lie in this book. Badgering you, no matter how politely, over the months and years with the same questions that you'll hear on the streets from complete strangers. Hear me when I say, you cannot let their beliefs shape your choices. Don't let their doubts and outdated data cloud your decision to do what's best for your child.

You won't believe the effrontery with which some people react when they find out you homeschool. Take the following stories of veteran homeschool Moms. Sherry took her three kids to the mall to get a picture with Santa during school hours. "Ho, ho, ho! Why aren't you in school today?" When the man in the red suit learned that these little darlings were homeschooled, he immediately started quizzing them. Instead of a magical moment with Santa, these kids received a rapid-fire oral test, "What's 5 x 6?" "Which war did America fight for independence?" "Spell reindeer" I don't think he did that to any of the public school kids that sat on his lap, do you? Bad Santa!

Tracey, a homeschool mother of three, was at her yearly exam with her OB-GYN. As she scooched on down to the edge of the table and put her foot in the stirrups, he asked what she did for a living. As soon as she told him that she homeschooled her children, he went into a diatribe of mis-facts about why homeschooling is bad for children—between the clanking of the metal speculum, he told her that her kids would lack socialization skills and fall behind grade level. Sounds like he's the one who lacked social skills! C'mon doc, who does that? Tracey was too shocked and ill-prepared to refute his misunderstandings, but you better believe that she never went back to that doctor. If it was me, I would've cited the research that homeschool students consistently perform better on reading and testing than their government and private school counterparts and there are many studies over many years that conclude it.[1] They also have better sleep hygiene[2], do fewer drugs, and have a deeper faith.

This next homeschool horror story from Amanda takes the top prize for jaw-hitting-the-floor audacity. Amanda, hospitalized with depression lay in a hospital bed struggling with the fatigue, pain, and sadness that plagued her battle. Uncertainty about her diagnosis worried her and on top of that, she missed her daughter Guinevere.

Her meddling Mother-in-law had the unmitigated gall to take little Guinevere-whom had never darkened the door of any educational institution in her life—and enroll her in public school...without Amanda's knowledge and certainly not her permission! If you're thinking, ok, she must've been in the hospital for months and the poor grandmother didn't know what else to do with the kid, no, don't. Amanda was only in the hospital for 10 days! As soon as she was better and collected Guinevere back home, her mother-in-law called DCF on her! This is a child that was part of a theatre club that literally put on Shakespearean plays. Voluntarily and joyfully the kids memorized the lines, rehearsed, and helped their dads build the set. Moms sewed costumes, babies crawled around and big kids helped take care of them. Dozens of families worked together creating a homeschool community in which the members were forever bonded.

When Amanda told me the story it was at least 12 years later. The kids have grown up. Some have gotten married and started their own families. Amanda's friend who sewed Guinevere's costume those many years ago would soon be a grandma. Guinevere's friend with whom she recited all those complicated Shakespearean lines would soon be a new Mama. Amanda and Guinevere attended the baby shower, which is where I met them. Obviously, these families built true and lasting relationships. Do you know who they're not going to see at a baby shower anytime soon? That wicked Mother-in-law.

"We don't talk to her anymore," said Amanda, with a dismissive eye-roll.

You are raising up a child in the admonition of the Lord, to help them find their God-given passion-filled path. When you know that you are a tool for the Lord in leading your kids to Himself, to discipleship and service through their life and career, I don't care if it's Grandma, Santa Claus, or your gynecologist,—as we say in the South, *They ain't got nothing to say to you.*

I met Julie, a sweet twenty-something mom of a toddler and six-year-old at my church. She decided to homeschool her eldest. Through excited texts, she shared with me many good things she was enjoying at the start of her homeschool journey. She and her son were both loving their unit study on race cars. I can still see the picture she texted of his excited expression, eyes bulging, mouth in a perfect O, when they measured out the length of a Formula One race car, nearly 19 feet in their hallway at home.

Not only was she bonding with him as she taught him, but she also stepped outside of her comfort zone and started a small business as a Mary Kay consultant to add to the household income. She was flourishing and growing right along with her son, who was enjoying being homeschooled thoroughly. That is until a meddling family member got a hold of her. Her husband's sister was decades into her teaching career and on the county school board. I'm not sure what she said to talk her out of homeschooling, but she was effective.

My heart broke when she told me that she put him back in school, "and he loves it." Because it's like taking a baby from the clutches of a loving mother and throwing him to wolves to raise. And so what, "he loves it"? Kids can be resilient and thrive in some really bad situations. They enjoy going to school, they like to eat ice cream for breakfast, they like to stay up late, like to skip baths and teeth brushings, like to watch scary nightmare-inducing movies, like to never eat their veggies, like to fit in with peers, like to try new drugs. Do you follow my reasoning here?

If you have family members that are already skeptical of your ability to parent or home educate then you will definitely feel the pressure of wanting them to respect your decision, of wanting them to think that you're just as capable as any state-certified teacher.

Silent prayers of "Please get it right, please get it right," screamed through my head when my father-in-law asked my third grader a multiplication fact. And of course, she did not.

"Come on! It was the fives facts; we skip count by fives like a banker! Have I taught you nothing?" My dropping heart wailed inwardly, feeling the incorrect answer a direct reflection of my unworthiness.

Instantly my imposter syndrome flared. *I'm incapable of teaching my child. I'm a terrible teacher. What am I doing wrong?* That snapshot of my home education program, my child's brain fart, if you will, was not an accurate picture any more than a mother's social media post about how wonderful her son, the neighborhood bully is because he picked up some trash from the side of the road. A closer analogy is that we are planting trees. Trees that we hope will bear fruit, 20, 40, 60, and 100-fold. It takes *years* for a tree to bear fruit, some citrus trees take up to 10 years! When you are years into this homeschool sojourn, you will start seeing things in your kids that you can directly attribute to being educated away from the masses. Learning about God, and good character on a regular basis without the snares of the world choking it out, you'll eventually see their faith start to mature and then flourish. Being with their siblings all day, every day without a peer group to steal their loyalty, you'll see bonds of closeness in your family you'd never known possible. With the flexibility of your own schedule, not having to stick to the county school calendar, you'll find many adventures to add memories and closeness.

At the time of my child's failed verbal pop quiz administrated by her Grandpa, I had no way of knowing what fruit would grow. But let's fast-forward to a beautiful moment on a beach eight years later.

We visited the historical Fort DeSoto on a blustery February morning in sunny Florida. Like all the other Forts that we've visited, this one is on the beach. After climbing through every bunker and cement-fortified hall of the fort we spread our blanket in the sand to enjoy the salty breeze, sea shells, and vitamin D. I taught my youngest son, Marett, how to properly throw a football, and with the wind carrying it, he was launching impressive distances. Little arching, rainbow, five-year-old spirals. It was so cute.

We scraped a picnic together with car snacks and "dry sandwiches" as my husband called them due to the lack of condiments. We all shared one tiny plastic spork from the on-the-go tuna can for the potato salad. There were lots of amazing family victories that day. But one thing happened that made this whole homeschool journey worth it. This one fruit let me know that all the years of bud-nipping, guiding, and encouraging are working.

We meandered along the tide line in the wet, hard-packed sand, millions of sea shells dotting our squishy walkway. Suddenly, we came upon a bright orange sponge with chubby round branches resembling the gnarled, bony hands of an old lady. We've been to the beach thousands of times, all up and down Florida's coastline, but we had never seen a creature like this.

"It's spongin!" said Piper, who's so interested in marine biology that *Shark Week* is her third favorite holiday. "These things are pretty neat. They act like an ocean filter. It sucks water into these holes here and it takes bacteria out of the water, it breaks it down, then sends the nutrients out to its cells."

Giving the spongin a little squeeze between her thumb and pointer, she held it out for her family to do the same as we all marveled at the creature and her demonstration. My heart about turned into a sponge, saturated with pride, as I watched her point out the pores and stem. In her element, she was a natural. Nonchalant, she was instantly a learned wildlife guide specializing in marine biology.

My son, Dash, begged to keep the sea creature. Heck, I wanted to keep it too, as a souvenir of this great homeschool moment, but my little marine biologist informed me that it would start stinking like dead fish as it dried out, so we reluctantly agreed it was best to leave it.

If you're sitting here thinking, "What's the big deal about that?" I ask you to imagine your own child demonstrating their self-taught wisdom in a useful, relatable way that brought others closer together in awe and wonder. This was a glimpse into her future, into the path along which God is calling her. The course which I'm honored to be her support and guide.

Now that homeschooling is becoming more mainstream and steadily increasing, we can liken it to the dorky-yet-cute-when-she-removes-her-glasses protagonist of an 80's rom-com that got a hot makeover, hurtling her popularity to homecoming queen status. The number of families that homeschool has tripled over the last two years, and is steadily increasing. Parents are waking up!

Even so, there will still be grandparents who disagree with it and doubt you. And you know what? I hope a fervent fire is lit in you to prove them wrong. Let that yearning get you through those months when flash cards aren't working and phonics aren't sticking, through the times when even *you* might doubt your capability. Remember what Paul tells us in his letter to the Galatians: let us not grow weary of doing good, for in due season we will reap, if we do not give up.

Assuredly, there will be tiring times for homeschooling parents. Who is going to be the one, when your child hits a learning roadblock, to read every book available, listen to experts on podcasts, and sift through mountains of curriculum so that she can overcome? Spoiler alert: it's not grandparents, aunts or uncles. It's you.

Key Point:
Many family members might not accept your decision to homeschool. Do it anyway.

Home Is Where the Truth Is:
If you want a zinger to throw at speculative relatives you can tell them this: 78% of 45 peer-reviewed studies found that "homeschooled students or graduates performed significantly better than their conventional or institutional school peers in terms of academic achievement, social, emotional, and psychological development, and success into adulthood (including in post-secondary education, college/university)."[1]

Action Item:
Prepare as a family what to say to the older generation when met with doubt, criticism, or judgment about homeschooling. Also, when doubts arise, know that this is important work and lean into the wisdom of Theodore Roosevelt who said, "Far and away the best prize that life has to offer is the chance to work hard at work worth doing."

LIE #15:

I Can't Homeschool My Child Because He Learns Differently.

"He did not say: You will not be troubled—You will not be tempted—You will not be distressed. But He said: You will not be overcome." —St. Julian of Norwich

"Now there are varieties of gifts, but the same Spirit; and there are varieties of service, but the same Lord; and there are varieties of working, but it is the same God who inspires them all in every one." 1 Corinthians 12:4-6

THE TEACHER AND SCHOOL inspector walk down the aisles of a small schoolroom, in a quaint, nineteenth-century Ohio village. Slowing their cadence as they walk by one boy's desk, "This one is addled," the teacher says loudly enough for the boy to hear. "It will do no good to keep him in school any longer."

After much long-suffering with his studies, this was the last straw for the poor child. Instantly, he bursts into tears, his chair scraping the floor as he fled the classroom running home to the safety and supportive love of his mother's arms.

It was then that he "found out what a good thing a good mother is. Coming out as his strongest defender, Mother love was aroused, Mother pride wounded to the quick."[1] With her brow furrowed, shoulders back, and chest puffed, she stormed back into the classroom with her son. Walking straight up to the teacher, eyes locked on his, finger pointing in his face she spewed her wrath, "You don't have any idea what you're talking about! Why, my son has twice the brains that you yourself have!"

Indeed, she was the most enthusiastic champion a boy ever had. And in that moment, as she continued to berate the teacher, that little boy determined that he would be worthy of her and show her that her confidence was not misplaced.[2]

Knowing what was best for him, the dedicated mother took her son home to educate him. This curious boy thrived at home, teaching himself many things through reading, even building a chemistry laboratory in his basement. Though the legitimate fear of chemical explosions loomed, she continued to let him discover and learn. This young man would grow up to be the most famous genius and prolific inventor of the nineteenth century, patenting 1,093 of his inventions which included the incandescent light bulb, the motion picture camera, and the electricity distribution system. He was Thomas Edison.

An innovator that learned differently than his peers, he was unfortunately placed in a school under a teacher who didn't know how to design instruction according to his needs and strengths. However, the learning environment that his mother provided for him at home ignited his genius and changed the world.

It would still be about a hundred years until Howard Gardner proposed the theory of multiple intelligences. His 1983 book "Frames of Mind," expanded the definition of intelligence and outlined eight variations of intellectual proficiencies. His work has been monumental in helping children realize their strengths, leading to confidence in learning and thriving careers because they honed in on their talents early and decisively.

GARDNER'S THEORY OF MULTIPLE INTELLIGENCES:

Linguistic (word smart)	Good at writing, reading, poetry, learning languages, attaining a wide vocabulary and telling great stories. Good listeners and conversationalists.
Logical/Mathematical (number or reasoning smart)	The main type of intelligence that comes to mind, includes being good at math, and using numbers in general, taking tests, critical thinking, reading graphs, as well as organizational skills.
Spatial (picture smart)	Adept in visualization, seeing things in their mind's eye, reading maps, or recognizing patterns of wide space such as pilots, navigators or architects would use.
Bodily Kinesthetic (bodily smart)	Good at maneuvering their own body, skillful at handling objects or balls and doing whatever they want with them. Skilled at working with their hands to create. Think dancers, sculptors, athletes, soldiers.
Musical (music smart)	Ability to interpret musical sounds, rhythm, tones, to play musical instruments or compose harmonic music.
Interpersonal (people smart)	These people are good at understanding others, reading their emotions and body language, and understanding social etiquette. Their strengths include, managing, motivating and working with people.
Intrapersonal (self-smart)	Understands themselves, their emotions, feelings, and capacities. Knowing their strengths and weaknesses, and regulating their own life accordingly.
Naturalist (nature smart)	Recognizing patterns, plants, animals in nature. Having a keen interest in the natural world or the outdoors.

If you want to learn more about the intelligences that you and your kids lean toward, there are online quizzes to help you. One that I like is at:

https://www.idrlabs.com/multiple-intelligences/test.php

Unfortunately, it seems that the school systems of America haven't gotten the memo that there are other ways to be smart than merely understanding words and numbers. The qualifying and ranking of children in government and private schools through standardized testing and checking off the benchmarks of multiple unrelated subjects leave children—who have a different set of smarts waiting to be uncovered and stoked to full potential—behind. Kids are made to feel stupid because they don't measure up to classmates who are linguistically and mathematically proficient. In the school system, the best-case scenario for these failing students is to get a diagnosis of a learning disability (if they don't already have one) so that family members, teachers and other advocates can design an Individualized Education Program (IEP) which will hopefully give them the tools they need to be successful. Also called accommodations, these tools are any methods and services that will help the child. Like allowing calculators or charts for math facts. For someone who has trouble seeing the whiteboard, their IEP will recommend sitting up front. Extended time to take a test is one of the most common accommodations.

Before we get into more accommodations, I'd like to recognize that the first thing many parents do when their child gets a learning disability diagnosis is to pull them out of school and start using the advantages of homeschooling to their child's favor. But others do not, and I fear that they've been bamboozled into thinking that keeping their child in the school system is the best way to implement IEP strategies.

You might know that your child needs special help, but don't think you can amply provide it. So not true!

There is not a single accommodation that you cannot do at home with your child— *and do it better* than any teacher in a classroom setting. Even the group project is doable for the smallest homeschool classroom of one teacher and one student. Group project, family project, tomato, tomahto. Seriously! Veritably, most learning adaptations mimic what conditions would *always* be at home!

Ahead are accommodations available that help with a slew of deficits pertaining to reading, math, spelling, penmanship, anxiety and depression, sensory issues, testing, and managing executive function disorder.[3] As I list these, you tell me if these aren't things that will easily and naturally occur at home.

They include but are not limited to:

- Extra time to complete the work or reading given.
- Preferential seating (sitting up front, closest to the teacher).
- Repetition of directions.
- Simple directions.
- Incorporating a child's personal interests into activities whenever possible (This sounds a bit like passion-driven learning, which I first explained in chapter four and should be one of the main objectives in your homeschool).
- Provide student with a choice of reading materials that match their interests and skill level.
- Shortened assignments.
- Providing a study carrel.
- Assignments and tasks given in segments.
- Redirection.
- Limit distractions.
- A "Hot pass" or "cool off card." A card the student gets so they can leave class, flash the hot pass to the

teacher, and go to the office, guidance counselor, or nurse (designated ahead of time) to cool off, if they feel a negative behavior coming on.

- Paraphrasing and rephrasing.
- Having someone read the material to them.
- Getting the child to explain things back in his own words and requiring the use of words different from the ones used in the initial explanation. (Also called narration, this one is straight from the Charlotte Mason Method, which I first mentioned in chapter 2.)
- For penmanship and writing deficiency: Reduce the volume of writing and copying, especially when it is not a critical component of an instructional task.
- Use a closure procedure on worksheets. In this method, the student fills in a blank rather than writing an entire sentence.
- Provide a peer buddy or monitor. (And who better than Mom, Dad or sibling?)
- Address their sensory issues.
- Make opportunities for turn-taking, initiating and terminating conversations, commenting, and asking questions. (ummm...#familylife).
- Visual prompts.
- A picture schedule.
- Gradually building the complexity of the task.
- Provide recorded books with appropriate pacing. (Yes, audiobooks we love you!)
- Give time to work independently.
- Positive or corrective feedback.
- Integrate several short, learning activities rather than a single long one into the session. (Another jewel from the Charlotte Mason method.)

- Permit retake spelling tests.
- Recognize effort and do not require the completion of the entire activity.

Did you notice how the vast majority of accommodations are instinctual to a mother? And you've already used plenty of them when you potty trained him, taught him to tie his shoes, brush his hair, sing the ABCs, or hit the ball off the tee. You're not so new to this teaching thing, after all!

Another thing you'll realize when you dig into these special learning strategies is how difficult it would be for a classroom teacher to incorporate them among their own 25-35 students. Even if they had only three or four students with an IEP, to give them what they need separately from the other students in their care would stretch a teacher even thinner. And what are they to do when one child's IEP calls for stimulation and bright colors, while another child's calls for no distractions, and quiet, calm surroundings? How are they going to pull that one off in the same small classroom? It's common for the administration to place students with conflicting IEPs with the same teacher making it impossible to give both students what their IEP calls for, because one negates the other. I'm sure that there are many capable teachers, that do a very good job of tailoring lessons for different learning needs, but with the average class size in elementary being over 20 kids per class, it's easy to see how many kids could get left behind. A one-size-fits-all approach...simply doesn't. Do you really want to throw your child's IEP to a game of chance?

With the many different types of intelligences, some learning *differences* (not disabilities) are actually blessings, not curses. Would you think it a blessing if you had a mind like Albert Einstein, Elon Musk, Ludwig Von Beethoven, or Jennifer Aniston? All of these people—the epitomes of success—are dyslexic. In her book, *Say Good-bye to "Dyslexia" and Embrace Full-Field Vision Learning,* Kathy Alford explains how parents can train the magnificent brains of their struggling learners. She also emphasizes the importance of removing the dyslexic label and replacing it with a more constructive one, *Full-Field Vision,* because of what she discovered working with dyslexic students for decades.

"Students with full-field vision have been shown to have a distinctive wiring of the brain, an extraordinary arrangement that can be used to the *student's advantage* in learning to read and write. However, because these same remarkable students often do not respond well to early phonics instruction, have difficulty keeping their place on the page, or reverse letters when they write, teachers and administrators over the years have tended to label these children as disabled. *Nothing could be farther from the truth!* In fact, during my 40+ years of teaching, I've seen just the opposite," Alford adamantly continues, "Should these individuals with full-field vision who make up about 20% of the population be labeled as having a learning disability simply because they see and learn in a different way from the other 80%? In my view *absolutely not!*"[4]

When Alford's daughter Sarah was six-years-old, she struggled with reading. 'I hate being in the lowest reading group,' she cried, tears magnifying her big brown eyes. Learning the tough spelling lists her teacher assigned added massive stress each week. Sarah was the youngest of five children, she was a bright child who loved learning and was highly attuned to plants, animals, and nature in general. However, Alford had recognized that Sarah, was exhibiting signs of dyslexia. As a third-grade teacher at a private school, Alford applied her expertise and worked every night with Sarah at the kitchen table, slogging through the first-grade homework. Despite Alford's knowledgeable efforts, by the end of the school year, Sarah still had inadequate gains. Second grade was not much better and at the end of that year, she still lagged way behind her peers in reading level.

Sarah's first three years of school brought so many learning challenges that when the time came to join her mother's classroom as a third grader it brought Sarah much enthusiasm. Despite her reading difficulties which had previously led to much embarrassment, she showed spunk, courage, and curiosity about the natural world. In class and out, Alford worked with her at her level, praising every progress. Sarah worked her hardest for her Mama. All the same, at the end of third grade, Sarah was still having a hard time with reading and Alford knew that sending her on to the rigor of fourth grade would lead to Sarah needing many accommodations and failure.

Alford was frustrated—not at her child but at herself—for not being able to get Sarah up to reading level. Alford prayed "intently, desperately, yet with hope in our Merciful Savior" asking him to guide her. After much soul-searching, Alford decided to quit her job teaching and homeschool Sarah. She vowed to search until she found new methods that would work for Sarah and started a tutoring business to help make ends meet. That summer Alford diligently scoured books, popular magazines, scholarly journals, and attended educational workshops. Finding some new methods and novel insights she gathered everything and started working with Sarah. The arduous quest paid off! Within three months Sarah was reading at grade level!

Here is what she discovered when working with her own child and the many others that she tutored: these struggling readers were actually seeing the whole visual field—or the whole page—all at once. Their eyes didn't move from left to right with ease, which is why the directionality of letters was so difficult for them. With some simple tools and exercises for training their eyes, Alford has had great success in teaching many dyslexic children how to use the brain that God gave them. She noticed that although they may have reading differences, full-field vision learners often grasp the big picture in science, math, and social studies. They think outside the box and are excessively creative which leads them to be some of the great inventors and innovators of history, like our hero at the beginning of this chapter, Thomas Edison.

Because of one mother's relentless determination in getting her child through her learning difference, we now have a new way to look at dyslexia—or rather "full-field-vision learning" and new methods in helping those kids achieve success. Can you feel that fire in yourself? To research, apply what you've learned, seek out help in your community and stop at nothing for the success of your own child? Whatever drive is in you, dear loving parent, is going to be greater than that of any other human being that your baby comes in contact with whether teachers, therapists, counselors or specialists.

If your child is struggling in some way and you suspect a learning difference or disability, you might want to have your child tested. It can be a huge relief to a full-field vision learner to know that they are not stupid, and why they can't read as some others do. Instead of struggling through exercises that won't work academically for them, you can help them find what does work without the pall of self-deprecating thoughts of *I'm just stupid lazy, and unmotivated,* plaguing them. With you as their advocate, you can embrace and overcome together.

Also, consider that if your child is diagnosed, they could be eligible for special education services provided by the school district for free. In at least 31 states, homeschoolers automatically qualify for special education services. Depending on where you live, you may apply for scholarships to use toward services or supplies or anything toward their education. Services vary from state to state, even district to district, so reach out to your local district to find out more information, or visit nationalschoolchoiceweek.com and search the article entitled, *How To Continue Your IEP, Even If You Start Homeschooling,* for information on a broad range of educational services for homeschoolers.

Whether your child has a learning difference or not, they are going to be stronger in some areas and weaker in others. Can we please stop making children work ad nauseam on their weaknesses as if that's the only way to be smart? That's so backward from what we do in the business world! Adults don't function from their weaknesses, instead, we thrive when we work from our strengths. Picture a Fortune 500 company that is growing, making innovations, and extremely successful. Do you think they have a staff that is functioning from its weaknesses? No! Instead, they've found people who are functioning in their wheelhouse— specialists or professionals who are constantly experiencing personal growth because they're working and building upon their *strengths*.

So what if your child's strength isn't Chemistry? I invite you to consider not forcing her to take Chemistry, where she can barely scrape out a passing grade even with a well-paid tutor. Take the money you would've spent on a tutor and invest it in what she is good at and loves to do. Maybe she spends hours listening to fantasy books bringing the mythical creatures she reads about to life in her sketchbook. I'm willing to bet that she would rather have drawing lessons and high-quality art supplies, then memorize the periodic table of elements. Which child is going to thrive and find her forte? The frustrated and confused chemist, or the happy and passionate artist who just downloaded a new book and has a shiny new 24-pack of Prismacolor colored pencils? Which parent-child relationship is going to flourish? The one in which a child is forced to learn something they'll never use again, or the one in which a parent supports and advocates for their child to develop their passions to such heights they may not have achieved on their own?

Now, am I saying that a child should never struggle with something that is difficult for them? Heck no! We shouldn't coddle them to the point that they're scared of failure. There'll be no resilience in that. We must teach them to have the right mindset. Renowned psychologist Carol Dweck found that your mindset has an acute bearing on what you are able to achieve. We want our children to have a *growth mindset*. Someone with a growth mindset sees a challenge as an opportunity to learn, grow, and better themselves. This mindset is based on the belief that if you work hard at something you'll improve. Your basic skill set when it comes to competence, intelligence, attitudes, and interests, does not determine your true potential! No matter what it is, no matter who you are. People who have a growth mindset know that the more they practice, the better they will become. They know that hard work—or grit—is the actual true determinant of success. As Alfred Binet, the inventor of the IQ test put it, it's not always the people who start out the smartest that end up the smartest.

In Dweck's book, *Mindset: The New Psychology of Success*, she lays out a very good argument that raw talent is a myth, although people may show natural talent above others in some areas, people who rise to the top of their profession, are actually the one's that put in the work to get better day after day, year after year. Think of people like Michael Jordan who didn't make the varsity basketball team until his junior year in high school, Leo Tolstoy, who was described as a normal child, or Albert Einstein who flunked his college entrance exam bombing the botany, zoology, and language sections. These icons did not have what hinders many bright, capable, athletic children today—a fixed mindset.

The fixed mindset says that you have a certain amount of intelligence and talent, and there's not much that you can do to change it. One student at Columbia University called it his "greatest learning disability—a tendency to see performance as a reflection of character and, if he could not accomplish something right away, to avoid the task and treat it with contempt."[5] Those with a fixed mindset think, "If this is hard for me, then I must not be smart, so I'm not even going to do it". They become afraid of challenges because risk and effort are a couple of things that might reveal that they aren't smart or skillful enough for the task. They see their mistakes as the fault of their lack of ability, something that they're incapable of changing.

Where those with a fixed mindset believe that their abilities are carved in stone, those with a growth mindset believe that they can cultivate theirs. Fixed mindset: Effort is a bad thing, because if you have to put in effort, that proves that you aren't talented because if you were you wouldn't need effort. Growth mindset: Effort is what *makes* you smart or talented. Whichever of these mindsets you hold will affect everything you undertake. Those with a fixed mindset think they constantly have to prove themselves so they are averse to anything that might show them as incapable. But people with a growth mindset see a challenge as a way to improve, learn something new, get better and reach their full potential.

Experts agree that a growth mindset is key in raising a self-motivated child. "Promoting a growth mindset is one of the best ways to improve your child's sense of control, to foster their emotional development, and to support their academic achievement."[6]

Praise effort, not intelligence.

Let's talk about some ways parents can foster a growth mindset. We start by praising effort, not talent or intelligence. A compliment from a parent such as, "You're so smart!" only gives a momentary boost of confidence. In the long run, it's actually going to hurt their motivation and performance. Because the minute they fail or struggle to understand a concept, they'll start to doubt themselves or think they're dumb. *If a good score meant I was smart, then a bad score means I'm stupid.* If our child scores really well on a test, we shouldn't say, "You're so intelligent!" Instead, we should say, "You studied really hard for that test, I'm proud of the effort you put in." Rather than saying, "Wow, you whacked that ball hard, you're a natural!" Say something like, "I can see you've been practicing your baseball swing, I'm proud of you for working hard."

As Dweck warns, we must be wary of the hidden messages in the praise we give our kids. See if you can find the hidden meanings in the following phrases.

"You understood that concept really quickly! You are sharp!"

"Listen to my daughter play this piano piece, Laurel. Isn't she the next Chopin?"

"Girl, you are a genius, you got an A and you barely even studied!"

At first listen, most parents would say these are confidence boosters, little ways to show our parental pride and support. But if you listen closely, you'll hear another message, the ones our children hear:

If I don't immediately grasp a concept, I'm not smart.

I better not try any hard piano music or they'll see that I'm no Chopin.

I better quit studying or they won't think that I'm a genius.

Or, *If I actually have to study, I must be dumb.*

After more than 30 years of studying the effect mindset has on a person, Dweck says, "If parents want to give their children a gift, the best thing they can do is to teach their children to love challenges, be intrigued by mistakes, enjoy effort, seek new strategies, and keep on learning. That way their children don't have to be slaves of praise. They will have a way to build and repair their own confidence."[7]

I know it's going to be hard to get out of the habit of lobbing those compliments that focus on smarts or talent instead of highlighting their growth mindset through persistence, practice, and good strategies. I still catch myself throwing them out there every once in a while. So, here are a few suggestions to get the growth mindset flowing:

"I saw the way you checked your work on that math problem, then went back and figured it out correctly! I'm so proud of you for taking your time and finding what worked!"

"I'm impressed that you picked that difficult recipe for your baking project. It's going to be laborious, and out of

your comfort zone to make, but you'll sure up your game as a baker making that one."

"That puzzle took a while to complete, but you stuck with it and finished it! I'm proud of you for concentrating for that long!"

Another way to foster a growth mindset is to acknowledge their work in ways that show we are genuinely interested in the energy they've put into it and their choices. For example,

"Oh wow, look at all the details that you've put in that drawing, tell me about this one."

"That was an exciting race, lots of competition! How'd you feel?" (This is appropriate whether they came in first, middle of the pack, or dead last.)

"You scored a goal tonight! All that practicing is paying off! Keep at it!

"I can see that you put a lot of effort into that essay, your strong verbs are getting stronger!"

Let's not forget about the kids who put in lots of effort and still didn't do well. Especially those that have a learning difference or disability, for them it's not only about effort but also about finding the right strategy.

"I see that you genuinely gave that your best effort, let's keep working and figure out what you don't understand."

"I understand this is tricky, we all learn differently. Let's keep trying to find a strategy that works for you,"

"It's ok that you haven't mastered this yet. You are working hard, that's going to make a difference. Keep trying and you'll see improvement."

Let's apply what we've talked about in this chapter into the life of a struggling learner who perhaps has just been diagnosed with a learning difference. Take them out of the institution, and bring them home to the calm environment in which they're most comfortable. Discover which intelligences they lean toward by taking an online multiple intelligences quiz. Instill a growth mindset. Pile on all the accommodations. Use special education services, if needed. Help them to discover their passions. And remember one more very important thing: God is their teacher.

This is what Charlotte Mason realized when she traveled to Florence, Italy. Beholding a Fourteenth-century fresco in a Spanish chapel that showed the Holy Spirit descending upon the minds of religious and secular men, she had what she called "The Great Recognition":

"The great recognition, that God the Holy Spirit is himself personally the Imparter of knowledge, the Instructor of youth, the Inspirer of genius, is a conception so far lost to us that we should think it distinctly irreverent to conceive of the divine teaching as co-operating with ours in a child's arithmetic lesson. But the Florentine mind of the Middle Ages believed that every fruitful idea, every original conception whether in Euclid or grammar, or music, was a direct inspiration of the Holy Spirit."[8]

Mason felt so moved that she hung a reproduction of the fresco in her school so that pupils and teachers alike could ponder God as their teacher in all things—even in "non-religious" subjects like math and grammar.

Key Point:

Students who learn differently will find success with the right accommodations. However, there is no accommodation offered by the school system that you cannot do at home for your child...and reap better results at that! The homeschool environment is perfect for helping struggling learners. Also, with so many different ways to be intelligent, we should be guiding our children to focus on what they're good at and to hone those strengths.

"It's not always the people who start out the smartest that end up the smartest." Alfred Binet, inventor of the IQ test.

Action Item:

To dig deeper into the importance of mindset, pick up "Mindset the New Psychology of Success" by Carol S. Dweck, Ph. D., so you can start your family on the growth mindset. Also, give your kids a multiple intelligence quiz to find which way they're leaning. An internet search will lead to a few. I like this one: https://www.idrlabs.com/multiple-intelligences/test.php

LIE #16:

I Can't Do It By Myself.

*"Just believe in yourself. Even if you don't,
pretend that you do and, at some point, you will."*
—Venus Williams

*"The eyes of the Lord are upon those who love
him, a mighty protection and strong support, a
shelter from hot wind and a shade from noonday
sun, a guard against stumbling and a defense
against falling." Sirach 34:16*

I CAN SEE YOU now, you're considering taking your eighth-grader out of government school before he dares to traverse the metal detector and wrought iron security gates of high school. Biting your nails, doubting, and praying, your mind races,

"What are we going to do all day?" Realizing you will be their sole teacher, you languish

"How can I teach my kid Algebra? It's been 25 years since I took that class!"

Or "How can I teach Spanish? *No hablo Español.*"

It's not just the upper-level courses that are intimidating. Other worries creep in. "Will my child miss out on sports and the camaraderie of other group activities, mainstays of government school life?" Besides, if you decide to homeschool your children, when will you ever have time for yourself? Time to take care of *you*?

No matter your child's age, we all have fears creeping in when it comes to the daunting task of educating them—

seemingly by ourselves. Maybe your kiddo is still in elementary school, some of my fondest childhood memories as a public school student were those rousing games of P.E. dodgeball. Instead of those upper-level course loads that are giving you doubts, it might be the concern that you don't want your child to miss out on team sports fun.

"Can I deny my kid the chance to pelt his classmate in the head with a maroon, medium-sized bouncy ball?" your doubting heart beseeches you.

"Sure, my spouse and I can make the kids run around the yard while pegging them with balls, but it's just not the same."

Another fantastic feature you might miss about having your kid hop on the big yellow bus and disappear for eight hours...all those glorious hours of free time when they go off to be taught by someone else. It's so easy to get a mani-pedi when the kids are taken care of by someone—*anyone* else. I've got hair and Botox appointments, facials, general upkeep, and maintenance to keep myself not looking war-torn. Just because I'm a homeschool mom, who seldom leaves the house Monday thru Thursday doesn't mean I'm giving up on myself. Indeed, that means I need *more* pampering. Can't I just have a few hours a week of personal time without 17 kids in tow?

Let me reassure you, as I explain an abundance of support structures available to homeschoolers, as well as new resources that are developing as homeschooling becomes increasingly mainstream. We've got conventions, co-ops, tutors, online learning platforms, homeschool hybrids, resource centers, online groups, even free college, and this list is continually growing. Your job is to find what works for you and your kids while deriving your main support from the Lord.

There are ways to make dodgeball games happen. You don't have to feel like your family has been exiled to a remote island, where everyone's weird, the women wear long skirts and we raise goats, scratching our way to survival—or our child's success. The latter having a strenuous and direct effect on our sanity and the longevity of our commitment as homeschool parents.

Twenty years ago, I might've said, OK, it's going to be a huge challenge. You're going to be the only homeschoolers in your town, not many people even know what homeschooling is, and you're going to be blazing a new trail, learning what works as you go. But we've come a long way since the looking-over-your-shoulder era of the illegal homeschool years when parents kept the curtains closed and didn't dare answer the door during school hours. Forty years after the complete legalization of homeschooling, there are at least 3.7 million Americans learning at home. [1] Post-pandemic, *every* American with school-aged kids has had a taste of it. It may be the fastest-growing form of education in the United States as well as around the world in places like, Australia, Canada, France, Hungary, Japan, Kenya, Russia, Mexico, South Korea, Thailand, and the United Kingdom.

Let me back up here with a little homeschool history. From the dawn of man up until the last 250ish years, the educating and training of children was the parent's job, save for the select few that were wealthy enough to afford special tutors and formal education. Government-run schooling is relatively new in society and started with the Prussians in the late 1700s when they began developing government-led compulsory education which I explained in chapter six. This model, still used today is an utter deprivation for all children with their natural curiosity. America followed suit with compulsory attendance laws starting in Massachusetts in 1852. By 1918 Mississippi was the last state to enact compulsory attendance making truancy illegal. Once this happened, the government had a monopoly on schooling until 1925 when the Roman Catholic church won the right in court to start its own schools. Later the Amish community also went to court for the right to educate their children, which tore down barriers and allowed other Christian denominations to open schools as well.

So, our great-great-grandparents and subsequent generations on down to ourselves may have only known government or private schooling, except for the few rogues that caught on to the benefits of keeping their kids home to learn in the late 70s and early 80s. Through the 1980s, legal battles were fought and won to make homeschooling legal in all 50 states.

Once homeschooling was legalized for every American, the "homeschooling movement" got well underway, and by the turn of the century around 3% of U.S. students were homeschooled. The pandemic-induced surge in the 2020-2021 school year shot that number to 63%. The number of homeschoolers the following year, 2021-22 was still significantly higher than pre-pandemic numbers, at around 46%.[2] While homeschooling used to be rare and oft chosen for religious reasons, the numbers and reasons for choosing it continue to grow. School violence and shootings, dissatisfaction with neighborhood schools, bullying, woke ideologies, and the lure of being able to tailor the education to fit the child all are beckoning parents in a mass exodus from school institutions.

Whatever your reason for finally coming to the powerful decision to homeschool, you can be sure that there is help and support out there for you as a homeschool family.

SUPPORT FOR YOU THE TEACHER

Did you know that there's a place near you where all the home education experts—I'm talking, authors, bloggers, podcast hosts, doctors of Family Psychology, mothers of multiples (and we aren't just talking 2 or 3 kids here—try 17 kids), and the very homeschool pioneers themselves gather for a weekend? Then they start bequeathing their homeschool experience to the parents currently in the homeschool trenches. I'm talking about homeschool conventions, which are quite like other conventions, except these are crawling with kids. Personally, it's my favorite school-focused weekend of the year. I get filled up spiritually and mentally rejuvenated as I learn parenting and teaching skills for the year to come. Conventions may be faith-based or secular, or a mix of both. If you choose a secular one there will be lots of great information, but I can't guarantee that spiritual strengthening. The Holy Spirit certainly does show up when He's invited, so I can't overstate the importance of attending a faith-based convention. It's like going on a spiritual retreat. The first convention I ever attended was so poignant for me that I could barely have a conversation— whether with a vendor or another mother—without my eyes filling with tears of joy and peace, knowing that I was making the best decision for my family. At a convention, you'll welcome the support in seeing others, like yourself that just want to do right by their kids, raising them in the ways of the Lord with an education tailored especially for them.

You'll look around the conference room, ballroom, church basement, or community center and see that you are not alone, nay there are hundreds of others of the same mind, and that alone will start to make your heart swell. Add in the motivational speakers, nuggets of wisdom to immediately take home, the general camaraderie, and you'll be giddy with rejuvenation. With keynote speakers, break-out sessions, curriculum expos, and Moms pulling mobile book carts, it can be a flurry of exciting learning for you and your spouse (even for teens and older kids that can attend sessions directed at them). But I must warn you, step lightly and quickly around the mobile book carts. Those things take corners wide, and I don't want you to get an ankle nicked in the cross traffic.

Conventions have childcare programs, teen programs, and vast curriculum expos. In 45-minute breakout sessions, I've learned how to get my kids to be obedient the first time I ask, mill my flour at home, teach math using card games, be a proactive parent, and lean into scripture for any parenting woe. The breakout sessions that I can't attend I download and listen to in the car over the entire year until the next convention. It's so much wonderful knowledge to absorb! A quick "homeschool convention" internet search will help you find the ones near you, and if you want a taste of the breakout sessions, you can probably purchase past audio files and start learning how to be an awesome homeschool family today!

The downside to conventions is that it can be expensive to stay on-site or eat at pricey food vendors and restaurants. Packing food and commuting from home helps offset costs. If you must bring the children, you can imagine how hard it is for them to sit through many sessions, no matter how many screens, books, hands-on activities, or toys you pack, so bring grandparents or a sitter to obtain your high score on break-out sessions. Also, it may be very crowded, the biggest homeschool convention in the country, put on by Florida Parent Educators' Association (FPEA) in Orlando, Florida attracts upwards of 15,000 people. The coffee line is insufferable, I always keep a pack of chocolate-covered espresso beans in my mobile book cart for that 2 p.m. bear that wants to jump on my back and drag me down. But I'm also not too proud to spend fifteen minutes in that serpentine line for a double shot espresso, straight to the head.

TUTORING/ONLINE LEARNING

You can choose to set your child up with online learning for all or part of their education. As a new homeschooling family, we had success with our state's online school, Florida Virtual School (FLVS). Each class that my daughter took had a teacher that she would talk with on weekly assessment calls. Learning at her own pace in the safety of our living room she received grades and feedback from a live person.

It can be daunting to think that *you* are the only lifeline between your child's misunderstanding and clarification on a certain subject. But even the greatest, genius, most dynamic teacher can't teach everything. So just give yourself some grace and accept that you'll need to lean on another's expertise. Whether it's depending on your spouse to strengthen your weak areas, or a tutor to get your kid through Algebra 2, help is out there.

There's a rescue for the confused learner or exasperated parent at sites like tutor.com, which provides free tutoring by connecting students to teachers in online classrooms. Sites like Kahn Academy offer dozens of courses that let students work at their own pace to take control of the gaps in their understanding. Any youth today knows that a YouTube search will uncover classes and teachers on pretty much anything you want to learn. Some library systems have entire databases of things to teach yourself and learn from experts. My county library offers mango.com free language learning. LinkedIn learning has over 10,000 courses on business technology to interpersonal skills. The free opportunities for your kids to teach themselves online are exhaustive.

ONLINE COLLEGE AND DUAL ENROLLMENT

Dual enrollment programs at the local college campus or online allow students to earn a postsecondary degree while still in high school, for free! That is exempt from payment of registration, tuition, and lab fees. Students simultaneously work toward completion of their home education program and associate degree. Dual enrollment broadens the scope of curricular options in which the parents and postsecondary institution work together in creating the schedule of courses.

YOUR KIDS WON'T MISS OUT, CO-OPS

If you're really interested in having your kids grow up with a community their age to lean on and are hesitant to pull them out of a government or private school for this reason, then a cooperative (co-op) could fill that need. Co-ops, have a band of homeschool parents running them and are great places to build relationships. Mom or Dad trades a skill or teaches a specific class. In return, their kids get to learn with a whole group of kids, one day a week. There will be a diverse range of ages. Depending on the structure, there will probably be class changes throughout the day, and your child could have 4-6 parent-taught classes. There will also be field trip days.

We participated in a co-op for one year, and it truly was a great experience. At the time, I had four kids ranging from 18 months up to 14 years old and we share great memories of that year. The year that someone else taught my daughter to read, (**chorus of angels sings Hallelujah**.)

I enjoyed teaching P.E., and with about 15 kids in my class, we were able to send balls pouncing at one another for the kid-favorite dodgeball game. I can still picture a priceless memory, watching my little 6-year-old daughter mow down everyone else as the last player standing for the dodgeball win! In the last moments of this riveting bout, she stood alone against four boys. One by one, she picked off three of the boys. The tallest kid in class, made a noble effort to take her out, hurling the ball at her head. She caught it! The whole class cheered her victory, excitement filled the gym! The truly special thing about her win was that her sister and mom both witnessed it, making reminiscing all the sweeter. Truly, we still talk about it, as legends do.

Some families participate in co-ops every year. The relationships that Moms build with one another and the friendships that students form last a lifetime. Seven years after leaving the co-op, we still see kids we met there at the library, park, and youth group, the co-op memories still holding tightly.

Our co-op adventure was only one year due to a couple of drawbacks. Co-ops can be time-consuming, especially if you have to plan lessons and organize materials for a class you teach. Also, the rigidity of the schedule can be a turn-off to people who love the idea of not being committed to something every week. And despite your efforts to avoid discipline problems in a traditional school setting, you and your kids are subjected to all the behavioral problems of other homeschool families. The beauty of being in charge of every aspect of your kids' education and social settings is that you feel out what season it works and when it doesn't, which season you want to go it alone, and when you want to lean into a community.

HOMESCHOOL RESOURCE CENTERS

If you are lucky enough to have one of these in your area, then I'll admit right now that I'm a tad jealous. This is a building with many classrooms, where learning and extracurriculars happen for homeschooled students. It's not a drop-off site, instead, it empowers parents by keeping them in control of their child's education and connecting them with teachers, tutors, the classes, and clubs their child needs. The Firmly Planted Homeschool Resource Center in Washington also has an Auditorium where theater club can hold their performances, and a coffee shop staffed by seasoned homeschool veterans in case you need some encouragement over a scone and latte. (Now, doesn't that sound lovely, caffeine with a dollop of wisdom?) It's a source of help and hope for many families and The Firmly Planted Ministry hopes and prays that they'll be able to expand by opening Homeschool Learning Resource Centers all over the country.

TUTORS, COACHES, FRIENDS, AND FAMILY

Don't forget the individuals in your family or community who can help ease the burden and ignite that passion-driven learning of which government schools are completely devoid. Every time we enroll in a sport, those coaches are helping me to mold my kids' character on and off the field (and get us a

PE credit whether they know it or not). I cannot sing, so I was no help to my daughter who was musically inclined. Instead, the cantor at our church gave her voice lessons. Oh, how I look forward to my heavenly reward of a beautiful voice to praise the Lord for all eternity. Thanks to our music minister, my daughter doesn't have to wait! Private tutors, art classes, and hobby clubs will help with rounding out your little ones and can serve as a weekly outing.

You may not have to look much farther than your own family for invaluable resources. My kids' Nana is a retired teacher and full-time tutor. I've jumped on her schedule many times when my kids were stuck and I just couldn't get them over the learning block.

During an aviation unit study, we took a two-hour road trip to my brother's Naval base where he was a flight instructor. On base, he gave us a backstage tour of old planes, new planes, big planes, and claustrophobia-inducing planes. The kids clambered into a P-8A Poseidon; an aircraft designed for anti-submarine warfare. Sitting in the cockpit they reveled at all the controls, marveling up-close at the millions of buttons, and at the aircraft's metal intestines, a plethora of tubes and wires that snaked out of the engines and under every panel. To top off an unforgettable learning experience, my brother took us through a secure room where we had to leave all of our watches, phones and electronics. Once we were safely vetted, we walked into a giant room filled the multi-million-dollar flight simulators that train America's Naval pilots. Literally, no one else but officers in uniforms with security codes and myself and my little precious kids. My daughters felt like they were following in the adventurous footsteps of their aviation heroine, Amelia Earhart, as they tried landing and flying their plane in all weather conditions and emergency situations. My son who was four at the time thought it was the best giant video game ever! It was truly one of our most awesome homeschooling adventures!

Unfortunately, I have to admit that if I wasn't in charge of their education, and I delivered them into the hands of the local elementary school, I probably never would've taken them to my brother's base. Such a sad thought, right?

Other free resources are nature centers, state parks, Junior Ranger programs, and hikes (both guided and unguided). A trip to a local preserve may have a volunteer expert waiting for a family of curious learners. Seeing your family will truly make their day as they enthusiastically share their expertise. America's state and national parks have learning pamphlets guiding young explorers through learning on-site. After finishing the activities, kids earn a badge and raise their right hand to be sworn in as an official Junior Ranger. To top off a season of studies on George Washington, Benjamin Franklin, and our nation's founding era, we traveled to the City of Brotherly Love, where it all happened. I held little hands in each of mine as we walked into the historically preserved Assembly Room, where the Constitution was debated, ratified, and signed. I can acutely remember my eyes welling with tears of patriotic pride, knowing I was handing this same feeling down for the sake of my posterity. We gawked at the Rising Sun Armchair that our great first president sat in as he presided over the Constitutional Convention. Outside of Independence Hall, my seven-year-old saw some litter on the ground. It was so stinkin' cute to see my little one picking up trash on the Philadelphia city sidewalk and throwing it in the proper receptacle. Her little chest puffed up proudly, peacocking her Junior Ranger badge and the statesmanlike loyalty that came with it.

HOMESCHOOLING OUTSIDE THE HOME.

I know that if you're reading this book and considering homeschooling in the slightest, your own free time is the least of your concerns. You mainly care that your child is getting an education that enlivens him and is being raised in the ways of the Lord. And good on you, Mom and Dad! That being said, those wonderful times when the children are busily working or gone for a short time can be just the recess we parents need to regroup, lesson plan, run a return up to UPS, or scratch the smallest thing off of our to-do list. Over the school years, you will hone this skill of etching out time for yourself, and we will talk about some more ideas in chapter 18. Ahead are some methods of lightening your educational workload as the teacher of your offspring.

HYBRID (HOMESCHOOL/SCHOOL)

Hybrid schools have many options, but essentially, it's working on the curriculum from a government, private, or Christian school at home. Also called virtual schooling at home, hybrid schools offer parents the option of sending their kids to school one or two days a week to a staff of teachers, and learning at home the rest of the week. Kids may not attend the school at all and do all of their learning online, it just depends on the hybrid school and the student. Typically, the best hybrid schools are much smaller than government schools and still focused on parent-led learning.

Moms and Dads find this model attractive because they see it as the best of all worlds. Parents don't have to come up with the materials and curriculum, the school takes care of that. Parents are there to guide the kids at home if they need help, and can add any ancillary materials as they see fit. With most hybrid schools, the kids have the opportunity to go to school in a group setting, even if it's only one day a week, therefore having the social interaction that new homeschool families find important. Built into the schedule, Mom and Dad, you'll have a few hours to get in some self-care and run errands. On top of that, these schools also keep students' records, produce transcripts, and administer standardized testing. (Depending on your state laws, homeschool students may not be required to take standardized tests, but parents can opt for them as a chance to see how their child stacks up, or for test-taking practice.)

UMBRELLA SCHOOLS

As a homeschool family, your state will require you to show some documentation like student evaluations, or standardized tests. At the very least you'll register as a homeschool student with the county. Umbrella Schools offer parents the option to take care of all that for them. Umbrella schools are considered private schools and they take care of enrollment, grades, and validating diplomas, while the child learns at home. Also called cover schools, they may not even be brick-and-mortar buildings that a student ever attends. Each one has its own registration requirements so it's important to do your own research when finding the right fit for you. Also note that kids registered under an umbrella school are considered private school students, not homeschooled, and therefore cannot play on the sports teams of government schools as homeschool students can.

HOMESCHOOL HUB

A newer mode of homeschooling that has emerged from the mainstream movement, the homeschool hub might be attractive for parents who want the homeschool life, but don't want to do all the work. It's a great transition from mass schooling that the government provides, to self-directed learning in a small setting with a flexible schedule. Hubs are comprised of a learning coach, an online curriculum, and a meeting place. Kids simply show up to the hub on their own schedule and do the online curriculum at their own pace, with the guidance of a learning coach and the other peers that attend. Families can take holidays when they wish but do still have an attendance requirement, about the same as the government school year requires, which is 34-36 weeks. Learning coaches direct students and students help one another. Parents have to get them there, pay their tuition, and hold them accountable. Therefore, the popularity of these hubs is growing like mushrooms after a rainy day.

I hope this exciting explosion of educational methods in and out of the home gets you closer to taking that step to withdraw your children from school. I've touched on tools that are accessible to everyone, but you have your own hopes and dreams that God has set on your heart for what your homeschool might look like. Perhaps you own a camper or sailboat and imagine the education that awaits your family as you drive coast-to-coast camping along the way, or sailing around the world. With the flexibility of schedule, the Lord to guide you, and the support that's out there, there are no limits! The homeschooling adventure awaits, my question to you is: *What are you waiting for?*

Key Point:

There is an abundance of support out there for homeschoolers. With the movement growing, more methods and support systems are popping up. Please don't ever think that you have to go it alone.

Home Is Where The Truth Is:

The homeschool population had been growing at an estimated 2% to 8% annually over the past several years, but it grew dramatically from 2019-2021. Approximately 6%-7% of school-age children in the United States are homeschooled.[1]

Action Item:

Start a running list of what you'd like your homeschool to look like on a day-to-day basis. For example, do you want a community of homeschoolers to meet up with? Does the hybrid model appeal to you? Does the ease of record-keeping under an umbrella school sound amazing? Will some of your student's time be spent with online learning? Jot down some ideas to pray about and research more deeply.

LIE #17:

Since They Aren't In School Around Their Peers, They Won't Develop Bad Character Qualities Or Ever Fight With One Another.

*"Hey and we pray, and we pray, and we pray,
and we pray Every day, every day, every day,
every day,"* —Bone Thugs-N-Harmony

*"Behold how good and pleasant it is when
brothers and sisters dwell together in unity."*
Psalm 133:1

THE COPPER RIVER VALLEY of south-central Alaska comprises 20,000 square miles of mostly untouched wilderness. Anywhere in this splendorous forest which you choose to point and shoot your four-lens smartphone camera will capture a photo worthy to grace the cover of any coffee table book entitled "America the Beautiful." Grand, eleven-thousand-foot snow-capped mountains peak over stratus clouds like grandparents gazing over their new descendant's crib. Lush green conifers stand as close as carpet fibers creating an emerald tapestry on the fertile land below, their beauty is matched only by their reflection in the Copper River named for the rich copper deposits and famous for the millions of salmon that come here to spawn. Don't let the fame and beauty of America's 10th-largest river lull you in for a quick dip on a warm day, because it will dish out hypothermia before you can say, "Ow, it feels like needles are stabbing me."

With the most frigid days in the region reaching 60 degrees *below* zero and so few denizens, you could be there for nine months without ever seeing another human. This makes most comfort-loving-tech-dependent Americans wonder why patriarch Billy Brown and his wife Ami chose this expanse as the place to raise their family. "Unlike any other family in America" and quite possibly my ultimate homeschool heroes, the Browns and their 7 children hunt, fish, and garden to survive off the secluded land of the Alaskan Bush. Salvaging junk like abandoned cars or boats they build their abodes and amp up their family compound. This Alaskan bush family might sound a bit familiar to you as they have over 95 episodes spanning 14 seasons on the Discovery channel. And although I cannot say that I've watched nearly all of the episodes, I can say that these parents had the right idea in keeping their family close-knit! Watching the show, I was more perplexed that the grown children chose to stay with their parents than the truly monumental feat of thriving in the unforgiving tundra. Is it the effect of an expansive wilderness that makes siblings want to stay together? Perhaps life-or-death adventure as a lifestyle? The call of the wild? So intriguing, right?

On a commercial break, I exclaimed, "That's how it should be! When our kids are grown, I don't want them to move away, across the country—or worse, to another country where we might only see them on the holidays, we need to stay together like the Alaskan Bush People!"

If not in the same house, on the same property, in a treehouse that we've fashioned out of old car doors and other discarded miscellany. A cul-de-sac compound? Maybe we can get our next-door neighbors to sell? Hub's reaction, a scoff, was not quite the aligned support I had hoped for.

I really can't blame him though, to think about that possibility right now is laughable for my family, not because my Florida behind wouldn't last two days in sub-zero temperatures, or because my gold-detailed Vince Camuto combat boots would get decimated in the Alaskan bush. I might be able to go six to nine months without seeing certain people, but my hairstylist Felicia is definitely not one of them. She is a balayage *artiste* and has ladies waitlisted for months merely for a consultation appointment, I can't just give her up like that.

My husband jeers at living the compound life with our kids because sometimes they just don't get along. They too would need tens of thousands of square miles for the five of them to spread out, lumped in with some heavy team-building activities like hunting and growing their own food for survival. Yeah, I'm sure that sibling bond gets real tight when your sister shoots a deer and all of a sudden you won't die of starvation. Right now though, our kids bicker, compete, and challenge each other as rivals to the point that they might want to see if the Browns have any more room in their 'wolf pack' for one of them.

As hard as fleshly desires are to control, my kids will brabble on about trifles to the point of parental insanity. About what things, you wonder? The shorter list is what do they *not* bicker about? We have assigned seats in the minivan so that they can't fight over the same coveted seat behind the driver. Even feeding the new kitten had them bumping chests. For the first few days, they literally quarreled over who would scoop the next poop out of the litter box! (Unfortunately, that wore off too quickly.)

When we have a weekend away at a hotel, we are on a meticulous rotating schedule of who gets to push the elevator buttons and use the key card to unlock the hotel room door. There we all stand, dripping wet, shivering in the frigid AC of the hotel hallway, which intensely increases your urge to pee. As the little six-year-old taps the key card reader, again and again, getting the red light, never the green, the 50-pound pool bag slides down my arm with a jerk. The baby bobbles on my arm, his chubby hand grabbing my bathing suit strap to keep from falling, like a cute little bull rider in a soggy diaper.

The impatient tween can't take it anymore, "Gawwwsh, just let me do it!". "No, it's my dayyyyyyy," the little one snaps back. Pee drips down my leg.

"Who's turn is it to sit by Daddy at dinner?" We have a calendar for that.

"Who's night for dishes?" Again, check the calendar.

Pouting over the pettiest things, incessant caterwauling, in this dynamic adventure of doing everything with your family, there can *and will* be lots of in-fighting and back-biting. If you've been accustomed to eight or so hours of quiet time during the school day, you can still relate. It's not long at all after they've thrown backpacks down and started to intermingle with their brethren that the fussing and fisticuffs start. As you transition into a homeschool family, you will be overjoyed when their loyalty shifts away from the school peer group back to their own family. The bond between homeschooled siblings will grow deeper the longer they are away from their peers, but I certainly must warn you that when you are all together 24/7, you may be battling siblings' squabbles on a daily basis. Why do they do it? And how do we combat it?

Sibling rivalry is as old as man. Literally, out of the first two siblings on earth, one killed the other.[1] It continues on down the generations with Jacob swindling Esau out of his birthright for a pot of stew and then stealing the blessing from his blind father while disguised as his older twin, with his Mom's help nonetheless! Having to run from Esau's anger and endure a 20-year exile gave him a chance to work out some of those personality foibles. He came back to Esau begging for forgiveness and paying restitution in the form of many livestock. However, even he couldn't have foreseen how savage this sibling rivalry can get. Jacob's eldest six sons go on to sell his favorite colorfully-cloaked son Joseph into slavery! In this fallen world, jealousy, resentment, and vying for parental attention, are all things that make it difficult for our children to always like each other. Throw in over-tiring schedules, annoying personality traits, and parents that are just as broken, and lose their temper. It can get pretty ugly. Even though God had a plan for Joseph and brought much good out of his brothers' deceit, we hope that our children don't throw one another into a pit over their differences. Granted, we don't show outright favoritism, by dressing one of our children in the fanciest designer clothes, while all the others wear scratchy animal skins, but I've got to ask myself: Is there something in my parenting methods that is contributing to the tumult? I certainly don't want them to carry their differences into adulthood. My hope is that they grow up to be buddies, confidants, and cool aunts and uncles to their nieces and nephews.

Growing up with an older sister and two younger brothers, I know it's hard to like your siblings, let alone love them. My sister and I were always warring. Being three years younger than she, I loved to push her buttons and tease her. She loved to tattle on me for everything. I mean, do you know how hard it is to have a skip party at your house during school hours when your older sister reports everything to your parents? Now, I was no angel, so I'm not blaming her for the chasm between us. It grew mutually. It's sad though that we only text once a year on our birthdays and see each other every third Thanksgiving even though we live only a half-hour drive apart. I don't want that for my kids! Ugh, it pulls my heartstrings just imagining it.

I want to know what I can do as a parent to remove rivalry or at least not incite it. I also want to give my kids the tools to work it out on their own, which will teach them necessary life skills, like negotiating and advocating for themselves. Plus, as I said before the most important point of homeschooling is to develop your kids' character qualities like humility, magnanimity, and benevolence-to-those-who annoy-you.

We've tried many band-aids to mitigate the blood sport between our kids. There was the super-effective *scrub a toilet if you antagonize,* which had our commodes sparkling, and made me hyper-vigilant to recognize antagonizing in the days leading up to a party. One mother of eleven children gave us the genius punishment *make the offender the victim's servant.* Yep, if you were on the receiving end of some foul treatment, you had a certain amount of time bossing that sibling around and making them do your dirty work.

Other parents suggest making the two offenders hold hands or sit nose to nose (awwwwwkward), select a chore from the job jar as soon as the bickering begins, run laps around the yard to blow off steam, or do something cooperative, like hold each other's feet down and each of you give me 50 sit-ups. Yeah, we parents can get pretty clever at doling out consequences that get tiresome to enforce. Then the kids build up immunity to the punishments which aren't addressing the root cause anyway, so they don't cure the problem.

It will help to take a look inside ourselves at what we, the grown-ups are doing because they're learning this behavior from somewhere. (Remember modeling sinful anger from chapter two?) For the tips I'm about to share, I tuned in to a duo more adept at squashing sibling spats than Starsky and Hutch were at crushing street rivalries, authors Adele Faber and Elaine Mazlish. They point out that parents *do* have the power to make a difference. "We can either intensify the competition or reduce it. We can drive hostile feelings underground or allow them to be vented safely. We can accelerate the fighting or make cooperation possible."[2] With the right set of tools, we can help lead our rivals to peace. Millions of desperate, tired-of-the-fighting parents have used the advice in their book, *Siblings Without Rivalry,* but I must admit, when I read it the first time, what they were telling me was counterintuitive, sounded impossible, and downright weird. Like, let one child say all the bad things they want about the other child. Never compare them even if it sounds like a compliment. One alarming suggestion made me say, *how could I ever stop doing that?* "Don't ever compliment one child in front of the other children, it's too much for them". Another one, the counter intuitive, *Don't focus on treating them equally.* Then there were the tips that made me say, "Uh-oh, I do that!" Like don't assign them to certain roles. Let's unpack these one by one.

THE BAD FEELINGS MUST COME OUT.

One thing that will change our parenting game when it comes to sibling rivalries is to stop gaslighting our kids. Gaslighting means: invalidating someone's feelings. It happens across political, and racial spectrums, as well as in intimate relationships and alas, even in child-parent relationships. I did it all the time to my kids before Faber and Mazlish brought it to my attention. For example, "I don't want to go to bed, I'm scared in my bedroom," said my four-year-old. "Oh, there's nothing to be scared of, you're ok, honey." *Now, go walk across the house, down a long dark hallway to an even darker bedroom, because I'm too tired to deal with your natural yet irrational fears,* is what I might as well have said. That's one of the many egregious examples with which I could fill a few pages of this book. It becomes harmful to both the parent-child relationship and sibling relationships when we make them suppress the bad feelings they will inevitably have toward one another.

We should acknowledge the negative feelings that one child has for another instead of dismissing them. When the formerly youngest child said that they wanted to "chop up the new baby and throw them in the trash," my reaction of, "That's a terrible thing to say, you should love your new sibling," was not the right one. Instead, I should've said something like, "Since the new baby got here you feel like

250

mommy spends a lot of time with the little thing, don't you? Sometimes you wish you could have mommy all to yourself?"

Once the feelings are acknowledged, they're more likely to overcome them, than if they've been shamed or blown off for feelings that are actually very natural. It will be hard to listen to, but when you're in private with them, let them pour their little hearts out to you about the woes of brotherhood. A helpful outlet for children is to have them draw what they're feeling, or write about it. If they can't do that yet, you can ask them to demonstrate their feelings using a stuffed animal or pillow. Clobbering a pillow is much preferable to lambasting little bro. The important thing is to allow them to get the bad feelings toward their sibling out, so that good ones can come in, and fewer animosities will grow.

NEVER COMPARE YOUR KIDS WHETHER FAVORABLY OR UNFAVORABLY

You would've thought rivalries were what I wanted with some of the parenting foibles that I committed on a regular basis. I thought that I was boosting my son's confidence when I told him during a math lesson, "Wow, I am so impressed with your number sense! Your sister couldn't do that math problem when she was your age!" (*game show buzzer*) Wrong answer Mom! I doomed him as a player in the detrimental comparison game where there are never any winners, no matter if it's a favorable comparison or unfavorable. Now he's thinking, "I'm better than my sister at math."

Lo and behold, when it was time for her math lesson, I would find him hanging around to see if he could compete on her level by answering any of her questions. The prize in this conjured-up competition was not only bragging rights, but a chance to make sis feel inferior if he figured it out before her, or flat-out stupid if she didn't know the answer and he did. What a payoff for a little brother, right? Especially if he's still smarting from his last sisterly tormenting. I would've been much better off to simply say, "Wow you are really grasping this math lesson! Thank you for concentrating!"

I probably justified it in my mind, it's a compliment to him, what can it hurt? But I immediately saw the repercussions. Unfavorable comparisons are even worse, I hope I never let one of these fly again: "Why can't you make your bed every morning like your sister, she's always so tidy?" I'm sure all that was going through that child's head was something to the effect of, "My sister's such a suck-up, I'll never be like her!" The better way to approach that kind of situation is to simply describe the problem. "I see a bed that needs to be made." If we can just describe what we see or feel as parents, instead of bringing other children into the equation we will reduce the competition that leads to strife. "I see a new toy that didn't get put away." Will create less of a matchup than "Can you be a big boy like your older brother and put away your toys?"

Now, if you're like my husband or any other sport-loving-business-minded-American-who-loves-to-win, then right now you are screaming at me, "What's wrong with a little healthy competition?! We live in a competitive society; shouldn't we give our kids a little taste of it so they can go out there and succeed in the real world?". Hey, you're talking to one of the most competitive women on the planet right here. When I was in pre-op for surgery, I asked the anesthesiologist out of all his patients that day who had the lowest resting heart rate. That's right, Booya! Right here, 42 BPM baby! I've made competitions out of egg dying at Easter (as a grown woman), and go ahead and ask any of my gym buddies if I'm fun to work out with because of the competitive push I bring to each workout. Still, the never-compare parenting tip makes sense to me. When I brought it up to my husband, he barely let me finish my thought before he cut in,

"Now you're just being hyper-sensitive, oh I can't even compliment my kid?" Always resistant to my newly acquired parenting advice which I am quick to throw his way after reading a great parenting book, he taunts, "Let me guess, you read it in a book, right? Well, I can go probably go find books that say the complete opposite."

So, I did an Amazon search on just that. Yes, I found a plethora of books on competition but they were aimed at the business and political spectrum. I was hard-pressed to find one written for parents to apply to their own kids. Competition can be great when it's cooperative. In healthy competition, opponents willingly come to abide by an agreed-upon set of rules. They'll defer to judges or referees while cooperating with their teammates. Unfortunately, that's usually not what tends to happen between siblings at home when incited by parental comments.

We must differentiate between good competition, *adaptive competitiveness,* and bad, *maladaptive.* "Adaptive competitiveness is characterized by perseverance, and determination to rise to the challenge, bound by an abiding respect for the rules."[3] These competitors will feel satisfaction from putting forth their best effort even if they lose.

On the other hand, maladaptive competitiveness is completely different. Demonstrated in someone who always has to prove himself the best at everything, he's the guy that'll shave reps off the workout, fudge his scorecard, or do whatever sinister little cheat that he can to win. He turns everything into a competition, provoking others until he sucks them into his sticky competitive web. He might take it as far as thinking his success means your failure. This is not only super-annoying, it's unhealthy, and he'll alienate himself from having any friends. We don't want our kids doing this when they grow up, or to each other right now because it invariably leads to fights and other maladies. Studies of people in the educational and business arena show that when competition becomes fierce, physical symptoms can develop, like headaches, stomach aches, and back aches. Emotional symptoms flare when those people became anxious, suspicious, and hostile.[4] These aren't things that we want to be a regular part of our home life. So yes, I do want my kids to be Uber-competitive in the sports arena or where cooperative, adaptive competition happens. But I want my home to be a respite from those aforementioned icky feelings betwixt siblings.

It made me uncomfortable, but I eventually had to accept that when I compliment one child in front of another child, I'm stoking their jealousy. Especially when I reflected on how often I had done it, like multiple times a day for years and years. It seems so natural when your child works really hard at achieving greatness, to automatically pour on the praise. If any of your other offspring are around, you might want to pump the brakes before belting out the verbal bouquets. Instead, experts suggest we simply acknowledge how that child must be feeling. For example, when one kid scores a hat trick in a soccer game, we should say something like, "You must be so proud!" Or "That must've been an exhilarating feeling!" But don't say, "I can't wait to tell Grampy, and post it to my social media! I'm so proud of you." You *can* say all that when the others aren't around, and you should! I know this is such a hard one to swallow, but consider that some children feel that it's a direct put down to themselves when they hear one of their siblings being complimented. When I became aware of this bad habit of mine, I started seeing the jealousy manifest immediately. "Oh wow, you picked out an awesome outfit," I say to one child. "Nice combo!" Then here comes a younger one to try and steal their thunder, "What about me mommy, did I pick a good outfit?"

DON'T TREAT EQUALLY, TREAT UNIQUELY.

After we stop gaslighting and comparing our children the next parenting paradigm we can ditch is thinking that they all need to be treated equally. Instead, focus on treating them *uniquely*. When we constantly try to keep everything even, we not only burn up our mental energy and drive ourselves nutty, but we are also teaching our kids to keep score against each other. How many times have I bought something for one child that they legitimately needed, like socks or undies, but then I'm so scared that I'm going to hear somebody whine, or make someone feel like they got shafted that the next thing I know, I'm roaming the aisles of TJ Maxx looking for other necessities to dole out to the other kids. Scrunchies for her, a board book for him, a church shirt for him, a candle for myself. Well, you know that last one was going in the cart regardless. But can you relate? It was so freeing when I simply said, "Indie needed socks. Everyone doesn't get something just because one person needs something."

Treating them uniquely was a game-changer for this homeschool mom with kids at five different levels pulling me in a hundred different directions. Trying to give everyone equal individual attention is a daunting task. However, giving attention according to their individual needs leads to a natural flow. It's not so stressful, but actually rejuvenating. My children quickly grasped the reality that one of their siblings might need more of my time when working on beginning reading skills, biology, or whatever. They know that when it's their turn to have individual time with me, I'll be focused on their specific needs whether it's throwing the football or math, they'll get unique, personal attention. Instead of, *I just spent 20 minutes with your brother, what would you like to do for 20 minutes*? I focus on what that child needs. *Hey why don't you read to me out of Tim Tebow's book for a few minutes, then we can play catch? (*See how I got him to read by dangling a carrot in front of him? Put that one in your tool belt for reluctant readers.) When we treat them singularly, they'll feel more cherished than if we are parsing out our time and attention according to a fairness flow chart.

Keep this in mind too for when they ask, *Who's your favorite?* Or *Who's cuter, me or so-and-so?* Which they will do at some point. Instead of the canned answer, "Oh honey, I love all of you the same." Try giving them some of the unique ways in which you love them, "Well, I love you because you like to snuggle with Mommy, and you always make me laugh with your funny jokes. Those are reasons that you're special to me." Letting them feel uniquely loved will work wonders in diminishing rivalries.

DON'T ASSIGN ROLES.

We must be aware of the fine line between treating them uniquely and casting them into roles. Assigning roles can be positive or negative at first, but beware of the lasting effect of these unpleasant parts in which we cast them in the family saga. It leads to bad feelings that create a tense environment, it may be the major reason they're fighting, and these roles can follow them into adulthood. Before I was privy to this being a thing, (and a stigmatic thing at that) I did it *a lot*. Whether I did it when I introduced them to the librarian, "She's my eldest, he's my middle child, and he's the baby." Or did it to boost their ego, "She's my logical thinker." I didn't realize the damage that I was doing and the underlying rivalries that I was inciting. I've said things like:

"Since you're our firstborn, you're a rule follower."

"She's my math whiz."

"He's the family comedian."

"You're my dedicated athlete."

"Cruz (the family cat) loves you so much because you always take the best care of him."

The list goes on, there are many reasons that parents do this to their kids, and kids do it to one another. When I find myself doing it, it's coming across as a compliment meant to bolster their ego—but that compliment comes at the expense of one of my other kids and adds undue pressure to the one receiving it. Perhaps I'm even boosting my own ego, living vicariously through a trait I saw in my own kid that I never had at that age. I might've called one of my children "The Organizer" because I was so amazed at how clean she kept her room even at a young age. Why so serious, you might be thinking, sometimes we assign roles as a light-hearted family joke. *You're always a Positive Patty, you balance out your sister who's a negative Nelly.* One of my children has a quirky sense of humor that has us laughing non-stop, we've called that child 'weird' one too many times. The more often we say that the more bizarre she becomes.

Siblings assign roles as a cut-down, hoping to make themselves feel better as the opposite, *You're such a baby, you need Mom to do everything for you.* Or they may have heard us assigning roles and just run with it, so they can reap some of the benefits of not having to be that. Like when I asked one of my children to organize the pantry, instead of the obedient *Yes ma'am* that I was hoping to hear, she retorted, "Shouldn't Piper do that instead of me, she's the *organized one*?" I did not succumb to her suggestion but encouraged her. She learned that she too can be organized if she only tries.

A harmonious household knows that it doesn't matter if one child shows prowess in one area, they don't corner the market to the point that other siblings can't try it too. *My daughter has a knack for music, but my son isn't musically inclined so we put him in basketball.* What? No! The kid might've had an interest to practice and a love of music, that is until he heard *that* comment.

No matter what the role is, positive or negative, a kid should be free to behave, develop, and change through the years without the pressure of being defined by a certain trait his whole life. Think about if you were labeled the cool-headed child, but in the frustrations of life sometimes you want to scream into a pillow to release some steam. And now you can't because, *What would mom and dad think of me if I had a temper, I'm supposed to be the calm one?* What if you're labeled as the straight-A student? Can you imagine the stress of not wanting to disappoint your parents by forgetting an assignment or scoring an 89 (*gasp*) on a test?

Throughout your children's lives, the world is going to try to put them into roles and they need to recognize it, refuse to accept it, or be defined by it. Just last night, as I sipped a glass of wine with my gorgeous grown-up daughter, she was bemoaning the 'back-handed compliments' she gets when people say things like, "I just have to tell you, I'm usually not attracted to dark-skinned women, but you are stunning." Or "You're the most beautiful mixed girl I've ever seen."

They think they're throwing her a line that'll make her melt, but she's not trying to play the role of "exotic queen" for the likes of them. She just wants to be appreciated for being herself. "It's so annoying, why can't I just be beautiful?" She said fluttering her eyelids in a sassy eye-roll.

GIVE THEM THE TOOLS TO WORK IT OUT.

When it comes to fighting, there are different levels of intensity and danger. If your kids are wailing on each other, and you worry about their safety because they really might hurt each other, besides immediately separating them, you may need to seek professional help to mediate the violence. The methods ahead can be applied to most other scuffles, like fights over property, or arguments that arise because one kid is annoying the other. When our children fight, we should try to stay out of it after we give them some tools and parameters to work it out between themselves.

Before going into the thick of the battle yourself, consider taking these steps:

1. Acknowledge the children's emotions toward each other. (Frustration, anger, wrath). This should start the calming down process.

2. Respectfully listen to both sides.
3. Let them know that you see both angles and it is indeed a difficult problem.
4. Encourage them in their ability to work out a mutually agreeable solution.
5. Leave the area.

A younger brother asks his older brother if he can play with his Bakugan collection.

"Sure, I'll play with you," the eldest says. "But you can't play with Dragonoid, he's my favorite. Or with Gilator either."

"But that's the one I want to play with, I'm telling Mommy, you're being mean!" (*younger one stomps off*).

"Mommy, I asked nicely to play with his Bakugans and he said yes and now he won't let me play with the one I want," the little one tattles.

"He's going to break it because he doesn't know how to transform it into a ball, and Dragonoid is special to me, I got it for my birthday," refutes big brother.

Without taking sides, the parent simply went along with the steps above.

"Well, yes this is frustrating for both of you.

To the younger child, she said:

"I can see you feel let down because he said you could play at first, but then he took the one you really wanted."

And to the other one:

"I can see that you are worried that your little brother might break your favorite one, so you gave him some others to choose from."

To both children, she says,

"I can see both angles, and this is really a tough situation. I bet if you put your heads together, you can come up with a solution that'll make you both happy." (*leaves the room*)

The solution they came up with might not have been the happy ending you were hoping for. Did big brother decided to share his favorite Bakugan and lovingly tutor the little brother on shaping him back into a ball? Nope, they just separated and played with different things. But hey, they solved it themselves, they weren't bickering anymore, and Mom didn't take sides which always leaves one kid feeling like the loser.

All these aforementioned tips are so hard, right? Parenting multiple children is like a tightrope walk and one misstep will send our kids' self-esteem plummeting into the dark abysm below. We have to constantly evolve as parents, making sure that what we say and do is not causing our children to hate each other while giving each one the unique attention they need. As they argue within earshot, we must cling to our last nerve without jumping in to mediate.

Teach them what good character looks like, by demonstrating it and keeping *our* temper under control. When we do lose our Christian composure, we must go to our children with a contrite heart and ask their forgiveness. It's a daily journey. Here's the thing though, we can do nothing by ourselves; *parents and kids* need the Holy Spirit, the Paraclete.

Look at the apostles, the men who walked with our Lord while he was on earth, sitting at his feet as he taught them for three years. They witnessed paralytics getting up and walking away, dead people coming back to life, and demons driven from the souls that they tortured. They went from fearing for their lives in a tumultuous storm at sea, to stupefaction as the Lord calmed it with three words, "Peace Be Still". They saw firsthand how he treated the lost, the poor, sinners, and the outcast. If anyone should know how to treat others, how to show brotherly love, should not they? Yet, Jesus' closest twelve friends couldn't't leave Capernaum without fighting like children. At least, not until they received the Holy Spirit at Pentecost. There were lots of apostolic shenanigans before tongues of fire changed their hearts and their ministries.

The first four disciples that Jesus called were two sets of brothers. First, Peter and Andrew, then James and John, the sons of Zebedee. What was Jesus thinking? Did he see the strengthening support of the brotherly bond as paramount to his ministry? Because these guys argued all the time about who was the greatest, walking from town to town, then at Zebedee's house, even at the last supper, after the institution of the Eucharist. *After they just broke bread with Jesus*, they go to quarreling about who is the greatest.⁵ Although the Bible doesn't mention it, I wouldn't doubt if they argued about who got to sit next to Jesus too. If they're like my kids, it went something like "Aw...Rabbiiiiiiii, John always gets to sit next to you!".

Before the last supper, Jesus' showed his frustration when they were powerless to cast out a demon that made a little boy unable to speak.

"Oh faithless generation, how long am I to be with you? How long am I to bear with you?"

Same, Jesus. I can't say the same words haven't crossed my mind. *How long until this kid leaves for college?*

After casting out the demon himself, the Lord told them that they needed to pray and fast some more.⁶ That's old-skool fatherly advice right there. Send the misbehaving little scoundrels to bed without any supper and tell them to pray and ask the Lord for forgiveness. (Has anyone done that since the Old Lady in the Shoe?)

St. Peter went from one of his biggest moments of triumph—a revelation from God that Jesus was the Christ, and being elected the first pope by Jesus himself, receiving the keys to the Kingdom and the authority to forgive sins or bind them—to "get-behind-me-Satan in about 2 minutes flat.⁷

Then here comes St. Philip, "Lord show us the Father and we shall be satisfied."⁸ C'mon Philip, don't you know him, after being with him all that time?

St. Peter brazenly chopped the servant's ear off, but when Jesus stifled that plan, it was like all of Peter's faith poured out like the blood from the high priest servant's ear. Later denying his Lord to the point of cussing the lady out for even suggesting he was a Galilean who knew Jesus. We all know what happened before the cock crowed that third time.[9]

It wasn't just Peter, they all fled in fear when Jesus got arrested. One of them even ran off butt-naked, possibly one of his best childhood friends Lazarus, whom he had raised from the dead.[10]

On the third day, when Jesus appeared to Mary Magdalene and her friends, did the disciples believe Mary Magdalene's story? Nope, even though they knew of her loyalty to him, they didn't believe her for one second.[11]

St. Thomas might've been nicknamed Thomas the Valiant because of the courage he showed when Jesus was going to raise Lazarus from the dead. A dangerous trip lies ahead on the way to Bethany, a small village in Judea. Some Jews in that region had just tried to stone Jesus. Thomas boldly said, "Let us also go, that we may die with him."[12] Exhibiting his headstrong determination after the washing of the feet, he prodded Jesus for more clarification on his teaching. "Lord, we do not know where you are going. How can we know the way?"[13] But since he was absent when Jesus appeared to the other eleven, he threw a hissy fit, doubting his brothers' eyewitness accounts, thus tagging himself through posterity with that dubious nickname.

Fast forward to dawn after a night-long blank fishing trip, those tired apostles were about to hit the Jewish fisherman version of the Powerball jackpot.

"Cast your nets to the other side!" Jesus called out from the shore.

Their nets were immediately filled with so many fish they could barely lift them into the boat. Peter, in his excitement, jumps in the water and swims a hundred-meter freestyle to greet his Risen Lord. This is when Jesus, being the loving and patient Son of God that he is, gave Peter the chance to make up for renouncing him, asking him three times, "Do you love me?"

"Lord, you know everything, You know that I love you," Peter answered.

"Follow me," Jesus beckons to Peter specifically as he calmly strolls away from the group of fishermen.

Peter and Jesus walk along the shore of the Sea of Galilee, after a freshly grilled fish breakfast cooked by the Messiah, back from the grave, breeze blowing through their hair, the sand working its way into their "mandals" (that's sandals for men) and between their toes. Jesus uses this alone time to have a serious chat about Peter's fate of martyrdom.

Seeing Jesus' favorite, the beloved disciple John following them, Peter immediately throws him under the proverbial chariot. "What about him?"

"What is that to you? Follow me," Jesus replies.[14]

How many times as a parent have I paraphrased that one? "Worry about thyself, Peter".

A lot like ourselves or our children when we want someone else to feel the pinch, I can think of times when I asked the Lord that same thing.

"What about them Lord, are you going to punish them justly?" My children when they want something that they can't have, like screen time or sugar. "What about so and so, they were on a screen, why do they get to be on a screen, but I don't?" "Why can't I have a cookie, I saw my sister eating one earlier?" Worry about yourself and follow Jesus.

Does it make you feel a little better to know that the apostles were quarrelsome, weak, doubting, and faithless until they received the Holy Spirit at Pentecost? The same is true for all of us, kids or grown-ups. Our best efforts are wretched, we all need the Holy Spirit's help. We must lean into him, with prayer and fasting to raise these brothers and sisters in harmony. Either that or move to the Alaskan tundra.

Key Point:

There are many reasons that siblings fight, including personalities, parenting methods, and vying for parents' love. There are some specific things that we can do as parents to make them feel more loved and less rivalrous. However, just like Jesus' apostles, we are all human and need the Holy Spirit's help in squashing squabbles.

Home is Where the Truth Is:

Some brothers and sisters truly love each other, take fifth-century Italian twins Scholastica and Benedict. They devoted their lives fully to God. Scholastica founded a religious community for women at Monte Cassino at Plombariola, five miles from where Benedict governed the nearby monastery. They visited each other once a year to pray and discuss spirituality. On their last visit, Scholastica sensed her death was looming. She begged her brother to stay longer, but he refused because he didn't want to stay away from the monastery overnight, which was against the rules. According to the *Dialogues of St. Gregory the Great*, Scholastica prayed that God would allow her brother to remain, and suddenly a severe thunderstorm burst forth, making it impossible for Benedict to return to the friary. Benedict cried, "God forgive you, Sister. What have you done?" Scholastica replied, "I asked a favor of you and you refused. I asked it of God and he granted it." They spent the remainder of the night in prayer and conversation, parting ways in the morning.

Only three days later, Benedict was praying in the monastery when he saw his beloved sister's soul ascending to Heaven in the form of a white dove.

Action Item:

Choose one of the parenting tips in this chapter that you feel will improve household harmony. Start employing it in your day-to-day parenting.

LIE #18:

"Me-Time" is More Important.

"We must often draw the comparison between time and eternity. This is the remedy of all our troubles. How small will the present moment appear when we enter that great ocean." —St. Elizabeth Ann Seton, founder of the Catholic school system.

"The apostles returned to Jesus and told him all they had done and taught, and he said to them, 'Come away by yourselves to a lonely place and rest a while.' For many were coming and going, and they had no leisure even to eat. And they went away in a boat to a lonely place by themselves." Mark 6:30-32

I F YOU FIND YOURSELF emerging from behind the beanbag chair cloaked in a loosely crocheted Afghan, on all fours, it probably means that you planned poorly. Possibly, it's time for the toddler to go down for a nap, but you've left their blanket only a few feet from the baby swing which is occupied by a droopy-lidded infant!

In this situation, you must do everything in your power to preserve the possibility of two little ones napping at the same glorious, blessed time. Remember a few things, one: Do NOT make eye contact with the near-sleeping infant through the holes in your disguise. Babies can smell Mama-down-time like a pit bull smells fear. They will lock on quick. And they're bred not to let go.

Second thing: celebrate your Machiavellic-self. Silently half-smile as the *Mission Impossible* theme song plays in your head, because it will. Lastly, and perhaps the most important of all, as the five-month-old watches the yarn lump that is you cross the room, do not do the aptly stupid thing I did and reach your hand out from under your camouflage like a Hungry Hungry Hippo. Instead crawl over the blanket that you are retrieving, in a Roomba-like fashion making the baby think that blankie-phagocytosis has just occurred and nothing else.

Gurrrl. I know that feeling of sleep deprivation, made worse by the spit-up-stained pajamas and messy bun that you've been rocking for days now. What mother doesn't? "Me-time" might be a mythical fantasy land to many busy parents, but we certainly need it. Most of us need more of it. I'm here to tell you some ways to still get it as a homeschool mom, who is with her kids every moment of the day.

Every one of us parents is going to get that frazzled, burnt-out feeling, no matter what. I know I'm getting close to meltdown if I start eyeballing that big yellow school bus rolling down my street collecting and keeping children for hours at a time. I start fantasizing about my kids hopping on, disappearing behind the folding doors, and the hours of quiet time it would afford me.

Unless you live in a tribe or small village as humans did throughout most of history, or have the means to hire a full-time nanny, that decompression time that keeps you from burnout just isn't there. Anxiety builds and before you know it, you're ready to uncork a bottle of wine at noon or pop an edible if that's your preference. I'm not here to judge, I've shot gunned a beer on a hot, stressful summer day standing in between the open refrigerator doors. Remember when you were in college and drinking made all those dudes a little cuter? It works on kids too. All of the sudden, my kids are a little more awesome. I can hear Mommy 12 times in a row and it doesn' even phase me. And while it's a temporary fix to loosening up, calming down, and not getting huffy when your kid can't read the word '*the*'; it's far from a permanent fix and will probably have you even more cranky when the buzz wears off.

I mean, It. Is. Hard. To keep focus, to keep them engaged, to keep pruning away the buds of poor character. You're battling that with poor sleep levels, perpetual piles of laundry, and you have to plan a pesticide-free, healthy dinner that everyone likes! That's a daily battle in itself, which gets super complicated with food allergies, picky eaters, and Taco Tuesday fatigue.

The Lord knew what his disciples needed; they took the boat out for some quiet, wind-down time. He knows what we need too, for the Bible tells us to "be strong in the Lord and in his mighty power." By putting on the full armor of God, we can take a stand against the Devil's evil schemes, whispering to us the lies that we deserve hours of downtime every day, that our kids are flourishing in the school system, and that they'll turn out just fine.

The armor of God consists of the belt of truth, the sports bra of righteousness (or breastplate if you're in ancient Greece), our feet fitted with the readiness that comes from the gospel of peace, the shield of faith for extinguishing the flaming arrows of the evil one, the helmet of salvation and the sword of the Spirit, which is the word of God. Adorned in these we are called to pray in the Spirit on all occasions with all kinds of prayers and requests.

Now, I'm not saying that the Lord hasn't perfectly equipped us for all of our daily battles, but I am forced to wonder if there's a modern update to this armor, Lord? Like how about some noise-canceling Bluetooth headphones up in that helmet of Salvation? Maybe a parent's lightsaber for reminding them to do their work? "Waw-waw-waw- flash the cards to master multiplication, you must." Let's notch that shield of faith up to a forcefield from bickering, a little cocoon of respite for Mama when the argy-bargy won't stop.

If you ask any mental healthcare professional about the importance of self-care, they'll affirm that it is truly essential for human beings to thrive. Mat and I have been seeing a marriage therapist for a few years. We visit her quarterly to work out any kinks and continually learn strategies in communication. One of the questions she asks us at the beginning of each session is "What are you both doing for self-care?" We have to be refreshed so that we can show up as our best for our family. Or, as I always like to echo in Mat's ear, "Happy wife, happy life."

Because anxiety trickles down to our children, they'll be greatly affected by the ways you invest in your rest. Up to half of the children of anxious parents develop anxiety disorders themselves.[1] Our behavior, our emotions, and even the smell of our perspiration have the potential to turn our offspring into stressed-out mini-mes.[2]

As early as the womb, babies are affected by their environment and can feel the mother's stress. In the first years of your child's life, stress is catching like an emotional virus. Even in the tiniest humans, the amygdala picks up on anxiety, fear, anger, and frustration. Then the pilot of the brain, the prefrontal cortex, replicates those feelings with mirror neurons. These neurons which imitate what they are seeing are imperative for empathy and key to helping kids learn through observation. When parents of newborns are stressed and frustrated, those mirror neurons start firing and babies cry and fuss more than when their parents exude confidence and calm.[3] While stress in utero on into the first year of life has the most impact on the developing brain, recent studies show that we can continue to hand down stress to our children through their adolescent years. If one parent is anxious about math, the child is more likely to develop math anxiety too, but only if that anxious parent regularly helps him with math.[4]

Now wait, don't you throw your hands up and yell, "See, I knew I was going to ruin my child!" Due to God's grand design, there's hope. Calm is also contagious. If we can learn to be a nonanxious presence for our children, then they'll have a safe landing place when the stresses of life overtake them. Perhaps you know someone who emulates calm composure. Like the Inuit parents that never yell at their kids, or perhaps the person you call when you are having a terrible day. They remain a poised sounding board, as you bounce your fears and problems off of them, slowly but surely all the friction is muffled by their imperturbability. Author Edwin Friedman, who coined the phrase "nonanxious presence" makes the case that we live in a chronically anxious and reactive society in which there are too few people leading our families, schools and organizations that can serve as a nonanxious presence. Groups work best when their leaders aren't overly anxious and worried because they don't pass the negativity on to others.[5] This is as true for giant conglomerates as it is for small families. Your kids need you to be a calm, composed presence in their lives.

There are other by-products that'll come when we are calm in our kids' presence, we should also exude joy and derive pleasure from their very being. Does your face light up when they come into the room? To genuinely feel loved for just being themselves is a boost to their self-esteem and their well-being. Shoot, when they were a baby all they had to do was lift their little bobble head slightly and we would just gush with love and encouragement. Fast forward ten years and getting that reaction from me isn't as easy. Sometimes, I'm so worn out, the minute they ask me for something, I throw my head back, slump my shoulders and let out an audible and exaggerated sigh.

Of course, my kids bring me joy and a love so deep that I would drop our nature journal and fist-fight a mama bear if we met one in the woods. So I don't need to be acting like that, especially since they pick up on our body language and facial expressions so adeptly from infancy. And you best believe that those mirroring neurons will have them doing that exact thing to you when you ask them to play with their younger sibling, remind them to switch their laundry to the dryer, or try to employ them in any other of the innumerable ways they make your life easier and better.

Let's talk about ways to keep your tank filled. Whether you are a homeschool mom, a career woman, or a stay-at-home mom, you have permission to do things for yourself. You can and *should* still dream. You shouldn't live life so beaten down, that you can't get your thoughts straight, set your own goals, and devote time and energy to those goals. I'd like to get you thinking about a few things that will not only help energize your life, but your whole family's life as you set to embark on this homeschool adventure together. These important things go hand in hand, self-care and your blue flame.

SELF-CARE

Since the widespread jump in mental health awareness, it's become quite the buzzword. Self-care encompasses nourishment for your mental health, physical health, energy levels, and emotions. You might think of self-care as a deep-tissue massage at your favorite spa, and it can be that. But it's much more than simply pampering yourself. It's about developing your self-awareness to figure out where you need nourishment. The right amount of self-care will help you keep your poise when meeting your children's educational, physical, and emotional needs. Oh, and we can't forget our spouse's needs too. Walking in our purpose is powerfully gratifying, but still, it's a lot.

In the manner that the small act of closing our eyes and taking a deep breath can settle our tensest moments, when we take time for self-care—even in its simplest form, we are making energy bank deposits, thus building up our own resilience in dealing with the demands of homeschooling and parenting. On our best homeschooling day when joyful learning abounds, complete with an exciting field trip and lunch at Subway, we're going to need a surplus of energy. Self-care is not about keeping your activities so low that your stress levels are also low, or even being happy all the time.

Our favorite teen, hack schooling phenom Logan Laplante, whom I introduced you to in chapter three, referenced Dr. Robert Walsh's Therapeutic Lifestyle Changes (TLCs) in his TED Talk. These are important aspects of self-care that can actually be as effective as either medication or psychotherapy for some common disorders such as depression.[6] TLCs are fun, inexpensive, free from harmful side effects, and proven over literally thousands of research studies to be beneficial to all. You will stay healthy in mind, body, and spirit when you sprinkle the following into your life keeping a nice balance: exercise, a healthy diet, time in nature, relationships, recreation, relaxation and stress management, religious or spiritual involvement, and service to others. Since I've already talked a lot about the religious and spiritual aspects, let's talk about the other TLCs.

EXERCISE AND TIME IN NATURE

Are you lessening your anxiety, depression, and insomnia because of regular exercise? Are your kids forming new neurons and learning better because they too are getting exercise? I'm not saying you have to go sign up for a marathon or bustle your kids to soccer practice five nights a week. I'm talking about regular movement and time in nature. Many children feel the stress of standardized tests and long school days stuck in the cinder block cubicle as early as first grade. Don't let your kids suffer from "Nature Deficit Disorder."

The health benefits that time in nature provides are astounding. Studies have shown that time in nature improves your memory and concentration, makes you happier, heals you faster, strengthens your immune system, and boosts your vitamin D production which helps prevent depression, cancer, osteoporosis, and heart attacks.[7]

The very act of getting outside to nature triggers the brain's "relaxation response." It'll click into cruise control because of the surrounding, arresting beauty of nature. Taking your family outside and doing nothing else but sitting on a blanket, causes blood pressure to decrease, and lessens production of the primary stress hormone, cortisol. Blood flow to the brain increases by 25 percent, and you'll enjoy heightened immunity and alertness, and less muscle tension.[8] When time in nature is a daily occurrence, the brain regularly goes into the relaxation response. As we know, working muscles makes them stronger, so it follows that the more often your brain goes into the relaxation response, the easier it'll be to switch it on when you really need it. Along with the plethora of other health benefits, regular time in nature sets the human brain up to handle stressful situations in a calm manner.

DIET

I love what Coach Julie at my gym says, "You can't out-train a bad diet." I'd like to take that a step further...you can't outlive a bad diet. Poor food choices lead to obesity, diabetes, fatigue and a slew of degenerative diseases. We all know that. Unfortunately, the standard American diet (the SAD diet, if you will) is pervasive and convenient. We can't perform our best while living on deep-fried fast food, even if it is from Chik-fil-a. It's essential to get in healthy proportions of lean protein, vegetables, fruit, and whole grains. Contrary to what many fad diets will tell you, you need a good balance of fat, protein, and carbohydrates. Take it from someone who has dabbled in every fad diet since the early 2000s, you can't cut major nutritional building blocks from your diet and expect your body and mind to function optimally. I cut carbs with the Atkins, quit starches with the South Beach, and nixed whole grains with the Whole 30. None of that gave me the body I wanted despite running marathons and lifting weights all the time. I finally started building more muscle, and feeling energized when I started focusing on getting enough fat, carbs, and protein. These macronutrients are essential for metabolism, energy production, lean mass and bone mass maintenance, immunity, health, and protection against damage at the cellular level. If you or your kids are athletes, macronutrients play a huge role, especially in endurance sports, injury recovery, and muscle loss prevention in aging. The importance of good nutrition can't be overstated. When the levels of macronutrients (fat, carbs, proteins) and micronutrients (vitamins and minerals) are optimized they can improve cognitive function, mental health, and well-being, particularly in aging.[9] In other words, food is fuel for your brain and body, *and* it keeps you young! If you eat junk all the time or allow your kids to, you are severely handicapping everyone in your family's potential.

We never leave the house without a bag full of healthy snacks that are high in protein and low on sugar, so we aren't tempted to pull into the drive-thru of a fast-food joint, or worse, grab sugary snacks from a convenience store. Our favorites for the road are grapes, bananas, protein bars of all brands and varieties, and peanut butter-filled pretzels (ok, and occasionally Cheez-Its make it in there too, but I did inform the kids that there was no Cheez-It bush in the Garden of Eden and therefore it's not real food). Don't forget the water. We ride around with a drink container that holds a gallon of fluid, sharing glugs from it whenever we're parched.

Hey, I know it's not exactly the most sanitary idea to be sharing germs by drinking after one another, but we eat pretty healthy, exercise regularly and stay adequately hydrated so we seldom get sick.

I'm not trying to come across as holier-than-thou on this one, because my kids subsisted on an alternating lunch of Tyson chicken nuggets and hot dogs for years. As parents, getting them to make healthy food choices is one of our most common battles. Indeed, it's a very important one, so we educate them on reading nutrition labels, and sticking to a serving size. We give them lots of options for real food—I'm talking about stuff that actually grew out of the ground. We've done a unit study on good nutrition, harped on the importance of protein in building muscle, logged our sugar intake, and bartered with the kids to, "Just eat five blueberries and then you can have some Mott's gummies." One of my greatest parenting victories occurred the other night at the dinner table when my five-year-old pretended to be a plant-eating dinosaur and I fed him lettuce leaf after lettuce leaf for ten minutes straight.

RELAXATION AND STRESS MANAGEMENT

Constant notification pings, multi-tasking, and the general needs of their family, are all hindrances to parents getting enough time to be alone with their thoughts—our brains need downtime. Did you know that in our culture many people are actually averse to sitting with their innermost psyche? One study found 67% of men and 25% of women would rather inflict electric shock on themselves than be left alone with only their brain to entertain them for an interminable stretch of time—fifteen minutes.[10] I admit, sometimes, I enjoy the fast-paced technology rhythm. The tires on my Chrysler Pacifica haven't even come to a complete stop at the red light before I'm grabbing my phone to check my texts. "It's green Mommy!" Is my queue to throw it back in the cup holder and perhaps finish sending the text at the next red light. I can try and keep up with life at that speed, or I could do something much more effective for my brain and niche out quiet time to reflect on all the day's happenings.

We need "radical downtime", a phrase coined by authors Stixrud and Johnson, which is a deep resting of the brain. It's a time to let our thoughts wander, to practice mindfulness. Similar to the childhood genius recipe that says imaginative play is great for developing minds, adults also need time for daydreaming, meditating, and sorting out their thoughts. We never grow out of that childhood need! It's absolutely critical for a healthy brain.[11] A daily generous portion is an effective antidote to over-stimulation that has us feeling like our brain is the fried egg in the this-is-your-brain-on-drugs commercial (which could be my brain after 3 PM on any given weekday).

There are certain parts of our brains that go dark when we focus on a task. Neuroscientist Marcus Raichle and his team at Washington University, mapped, grouped, and named these parts of the brain: the default mode network (DMN). When we blink the DMN activates. It's also active when we are alert but not focused on a task. We need to get the DMN activated so that our brain stays healthy. There are lots of ways that we can unwind with a focused task like scrolling social media, watching YouTube, reading a book, journaling, or my personal favorite, working on a jigsaw puzzle, but these don't qualify as the downtime our brains need to process all the information that inundates our daily grind.

Have you ever been on a long drive and allowed Siri or Google Assistant to read all of your backlogged text messages—you know, the ones that notify you of your Walmart grocery delivery, doctor appointments, favorite brands' flash sales, and others that got buried in the melee of messages? Once we've sifted through all the notifications on our phone, we're better able to receive the actual important messages from loved ones quicker, easier, and with more clarity.

Activating the DMN allows your brain to sift through all of its notifications. Meditation, unfocused downtime, self-reflection, sitting in a quiet room with your thoughts...whatever you want to call it, helps your brain process the tasks, interactions, stresses, and frustrations of the day. It's seldom during a focused task that we have an aha moment, conversely, in the DMN lots of them can occur. You will be honing self-awareness, creative incubation, autobiographical planning, consideration of the meaning of events and interactions, taking another person's perspective, reflecting on your own and others' emotions, and moral reasoning.[12] We could take a cue from Einstein on this one, his breakthrough in the theory of relativity came after a year hiatus in Italy "loafing aimlessly' and popping in on a lecture every now and then.[13]

Amidst my little lovelies caterwauling 'mommy' three hundred sixty-seven times a day, my aha moments are few and far between if I don't get some silent time. As would be any wisdom that comes from the Lord in the form of spiritual revelations. Look at Jesus' earthly father, St. Joseph, a silent man who doesn't utter one word in sacred scripture. He married the mother of God, humbly lead his family, and saved the God-child from massacre by fleeing to Egypt all because he was open to God's voice through his profound interior life.

How can *we* know where God is calling us if we don't sit in silence and listen? Sure, we can hope for other signs, reading scripture, and listening to the people that the Holy Spirit sends our way. Occasionally, the Lord blatantly opens a door making it clear what our next step should be. His voice won't be in the great wind caused by the flurry of activities, or in the earthquakes of our life's mishaps, or even in the dumpster fire of a lesson plan gone awry. If we are opening daily a pathway of communication by waiting in silence and listening for him, when he does speak in that still, small voice, we'll hear him.

If you're one of those people that would rather self-administer shock, then meditate, start small and try it for one minute. Then build up from there, shooting for a few minutes every day. One more important benefit to activating the DMN, is that you are helping your mind to stop racing so that your body can follow.

My family found a significant help in relaxing our minds and bodies before bed. The app, *Pliability*, leads users through a series of three to four-minute stretches lasting about twenty minutes. As our muscles relax deep into the stretches, it improves our mobility and flexibility. While the kids' muscles are still supple, Mat and I have gotten stiff in our forties. Stretching has improved our muscle recovery and keeps our bodies and joints feeling like they did when we were much younger. We are less sore in general, and have felt athletic gains because we better execute basic movements like squats and barbell work. When I gaze across the dimly lit room and behold my entire family stretching in unison as any athletic team does, I'm proud to be a part of this family, grateful that God entrusted them to us. When it's over we all lay there on our backs, quietly relishing in the relaxation of a good stretch. We pray our bedtime prayers aloud and go off to bed for a deeper night's sleep than if we hadn't stretched.

Spouses and children will absolutely thrive on a couple of monotonous boundaries. Establishing a nighttime routine such as a family read-aloud or stretch session will bolster your sanity and wind everyone down for a good night's sleep. Maybe a morning routine would be better for your family. Breakfast with a scripture reading and then a brief walk outside to get the blood flowing can signify to the brain that it's time to get focused and start school. Rituals like this become the oil in the many moving parts of the family machine, minimizing friction, helping it to run cleanly, and preventing unnecessary loss of power.

RECREATION AND RELATIONSHIPS

While too much time with tech isolates us, doing fun things with loved ones helps us flourish. Ancient wisdom says surrounding yourself with good friends and people you love adds to a healthy and happy life. With the homeschool schedule, you literally have time with your kids all day, every day. When you're out from under the restrictive school-year calendar, your days are all yours and no one gets to tell you where you have to be. That's going to be a mood booster in itself!

Of course, you'll have to schedule time with your girlfriends, get at least one date night a month, and do other adult activities or you might start to feel like you're on an island, remote, cut off from the outside world. I remember one particularly long drudge without any break from the little ones, I was so desperate for friends. When the UPS and Amazon couriers pulled into my driveway at the same time, I passed out Gatorades and felt like I was throwing a block party. I was on a bit of a social high until I realized I was wearing the same shirt that I had on yesterday when Amazon delivered. Oh well, come to think of it he was wearing the same shirt yesterday too.

YOUR BLUE FLAME

Making self-care a priority to keep ourselves refreshed is essential. But engaging in your blue flame will energize and motivate you. There is something inside you, that you are meant to share with the world, that will absolutely make you come alive, especially when you use it as a way to give love to the world. It might be a skillset, a passion, or a hobby and when you do it your brain is flooded with dopamine—the neurotransmitter that is critical to the physiological processes including movement, motivation, reward, and pleasure. Perhaps you know what it is already, or it might be just below the surface, it could be baking, writing, public speaking, decorating, traveling, drawing, mechanics, growing bonsai trees, or whatever. You've got to find your *blue flame.* Have you ever been so absorbed in a hobby that time stood still, you had complete focus, with zero stress? This is called getting into "flow". [14] If you've ever experienced flow, think about what you were doing. This could be your blue flame and as you pour love into the world through a joyful activity such as this, your life is infused with flow *and* purpose.

Author, stand-up comedian, and mother of six, Jennifer Fulwiler knew that writing was her blue flame. She rebelled against conventional wisdom that said, "You have three kids in diapers, don't over-work yourself. You're too busy to focus on anything else." Instead, she started a blog about her conversion from Atheism to Catholicism. She couldn't have fathomed the immediate metamorphosis she underwent when she started using her blue flame.

"My whole life changed when I realized that instead of sapping my energy, my blue flame gave me energy. When I would take time to write, it was like taking a caffeine pill. I was infused with a burst of inspiration and joy that would help get me through the rest of the day," Fulwiler continues. "The kids noticed that I was smiling more. Joe noticed that I was up for pleasant conversation when he got home from work, instead of my old habit of throwing my hands up and saying, 'Ugh, I'm out!' And stomping upstairs as soon as he walked in the door."[15]

Fulwiler realized that she was doing her family a favor by making time for her passion. Depending on God's guidance while harnessing her blue flame, over the next few years she realized her lifelong dream of becoming a published author and had the courage to self-produce her nationwide comedy tour using the family credit card! Her family is living their best life in what she calls the *village hustle*, which is being a 'hot girl, girl boss who knows that love, family, and community are the foundation of all true success'.

If you want to figure out your blue flame, Fulwiler suggests asking yourself these questions and jotting down the answers.

- When have you felt truly alive?
- What did you do for fun as a kid?
- How have you helped others?
- What is something that you're good at, but your friends are not?
- Whose life do you envy?
- Whom do you admire and what is it about them that makes you feel that way? Somewhere in your answers to this query lies the clues to your blue flame.

I got a clue to my blue flame when I thought about one of my earliest memories. My dad told me to get a nice outfit on because we were going to dinner at the pizza joint he managed. I remember running upstairs, rummaging through my middle drawer, and plucking out a striped shirt. Slamming that drawer, I moved down slid open the bottom one and grabbed my pine green corduroys to match. When my three-year-old little self came down those stairs, my parents were so impressed with my clothing choice, you would've thought I had solved an algebraic equation. "Wow, Maeve that outfit matches perfectly," Dad gushed. My mom chimed in, "Oh yeah, that's remarkable that you chose a matching outfit all by yourself!" This nostalgic memory is seared in my mind so vividly that I can still visualize the inch-wide green and white stripes with red pinstripe detail, down to the little white lint dotting my corduroys.

When I was only a couple of years older, I remember asking my mother what size I wore, so I could peruse the Walmart rack myself.

"You're about a 6X, honey," she said.

That's at five, six-years-old max that I was turning myself loose in the clothing department. All my life, I knew fashion savvy was a gift from God to me, a creative outlet, a form of self-expression.

Even when I was in the throes of having babies, changing diapers, and homeschooling the kids, I still yearned for something of my own. I needed to let my creative juices flow, a hobby that didn't involve children, perhaps even a way to make a little extra cash. Anything that would give me a break from the day-to-day. Maybe I could sell my homemade decor or throw pillows at the Friday night artisan market in our hometown. I remember praying, "Lord send me something to do, even better if it could be a side hustle." Gah, that expensive lamp I was drooling over in the Serena and Lily catalog would not stop haunting me.

A couple of days after I prayed that prayer, my friend called me about an opportunity to serve women through the vehicle of fashion through a clothing brand with which I was already obsessed. As the stylist, I would bring the collection of blouses, slacks, jeans, dresses, skirts and accessories into women's homes using a folding clothing rack on wheels. The host has gathered her friends, and put out a simple spread of wine and appetizers. A collision of the best of all worlds— wine, girl time, and shopping. Guests delight in fashion tips through a presentation similar to what a buyer for a New York boutique would enjoy. Then for the finale, they try on clothes with the opinions of trusted friends and a personal stylist.

It was a perfect fit, serving women through my love of fashion. I did all that was required to build my clientele, made phone calls, put in orders, posted to social media, and followed up with clients to make sure they loved their new clothes. I focused on serving these women. Seeing how I was changing their lives kept stoking my blue flame. You might be like one of the many women whom I served who stood in their closets, surrounded by cherry-picked clothes with nothing to wear. Under my tutelage, they'd learn how to dress for their body type and leave a changed and confident woman. Fall collection after spring collection for many years I helped women create a wardrobe that they loved, got discount designer clothing, and made lasting friendships.

It gave me so much drive and energy, that when I reflect on those years, I'd say "How did I ever have time for that? How did I muster the energy?" Now I realize the empowerment that came from using my blue flame.

Your blue flame might not ever earn you any money, but it's still going to be effective in breathing freshness and vigor into your life as you give love to the world. My dad found his blue flame—surfing—at the age of 58. Twenty years later, he's literally one of the fittest baby boomers on the planet, surfing for hours at a time, three to four times a week. He's found many ways to love others through surfing. Do you want to learn to surf? No matter how old or how young, he'll teach you. He keeps a twelve-foot wooden cross atop the surf racks on his rust-kissed Toyota Rav 4. That cross is a reminder of Jesus' sacrifice which he plants in the sand beside his truck before he paddles out. An eighteen-year-old local recently told us that all his life, he's used that cross as a visual marker to know how far he's drifted with the ocean current during each surf session.

My dad hands out religious articles like Miraculous Medals and spiritual books on the beach and started a Catholic surf club. He has many stories of the surfers' lives whom God has changed through my Dad's presence in the surf community. One spring, a self-proclaimed Satan worshipper with face piercings and tattoos walked up with a lighter trying to burn the cross. Before he walked away, my dad told him the grave fate that awaited him for all eternity if he didn't turn away from Satan. The next spring, the same man, sans face jewelry, gave my dad a thumbs-up and a smile.

The locals call my Dad 'Preacher George', but he's not an ordained minister, just someone letting God use him through his blue flame.

You might be thinking, "I'm about to start homeschooling, I can't possibly start a new hobby or side gig." I hear you; it will definitely take some time to figure out your new normal. Like any transitional season, you'll want all your energy focused on optimization. What I'd like to iterate is that burnout will be on the horizon if you don't consider yourself and your needs, so it's advantageous to at least start thinking and praying about your blue flame now. There will be time for you to focus on yourself and your goals. Finding little ways to serve others while using your blue flame will pump enthusiasm into your whole family's life. One of the best ways that kids learn is through observation. Show them what it is to become the best version of yourself, achieve personal goals, and love others. Heck, you might even find that teaching is your blue flame which would be a win-win for your whole family.

Whether you are trying to find your blue flame or thinking about diving into the homeschool world, you are going to come up against forces that don't want you to do it. It might be self-doubt, pushback from people you love, fear, or even the devil himself. When you try to take your children back from the devil's clutches, he's not going to give up without a fight.

Homeschooling is the Lord's work, and the enemy hates anything that brings people closer to God. He will stoke stress into fear into burnout into blowup, hoping you'll quickly get fed-up and send them back to government schools. That's why it is so important not to give in to fatigue and frustration. The devil and the evil forces of this world will have far fewer chances to seduce your children when you are their main influencer. Keep your focus, you know in your heart of hearts that this is the right, best thing for your kids. God sees and blesses each sacrifice that you make to teach them because this is how he intended families to learn, because the schools are broken, because the agenda of indoctrination is intolerable.

No amount of daytime mani/pedis, girlfriend lunches, not even extra time to volunteer for a noble cause is worth sending your kids away to a place where human traffickers hang out to recruit them, and the grown-ups in charge sexualize and indoctrinate them with a Godless, divisive, life-destroying, America-hating agenda. The many wasted hours away from your loving care are spent numbing their minds, sucking all passion for learning right out of them, force-feeding them needless facts, and thwarting all critical thinking. If all of that wasn't damaging enough, you can be sure that over the 25,000 hours that they are gone from you during these critical years of development they will shift their loyalty from the ones who gave them life and sustenance, to the people who are so renowned for manipulating them to do the inadvisable that they have their own maxim—*peer pressure*!

Your kids need you to do this. America needs you to do this, I need you to do this! At the next homeschool convention, I want to smile as I watch you and your little stair-step ducklings trailing behind you, baby in the Bjorn, mobile folding cart packed with lunches, books, and school supplies.

Let's pray together that our grown kids will one day meet each other on a college campus or in the workplace. They'll be bubbling over with enthusiasm for life because we helped guide them to their passionate, anointed path. They'll be like-minded sisters and brothers in Christ who know that truth is objective, and how to defend it. My kid will have your kid's back when he starts sharing the saving message of the Gospel with a lost and confused, government school graduate. I can see it now; our kids are going to grow up to do great things together for the Kingdom.

Then you and I, when we stand before the Lord at the end of our lives can say, "I sacrificed, I taught, I never relented for you, O Lord."

My mission field: my living room. My disciples: my kids.

Key Point:

Parents do need me-time, quiet time away from the children. Self-care should be a priority and should include time for introspection so that we can nourish ourselves in the areas we are depleted.

When we use our God-given gifts to add love to the world, we will experience a jolt of freshness and energy.

> *"You are the CEO of your life. If you have kids, you are the CEO of your family. You have a duty to dream. It's your job to set the vision, to look up from the ground and out to the horizon and imagine what might lie beyond."*
> *—Jennifer Fulwiler*

Action Item:

Let your child sleep in tomorrow as you research your state's requirements for starting your homeschool journey. Visit HSLDA.org., the information is listed for every state. Once you know if you can meet the state requirements, it could be as simple as keeping them home from school, or filing a letter of intent to homeschool. Even if your state requires a notarized affidavit and home instruction plan the sooner you start working on it, the sooner your homeschooling adventure can begin!

ACKNOWLEDGMENTS

*"Adhere to your purpose and you will soon feel as
well as you ever did. On the contrary if you falter
and give up, you will lose the power of keeping
any resolution, and will regret it all your life." —
Abraham Lincoln, letter to Quintin Campbell,
June 28, 1862*

*"This, then, is how matters turned out with
Nicánor. And from that time the city has been in
possession of the Hebrews. So I too will here end
my story. If it is well told and to the point, that is
what I myself desired; if it is poorly done and
mediocre, that was the best I could do."
2 Maccabees 15:37-38*

FIRSTLY, I WANT TO thank my Lord and Savior, Jesus
Christ, for putting this mission on my heart, for using
me to get a message out, and for his guidance in doing
it—even if I am a bit dense in receiving the message
and slow to act in obedience. Why would he choose me, an
impatient parent who suffers from misophonia and severe
ADD? Because I was willing. I apologize to you the reader if
there are any mistakes or mis-facts in this book. To share
these truths with parents, I've worked tirelessly at my home
office, in the camper, while my kids jumped at the trampoline
park, and on the sidelines of sporting venues all across
Florida. It was my purpose to present solid research from
reliable sources. But with my neurodivergent brain, there

could be one or two in here. If you find a mistake or an omission, please email me at info@maevejemison.com and let me know about it.

Secondly, Thanks for reading this far! You're holding this book in hand, not only because the Lord inspired your aunt, friend, or mom to give it to you, but because he called me to write it. Of course, not before he called me to homeschool, nor before he called me to marry Mat years before that. My gratitude to God for my journey cannot be overstated. Now, thank you for putting so much thought and prayer into your family's journey. Big props to you for being a caring parent and for wanting to provide the best education and faith foundation for your children.

To my young kids, thanks for supporting me on the fulfilling journey of writing a book, and more importantly: getting the message out to others about how wonderful this family adventure of homeschooling truly is. If even one family decides to homeschool because of this book, then the innumerable fend-for-yourself nights were worth it! Keep digging into the history and Truths of our faith and your relationship with God will continue to get deeper. The more you learn, the better you'll be able to teach the truth. We can't have any of my great-grandkids joining the wrong side of Armageddon. I love our Friendly Defender Fridays, morning Bible readings, and your questions of faith (especially when they're too deep for me to answer and we have to ask Grampy)! What a joy to guide you toward your passions, and cheer you from the sidelines!

To my grown daughter and friend, Damaris. Because of you, I had to get my life going in a good direction, had to start setting goals and achieving them. I love you and am super proud that now I get to watch you crush your goals.

Mat, thanks for choosing me. Your daily outpouring of affection gives me the confidence to chase goals and tell a joke in a big room. I'll always hand off the baton so you can execute a funnier joke than I would have, so long as you carry me on all the partner WODs that have heavy back squats. You're forever my security, my sounding board, my love.

Dad and Kathy, having two giants of the faith like you as parents is like hitting the ancestral lottery. Nowhere could anyone find a better, more loving example of servants of Christ than you two. I'm so grateful to you for entertaining grandkids, tutoring, editing, holy pep talks, and encouragement. When I doubt myself, you're the first place I turn. Thanks for believing in me and cheering me on in everything that I do.

My friend TK who is strong, fit, and smart, you've been an amazing friend over the years, over the miles, and through the process of writing this book. I'm sure it got tiresome hearing how many words I was up to, but you never let on! Thank you for your perspective, afternoon coffee vid-chats, and for living out 1 Thessalonians 5:11, "Therefore encourage one another and build one another up."

Speaking of encouragement, Belinda, I've always known that was your spiritual gift. And wow, did it benefit me through this process! Thanks for the confidence your words always deliver and of course, for all the belly laughs when we're together.

Erica Carter, thanks for your wise and adept editorial skills which were a huge help. Your supportive feedback gave me courage and confidence. I'm grateful for your experience and friendly support.

Heidi St. John and Jen Fulwiler, you don't know me *yet,* but one day we will probably be besties. I've read your books, listened to your podcasts, and been encouraged to walk out my purpose by getting into the cultural battle for our future. You've made me laugh, encouraged me to achieve big audacious goals, and continually pour messages of hope and inspiration into my quiet life. I know that it might sound a little creepy and weird putting you in my acknowledgments since we haven't met, but I'm willing to be that so long as you know the far-reaching effect of your ministries and the difference they've made in my life.

And finally, to all the homeschool moms, new ones, future ones, and the veterans. Y'all are supportive *for real*! Every one of you that I told about this book boosted me up, agreed on the importance of the message, told me horror stories, or was simply there with wisdom and love to help another mother in the homeschool trenches. I hope that this book encourages you as much as you all encourage me!

NOTES

Introduction

[1] Curran, E. J. (2023, February 13). *7 unexpected benefits of eating together as a family, according to science*. Parents. Retrieved February 19, 2023, from https://www.parents.com/recipes/tips/unexpected-benefits-of-eating-together-as-a-family-according-to-science/

[2] Vaughn, Michael G., et al. "Are Homeschooled Adolescents Less Likely to Use Alcohol, Tobacco, and Other Drugs?" *National Library of Medicine*, PubMed Central, 21 Aug. 2015, https://www.ncbi.nlm.nih.gov/pmc/articles/PMC4652803/.

[3] Elflein, John. "Major Depressive Episode Youths by Gender U.S. 2004-2021." *Statista*, 23 Jan. 2023, https://www.statista.com/statistics/252323/major-depressive-episode-among-us-youths-by-gender-since-2004/.

[4] Pryor, John H., et al. "National Norms Fall 2010." *UCLA*, 2010, https://heri.ucla.edu/PDFs/pubs/briefs/HERI_ResearchBrief_Norms2010.pdf.

[5] Elflein, John. "Major Depressive Episode Youths by Gender U.S. 2004-2021." *Statista*, 23 Jan. 2023, https://www.statista.com/statistics/252323/major-depressive-episode-among-us-youths-by-gender-since-2004/.

[6] Sabina, C., Wolak, J., & Finkelhor, D. (2008). The nature and dynamics of internet pornography exposure for youth. CyberPsychology & Behavior, 11(6), 691-693. doi: 10.1089/cpb.2007.0138

[7] Common Sense Census: Media Use by Tweens and Teens 2019. https://www.commonsensemedia.org/research/the-common-sense-census-media-use-by-tweens-and-teens-2019

[8] Ray, B. D. (2019). Research facts on homeschooling. National Home Education Research Institute. https://www.nheri.org/research-facts-on-homeschooling/-Australian Broadcasting Corporation. (2019)

LIE #1: Your Children Won't Be Adequately Socialized.

[1] William Z. Foster, "Toward Soviet America," Marxists.org, accessed May, 12, 2022, https://www.marxists.org/archive/foster/1932/toward/06.htm

[2] John Dewey, *Impressions of Soviet Russia and the Revolutionary World*. Teacher's College: Columbia University, 1964), p.78.

[3] Mering, N. (2021). *Awake, Not Woke: A Christian Response to the Cult of Progressive Ideology*. TAN Books, p. 178.

[4] Mason, C. A., & Narad, M. E. (2015). *Homeschooling and the use of alcohol and other drugs: What research tells us*. Journal of Drug Education, 45(1), 1-14. doi: 10.1177/0047237915572396

[5] National Home Education Research Institute. (2019). *Gen2 Survey: A Spiritual and Educational Survey on Christian Millennials.* Retrieved from https://www.nheri.org/Gen2SurveyASpiritualandEducationalSurveyonChristianMillennials.pdf.

LIE #2: I Could Never Homeschool, I Don't Have the Patience.

[1] James 1:19-20 (Revised Standard Version Catholic Edition). Italics added.
[2] Proverbs 15:1(Revised Standard Version Catholic Edition).
[3] Hubbard, Ginger. *"Biblical Parenting Podcast Episode 19."* (2021). Parenting with Ginger Hubbard. Apple Podcasts.
[4] Ibid.
[5] Briggs, Jean. (1970). *Never in Anger: Portrait of an Eskimo Family.* Pg. 154. Harvard University Press.
[6] Doucleff, Michaeleen. (2021). *Hunt, Gather, Parent.* Penguin Press, p. 144.
[7] Ibid. pg. 146

LIE #3: The Highest Priority Is Getting Our Schoolwork Done.

[1] Matthew 16:36
[2] Lucado, M. (2006). The Oak Inside the Acorn. Thomas Nelson.

LIE #4: You Have to Follow A Certain Curricula to Succeed. There's a Perfect One Out There For You. All You Have To Do Is Find It.

[1] Lawson, M. A. (2012). The Real Power of Parental Reading Aloud: Exploring the Affective and Attentional Dimensions. Reading Teacher, 66(4), 287-296. https://doi.org/10.1002/TRTR.01090
Theories of language and language development help to illuminate the auditory dimension of language and literacy learning. This article proposes that the power of parental reading aloud may be underestimated. While shared storybook reading enhances children's pre-reading skills, uninterrupted listening to narratives may assist children both to acquire the underpinning prosodic sensitivity that accompanies expressive reading aloud and to develop the auditory attention systems that are associated with academic achievement.
[2] Trelease, J. (2013). The Read-Aloud Handbook. Penguin Books, p. 4.
[3] Ibid pg 5.
[4] American Library Association. (n.d.). Children who are consistently read to or listen to audio books become older kids who like reading. Retrieved from http://www.ala.org/alsc/publications-resources/for-parents/parent-tips/reading-aloud
[5] McCurdy, H. G. (1957, November). The Childhood Pattern of Genius. Journal of the Elisha Mitchell Scientific Society, 73(2), 448-462.

[6] Sir Ken Robinson. (2006, February). Do schools kill creativity? Video file. TED Conferences. Retrieved from https://www.ted.com/talks/ken_robinson_says_schools_kill_creativity

[7] Gatto, J. T. (2001). The Underground History of American Education: A School Teacher's Intimate Investigation Into the Problem of Modern Schooling. Oxford Village Press.

[8] Robinson, K. (2006, February). Do schools kill creativity? Video. TED. https://www.ted.com/talks/ken_robinson_says_schools_kill_creativity?language=en

[9] Ibid.

[10] Boyack, C. (2014). Passion-Driven Education: How to Use Your Child's Interests to Ignite a Lifelong Love of Learning. Libertas Press.

[11] Stixrud, W. R., & Johnson, N. (2018). The Self-Driven Child: The Science and Sense of Giving Your Kids More Control Over Their Lives. Penguin Books.

[12] Stixrud, W. R., & Johnson, N. (2018). The Self-Driven Child: The Science and Sense of Giving Your Kids More Control Over Their Lives. Penguin Books.

[13] World Economic Forum. (2018). Data Science in the New Economy: A White Paper. Retrieved from https://www3.weforum.org/docs/WEF_Data_Science_In_the_New_Economy.pdf.

LIE #5: At Least I Know They're Teaching the Right Things In School.

[1] Kaushik, N. (2018, August 7). What is the Difference Between Education and Indoctrination? DifferenceBetween.com. https://www.differencebetween.com/what-is-the-difference-between-education-and-indoctrination/

[2] Zoe Karen Hill, Majority of Americans Hold Negative View of Critical Race Theory Amid Controversy. https://www.newsweek.com/majority-americans-hold-negative-view-critical-race-theory-amid-controversy-1601337. June 16, 2021

[3] Jordan Boyd, Loudoun County Dad Smeared As 'Domestic Terrorist 'Says School Covered Up Daughter's Rape By Boy In Girls 'Bathroom. https://thefederalist.com/2021/10/13/loudoun-county-dad-smeared-as-domestic-terrorist-says-school-covered-up-daughters-rape-by-boy-in-girls-bathroom/. October 13, 2021

[4] American News. "Trans-Identified California High School Track Star Blows Out Female Competitors, Costs Women Athletes Their Awards." The Post Millennial, May 22, 2023, https://thepostmillennial.com/trans-identified-california-high-school-track-star-blows-out-female-competitors-costs-women-athletes-their-awards

[5] Today Story. (Accessed Nov. 21, 2023) High School Girl's Feld Hockey Player Loses Teeth, Injured By Shot From Male Opponent. Retrieved from https://www.youtube.com/watch?v=2ebjipWT8JQ

[6] California Teachers Association, Report of Board of Directors, Committees, and items of new business, State Council of Education, June, 1-2, 2019. Los Angeles, CA.

[7] DefendingEd. (n.d.). List of School District Transgender & Gender Nonconforming Student Policies. DefendingEd. Available: https://defendinged.org/investigations/list-of-school-district-transgender-gender-nonconforming-student-policies/. Accessed: August 2, 2023.
[8] Natashja M. de Graaf et al., "Sex ratio in children and adolescents referred to the gender identity development service in the UK (2009-2016)," *Archives of sexual behavior 47, no.5 (April 2018):1301-4,* https://www.researchgate.net/publication/324768316_sex_ratio_in_children_and_adolescents_referred_to_the_gender_identity_development_service_in_the_U K_2009-2016
[9] Marjorie King. Queering the schools. (https://www.city-journal.org/html/queering-schools-12411.html) Spring
[10] California Healthy Youth Act, AB 329, Section 51932(b), https://leginfo.legislature.ca.gov/faces/billNavClient.xhtml?bill_id201520160AB 329.
[11] See California Healthy Youth Act, AB 329, Section 51932(b), Chapter Three.
[12] Shrier, A. (2021). Irreversible Damage. Regnery Publishing.
[13] FLASH. (2011). Middle School FLASH, 2nd Edition, Lesson 2 Sexual orientation and gender Identity Curriculum. Public Health - Seattle & King County.
[14] Advocates for Youth. (2017). Rights, Respect, and Responsibility Curriculum. Advocates for Youth.
[15] MA Family Institute. (2023, August 18). Sex is on the School Calendar All Year Long. MA Family Institute. Retrieved from https://www.mafamily.org/2023/08/18/sex-is-on-the-school-calendar-all-year-long/
[16] Shrier, A. (2021). Irreversible Damage. Regnery Publishing. Pg. 69.
[17] Shilts, R. (1982). The Mayor of Castro Street: The Life and Times of Harvey Milk (p. 24, 180). Saint Martin's Press.
[18] Ibid (p. 237-238)
[19] Ibid (p. 78-79)
[20] Flynn, D. J. (2018). Cult City: Jim Jones, Harvey Milk, and 10 Days That Shook San Francisco. Encounter Books.
[21] J. Ristori and T. D. Steensma, "Gender Dysphoria in Childhood," *International Review of Psychiatry* 28, no.1 (2016): 13-20, 10.3109/09540261.2015.1115754
[22] He did this in his capacity as chair of the American Psychiatric Association's workgroup on Sexual and Gender Identity Disorder.
[23] "Transgender Kids: Who knows Best?" *This World;* See J. Ristori and T.D. Steensma, "Gender Dysphoria in Childhood" *International Review of Psychiatry* 28, no, 1 (2016) 15, Table 1
[24] In 2018 the hospital that shut down his clinic and fired him apologized publicly to Dr. Zucker for having misrepresented his work and smearing him with unsubstantiated accusations, the hospital paid him almost $550,000 plus legal fees in compensation.
[25] See, e.d.C. Dhejne et al, "Mental Health and Gender Dysphoria: A Review of the Literature," *International Review of Psychiatry 28*, no. 1 (2016): 44-57,

https://www.ncbi.nlm.nih.gov/pubmed/26835611; M.S.C.Wallien et al., "Psychiatric Comorbidity among Children with Gender Identity Disorder," *Journal of the American Academy of Child and Adolescent Psychiatry 46*, no. 10 (2007):1307-1314.

[26] Lisa Littman, "Parents reports of adolescence and young adults and perceived to show signs a rapid onset Gender Dysphoira,"*PLoS One* 14. No. 3 (August 16, 2018),Fig.1, https://journals.plos.org/plosone/article?id=10.1371/jurnal.pone.0202330.)

[27] Ty Turner "How to Tell if You're Transgender," YouTube, feb. 20, 2015, https://www.youtube.com)

[28] Marcus Evans (https://quillette.com/2020/01/17/why-i-resigned-from-tavistock-trans-identified-children-need-therapy-not-just-affirmation-and-drugs/)

[29] Cecilia Dhejne et al., "Long-Term Follow-Up of Transexual PersonsUndergoing Sex Reassignment Surgery: Cohort Study in Sweden," *PLoS One 6,* no. 2, (February 2011), https://doi.org/10.1371/journal.pone.0016885.

[30] See "Board of Directors Part One: Agenda and Papers of a Meeting to be Held in Public, "The Tavistock and Portman NHS Foundation Trust, 53, The table on "Self-Harm" on page 54 shows that administering puberty blockers had no positive impact on gender dysphoria.

[31] Osteen, Joel https://www.joelosteen.com/en-US/how-to-watch/Messages/2018/04/09/20/26/Loving%20Unconditionally. Accessed September 8, 2022.

[32] Jordan Boyd "Sexual Assault In the Girls' Bathroom (https://thefederalist.com/2022/01/13/cross-dressing-loudoun-teen-convicted-of-assaulting-female-students-sentenced-to-life-on-sex-offender-registry/)

[33] Michael Cook, "13-Year-Olds Given Mastectomies at California Clinic," BioEdge, Sept. 15, 2018, https://www.bioedge.org/bioethics/13-year-old-girls-given-mastectomies-at-california-clinic/12816.

[34] Massachusetts Family Institute. (2020, January 17). Pornographic Comprehensive Sexuality Education in Massachusetts Public Schools. https://www.mafamily.org/2020/01/17/pornographic-comprehensive-sexuality-education-in-massachusetts-public-schools/

[35] Our Whole Lives. P. 264 Unit 5, Workshop 16: Redefining Abstinence.

[36] The Sex Lives of Sex Researchers.. https://doi.org/10.1177/1536504214558215

[37] Private Acts/Public Policy: Alfred Kinsey, the American Law Institute and the Privatization of American Sexual Morality.. https://doi.org/10.1017/s0021875800024889

[38] If you want to read more about this, search "David Reimer". I must warn you it is a tragic and gut-wrenching story that will stay with you. I could not bring myself to write details here because of the depressing effect it would have on readers.

[39] Grossman, M. (2009). You're Teaching My Child WHAT?: A Physician Exposes the Lies of Sex Education and How They Harm Your Child. Regnery Publishing.

40 Grossman, M. (2013, July 16). A Brief History of Sex ed, How we Reached Today's Madness. The Public Discourse. https://www.thepublicdiscourse.com/2013/07/10408/

41 DeSantis, R. (2021, June 22). Florida Governor Ron DeSantis Holds Press Conference in Fort Pierce, FL. C-SPAN. https://www.c-span.org/video/?513947-1/florida-governor-ron-desantis-holds-press-conference-fort-pierce-fl

42 Stewart, J. (2021). The Big Ideas Behind Critical Race Theory. Ebook.

43 Horkeimer, M Critical Theory: Selected Essays, (Bloomsbury Academic, 1982), p. 244.

44 Stewart, J. (2023). Confronting the confusion of critical race theory with clarity and truth Lecture. FPEA Convention, Orlando.

45 Genesis 1:26-27

46 Stewart, J. (2021). The Big Ideas Behind Critical Race Theory. Ebook.

47 DiAngelo, R. (2018). White Fragility: Why It's So Hard for White People to Talk About Racism. Beacon Press.

48 Oluo, I. (2018). So You Want to Talk About Race. Seal Press

49 In CRT, "lived experience" is sometimes also called "second sight."

50 Oluo, I. (2018). So You Want to Talk About Race. Seal Press, p. 14-15.

51 Stewart, J. (2021). The Big Ideas Behind Critical Race Theory. Ebook.

52 Stewart, J. (2023). Confronting the confusion of critical race theory with clarity and truth Lecture. FPEA Convention, Orlando.

53 This list is taken from: Peterson, J. B. (2017, November 10). The Lie of Diversity. Jordan B Peterson. https://www.jordanbpeterson.com/blog-posts/lie-of-diversity/

54 Mering, N. (2021). Awake, Not Woke: A Christian Response to the Cult of Progressive Ideology. TAN Books.

55 Yglesias, M. (2019, April 1). The Great Awokening. Vox. https://www.vox.com/2019/4/1/18290620/great-awokening-white-liberals-race-polling-trump-2020. Emphasis added.

56 Rufo, C.F. (2020, August 12). "Nuclear Consequences," (blog) https://chrisopherrufo.com/national-nuclear-laboratory-training-on-white-privilege-and-white-male-culture/.

57 Yglesias, M. (2019, April 1). The Great Awokening. Vox. https://www.vox.com/2019/4/1/18290620/great-awokening-white-liberals-race-polling-trump-2020

58 Patterson, O. (2002). The Ordeal of Integration: Progress and Resentment in America's "Racial" Crisis. Civitas/Counterpoint.

59 Centers for Disease Control and Prevention (CDC). (2021). Births: Final Data for 2019. National Vital Statistics Reports, 70(13). https://www.cdc.gov/nchs/data/nvsr/nvsr70/nvsr70-13.pdf

60 Mfume, K. (1995). Speech at the Million Man March. Washington, D.C.

61 The Success Sequence is often cited as a way to battle poverty, as it suggests that individuals who follow the three steps of graduating from high school, getting a full-time job, and getting married before having children are more likely to achieve financial stability and avoid poverty. Research has shown that

individuals who follow the Success Sequence are more likely to have higher incomes, lower rates of poverty, and better health outcomes compared to those who do not follow the sequence.

For example, a study by the Brookings Institution found that individuals who followed the Success Sequence had a poverty rate of just 2%, compared to a poverty rate of 76% for those who did not follow the sequence. Another study by the American Enterprise Institute found that individuals who followed the Success Sequence were 55 times less likely to be in poverty than those who did not follow the sequence.

Overall, the Success Sequence is seen as a way to promote economic mobility and reduce poverty by providing individuals with a clear path to financial stability and success.

[62] Carson, B. (2022). Created Equal. Penguin Books, p. 27.

[63] Stewart, J. (2023). Confronting the confusion of critical race theory with clarity and truth Lecture. FPEA Convention, Orlando.

[64] Carson, B. (2022). Created Equal. Penguin Books, p. 250.

[65] McCollum, C. (2022, March 12). Utah principal says there's no truth to rumor of litter boxes for student said to have sensory issues. The Herald Journal. https://www.rexburgstandardjournal.com/news/national/utah-principal-says-theres-no-truth-to-rumor-of-litter-boxes-for-student-said-to/article_de528d8c-c2b6-5c17-801b-fb0db2cd025f.html

LIE #6: Private or Christian Schools are Just As Good as Homeschooling, If Not Better.

[1] National Center for Education Statistics (2018). National Teacher and Principal Survey (NTPS) Public School and Private School Documentation. https://nces.ed.gov/surveys/ntps/documentation.asp

[2] Phys.org. (2020, June 29). Private school students report higher self-esteem than public school students. https://phys.org/news/2020-06-private-school-students-social-emotional.html

[3] National Catholic Educational Association. (2023). Catholic School Data. https://ncea.org/NCEA/Who_We_Are/About_Catholic_Schools/Catholic_School_Data/NCEA/Who_We_Are/About_Catholic_Schools/Catholic_School_Data/Catholic_School_Data.aspx?hkey=8e90e6aa-b9c4-456b-a488-6397f3

[4] Meritocracy's Miserable Winners. The Atlantic. https://www.theatlantic.com/magazine/archive/2019/09/meritocracys-miserable-winners/594760/

[5] (2009). Homeschooling: A Growing Option in American Education. Home School Legal Defense Association. https://www.hslda.org/docs/news/200908100.asp.

[6] Ware, O. (2020). Fichte's Moral Philosophy. Oxford University Press. https://doi.org/10.1093/oso/9780190086596.001.0001

[7] Ibid.

[8] Greene, J. (2012). How to Break Free of Our 19th-Century Factory-Model Education System. The Atlantic.

https://www.theatlantic.com/business/archive/2012/05/how-to-break-free-of-our-19th-century-factory-model-education-system/256881/

[9] Truthnet (2018). What Type of Educational System is Taught in the US?. https://steemit.com/education/@truthnet/what-type-of-educational-system-is-taught-in-the-us

[10] Jetset Magazine (2019). A Nation of Workers: Is Public Education Dummying Down the Labor Force?. https://www.jetsetmag.com/exclusive/business/nation-workers-public-education-dummying-labor-force/

[11] General Education Board. (1902). The country school of to-morrow. Occasional Papers, No. 1. New York: General Education Board.

[12] Newsweek (2022). Even Republican Private School Kids Are Being Taught CRT, Our Research Finds | Opinion. https://www.newsweek.com/even-republican-private-school-kids-are-being-taught-crt-our-research-finds-opinion-1784753

[13] Accuracy in Media (2023). Indiana educators brag about slipping in CRT and DEI instruction 'under the radar'. https://www.aim.org/aim-column/indiana-educators-brag-about-slipping-in-crt-and-dei-instruction-under-the-radar/

[14] Mering, N. (2021). Awake Not Woke. Penguin Books, pg. 27.

[15] Ibid. pg 174.

[16] National Fatherhood Initiative. (n.d.). Father Absence Statistics. Retrieved from https://www.fatherhood.org/father-absence-statistic

[17] McCants, P. Campus Renewal, Campus Ministry, p. 1, https://www.campusrenewal.org/wp-content/uploads/2016/09/Campus-Renewal-Campus-Link-Grant-Proposal.pdf.

LIE #7: It's The Youth Pastor or Catechist's Job To Teach My Child The Faith.

[1] Catholic Church. (1994). Catechism of the Catholic Church. Vatican City: Libreria Editrice Vaticana. Paragraph 1666.

[2] Christian News Network. (2015, February 16). Study Finds Homeschoolers Less Likely to Leave Faith Than Public/Private Schooled Students. https://christiannews.net/2015/02/16/study-finds-homeschoolers-less-likely-to-leave-faith-than-public-private-schooled-students/

[3] Barna Group. (2019). Resilient Disciples. https://www.barna.com/research/resilient-disciples/

[4] Lifeway. (2007). Reasons 18-22 Year Olds Drop Out of Church.

[5] Ham, K., Beemer, B., & Hillard, T. (2009). Already Gone: Why your kids will quit church and what you can do to stop it. Master Books.

[6] Ferrer, H. M. (2019). Mama Bear Apologetics. Harvest House Publishers.

[7] Pastor Tim. (2007, May 15). Tattooed for Christ. Christianity Today. https://www.christianitytoday.com/pastors/2007/fall/10.15.html

[8] The Holy Bible: Revised Standard Version Catholic Edition. (2006). Romans 2:15.

[9] Fox News. (2022, July 22). 180-million-year-old sea monster found with skin and blubber. https://www.foxnews.com/science/180-million-year-old-sea-monster-found-with-skin-and-blubber. (Accessed July 22, 2022).

[10] Snelling, A. A. (2009). Geologic Evidences for the Genesis Flood. Answers in Genesis. https://answersingenesis.org/the-flood/geologic-evidences-for-the-genesis-flood/. (Accessed July 23, 2022).

[11] Leviticus 18:22

[12] Catechism of the Catholic Church. (n.d.). Paragraph 2358. Vatican.va. http://www.vatican.va/archive/ccc_css/archive/catechism/p3s2c2a6.htm.

[13] Generations with Vision & Brian D. Ray. (2015). A Spiritual and Educational Survey on Christian Millennials. http://www.nheri.org/Gen2SurveyASpiritualandEducationalSurveyonChristian Millennials.pdf

LIE #8: Homeschoolers Are Weirdos.

[1] National Center for Education Statistics. (2019). Bullying.https://nces.ed.gov/fastfacts/display.asp?id=719.

[2] National Center for Education Statistics. (2022, June 28). New NCES Data Show Increases in School Shootings and Cyberbullying in K–12 Schools Over the Last Decade. https://nces.ed.gov/whatsnew/press_releases/06_28_2022.asp

[3] K12 Dive. "School shootings reach unprecedented high in 2022." Accessed June 2023, https://www.k12dive.com/news/2022-worst-year-for-school-shootings/639313/.

[4] Knoll, J. L. (2018). Is the Plague of Mass School Shootings in the US Here to Stay? Psychiatric Times. https://www.psychiatrictimes.com/view/is-the-plague-of-mass-school-shootings-in-the-us-here-to-stay-. (Accessed July 14, 2022).

[5] Koch, K. (2017). Raising Resilient Kids. Moody Publishers.

[6] Ibid. Pg. 62.

[7] CNBC. (2019, April 3). Self-made billionaire Spanx founder Sara Blakely sold fax machines before making it big. https://www.cnbc.com/2019/04/03/self-made-billionaire-spanx-founder-sara-blakely-sold-fax-machines-before-making-it-big.html.

LIE #9: They'll Miss All of Their Government School Friends.

[1] Koch, K. (2015). Screens and Teens: Connecting with Your Kids in a Wireless World (pp. 38-42). Moody Publishers.

[2] Huerta, D. P. (2019). Seven Traits of Effective Parenting. David C. Cook. Colorado Springs.

[3] National Center for Missing & Exploited Children. (n.d.). Dr. Carpenter's Study. https://www.missingkids.org/footer/media/DrCarpentersStudy.

[4] Willard, J. Jenna Willard. (2022, September 18). Interview with Jenna Willard Video. YouTube. https://www.youtube.com/watch?v=LAXn3_WPuIw.

LIE #10: You Should Teach According to the Government Benchmarks Instead of Igniting Their Passions and Tailoring Their Education.

[1] This teacher's name was changed.

[2] Kathy is also my Dad's wife, Nana to my kids, and has been a caring, loving, mother to me in my adult years since she came into my dad's life after the death of my biological mother.
[3] Plato. (1973). The Republic and Other Works (p. 229). Anchor Books. New York.

LIE #11: I work, Therefore I Can't Homeschool.

[1] Responsible Homeschooling. (n.d.). Parent participation in the labor force. Retrieved from https://responsiblehomeschooling.org/research/summaries/homeschool-demographics/
[2] Gray, P. (2011). The Special Value of Children's Age-Mixed Play. American Journal of Play, 3(4), 500-522.
[3] United States Census Bureau. (n.d.). United States Census Bureau. Retrieved from https://www.census.gov.
[4] Federal Reserve Bank of New York. (n.d.). Household Debt and Credit Reports. https://www.newyorkfed.org/microeconomics/hhdc.html

LIE #12: You're Not Doing Enough.

[1] Proverbs 14:30
[2] Gatto, J. T. (1991, July 25). I Quit, I Think. Wall Street Journal.
[3] Gatto, J. T. (2002). Dumbing Us Down: The Hidden Curriculum of Compulsory Schooling. New Society Publishers.

LIE #13: I Don't Have The Organizational Skills.

[1] Fox 8 News. (2019, March 6). Survey: 28 percent of kids today have to do chores. https://fox8.com/morning-show/nineam/survey-28-percent-of-kids-today-have-to-do-chores/
[2] Daily Mail. (2018, March 16). Most children don't do household chores, according to new report. https://www.dailymail.co.uk/news/article-5514215/Most-children-dont-household-chores-according-new-report.html
[3] Harvard University. (n.d.). The Grant and Glueck Study. The Study of Adult Development. https://www.adultdevelopmentstudy.org/grantandglueckstudy

LIE #14: Other Family Members' Opinions Actually Matter In This Decision.

[1] (Meltzer et al., 2014; Tribby and Berrigan, 2021; Martin-Chang et al., 2011; Brewer and Lubienski, 2017; Morse and Bell, 2018; Sadorra, 2023; Yu et al., 2016; Valiente et al., 2022).
[2] Meltzer, L. J., Shaheed, K., & Ambler, D. (2014). Start Later, Sleep Later: School Start Times and Adolescent Sleep in Homeschool Versus Public/Private School Students. Behavioral sleep medicine, 12(5), 343-354. https://doi.org/10.1080/15402002.2014.963584

LIE #15: I Can't Homeschool My Child Because He Learns Differently.

[1]T.P's Weekly. (1907, November 29). Edison's Resting Place. Retrieved from https://www.newspapers.com/clip/105758/edisons-resting-place-tp-weekly/.
[2] Ibid.
[3] A Day in Our Shoes. (n.d.). IEP Accommodations and Strategies Printable. Retrieved from https://adayinourshoes.com/wp-content/uploads/IEP-Accommodations-and-Strategies-printable.pdf.
[4] Alford, K. (2019). Say Good-by to "Dyslexia" and Embrace Full-Field Vision Learning. Vision Dynamics LLC.
[5] Dweck, C. S. (2006). Mindset: The New Psychology of Success. Ballantine Books. (p. 179)
[6] Stixrud, W. R., & Johnson, N. D. (2018). The Self-Driven Child: The Science and Sense of Giving Your Kids More Control Over Their Lives. Penguin Books. (p. 109).
[7] Dweck, C. S. (2006). Mindset: The New Psychology of Success. Random House.
[8] Gore, L. (2019). Charlotte Mason the Teacher Who Revealed Worlds of Wonder. CreateSpace Independent Publishing Platform.

LIE #16: I Can't Do It By Myself.

[1] National Home Education Research Institute. (2022). How many homeschool students are there in the United States during the 2021-2022 school year? https://www.nheri.org/how-many-homeschool-students-are-there-in-the-united-states-during-the-2021-2022-school-year/
[2] Fortune. (2022, April 14). Pandemic homeschooling surge leads to US school reopening. https://fortune.com/2022/04/14/pandemic-homeschooling-surge-us-school-reopening/

LIE #17: Since They Aren't In School Around Their Peers, They Won't Develop Bad Character Qualities Or Ever Fight With One Another.

[1] Genesis 4:8
[2] Faber, A., & Mazlish, E. (1998). Siblings Without Rivalry: How to Help Your Children Live Together So You Can Live Too. W. W. Norton & Company.
[3] Bronson, P. (2013). Top Dog: The Science of Winning and Losing. (Pg. 10)
[4] Kudielka et al. (2004). Why do we respond so differently? Reviewing determinants of human salivary cortisol responses to challenge.. https://doi.org/10.1016/j.psyneuen.2003.09.001
This review article discusses the various factors that can influence an individual's stress response, including competition, and how this can lead to physical symptoms such as headaches, stomach aches, and back aches.
Selye (1976). The Stress of Life. McGraw-Hill.
This classic book by Hans Selye discusses the concept of stress and its effects on the body, including physical symptoms such as headaches, stomach aches, and back aches, which can be caused by competition and other stressors.
[5] Luke 22:24-27
[6] Mark 9:14-38

[7] Matthew 16:16-23
[8] John 14:8-10
[9] Luke 22:54-62
[10] Staples, T. (2018). Another Theory for That Naked Man in Mark. Catholic Answers Magazine. https://www.catholic.com/magazine/online-edition/another-theory-for-that-naked-man-in-mark
[11] Mark 16:11
[12] John 11:16
[13] John 14:4
[14] John 21:6-23

LIE #18: "Me-Time" is More Important.

[1] Stixrud, W. and Johnson, N. (2018). The Self-Driven Child: The Science and Sense of Giving Your Kids More Control Over Their Lives. Penguin Books, p. 83.
[2] Ibid p.84.
Epigenetics is a rather new field of study which refers to the ways that experience affects genes by turning the function or specific genes on or off.
[3] Ibid p.86.
[4] Maloney, E. A., Ramirez, G., Gunderson, E. A., Levine, S. C., & Beilock, S. L. (2015). Intergenerational effects of parents 'math anxiety on children's math achievement and anxiety. Psychological Science, 26(9), 1480-1488. https://doi.org/10.1177/0956797615592630.
[5] Friedman, E. (2007). A Failure of Nerve: Leadership in the Age of the Quick Fix. Seabury Books.
[6] Walsh, R. (2018). Lifestyle and Mental Health. California Psychologist, 51(4), 16-18. https://drrogerwalsh.com/wp-content/uploads/2019/08/LMH-Summary-for-California-Psychologist-2018-12-20.pdf.
[7] SelectHealth. (2019, July 22). 10 Reasons Why Being in Nature Is Good for You. SelectHealth. https://selecthealth.org/blog/2019/07/10-reasons-why-being-in-nature-is-good-for-you.
[8] Khalsa, D. S., & Stauth, C. (1997). Brain Longevity: The Breakthrough Medical Program That Improves Your Mind and Memory. Warner Books.
[9] Rehabilitation Nutrition for Injury Recovery of Athletes: The Role of Macronutrient Intake.. https://doi.org/10.3390/nu12082449
[10] Wilson, T. D., Reinhard, D. A., Westgate, E. C., Gilbert, D. T., Ellerbeck, N., Hahn, C., Brown, C. L., & Shaked, A. (2014). Just think: The challenges of the disengaged mind. Science, 345(6192), 75-77. https://doi.org/10.1126/science.1250830.
[11] Raichle, M. E. (2010). The Brain's Dark Energy. Scientific American, 302(3), 40-49.
[12] Singer, J. L. (1966). Daydreaming: An introduction to the Experimental study of Innerexperience. Random House.
[13] Rovelli, C. (2016). Seven Brief Lessons on Physics. Riverhead Books, pp. 3-4.
[14] Csikszentmihalyi, M. (1990). Flow: The Psychology of Optimal Experience. Harper & Row.

[15] Fulwiler, J. (2021). Your Blue Flame: Drop the Guilt and Do What Makes You Come Alive. Zondervan.

www.ingramcontent.com/pod-product-compliance
Lightning Source LLC
Chambersburg PA
CBHW030402130626
46549CB00004B/1603